A COMPREHENSIV[E]
for Depression Recovery and Prevention

Your

HAPPINESS
TOOLKIT

16 *Strategies for*
OVERCOMING
DEPRESSION

And Building a Joyful, Fulfilling Life

CARRIE M. WRIGLEY, LCSW

MORNING LIGHT
P U B L I S H I N G

Cover and Interior Design by Najdan Mancic

This book contains the ideas and opinions of the author. It is intended to provide helpful and informative material on the subjects addressed in the publication. It is not intended as formal treatment. If the reader requires professional services, a competent mental health professional should be consulted. The author and publisher specifically disclaim all responsibility for any liability, loss, or risk that results from application of any of the contents of this book.

Printed in the United States of America
Morning Light Publishing
9055 S. 1300 E.
Sandy, Utah, 84094

Your Happiness Toolkit:
16 Strategies for Overcoming Depression, and Building a Joyful, Fulfilling Life

Library of Congress Control Number: 2019907568

ISBN: 978-1-7331175-0-0 Paperback Edition
ISBN: 978-1-7331175-1-7 Kindle Edition
ISBN: 978-1-7331175-3-1 Ebook Edition
ISBN: 978-1-7331175-2-4 Audiobook Edition

For more information, visit **CarrieWrigley.com**

*Dedicated to those who struggle,
those who are trying to help, and those
who simply seek to remain happy and
hopeful in a challenging world.*

TABLE OF CONTENTS

—

FOREWORD

The tools described in this book have the power to help you overcome depression. *BUT* - in order for them to work for you, *you* need to work them.

You might be a little disheartened by that last statement. But that's actually the very thing that makes this book so hopeful— *it gives YOU the power*. Taking responsibility, as Carrie Wrigley has written, *"puts you in a position of significant power and control within your own life."*

As someone who has often struggled with depression, I used to bristle at the mere suggestion that I might somehow be responsible for it. I'd get defensive if someone tried to tell me to just "snap out of it," or "be more grateful," or try some newfangled therapeutic approach.

It was as if they believed I wasn't a victim of my depression—that it was somehow within my realm of control. *It wasn't!* No one wants to feel depressed. No one wants to feel suicidal. I didn't choose these feelings, they chose me! *Depression—I thought— was caused by forces completely outside of my control.*

But that kind of mentality only strengthened and perpetuated my depression. Because—and this is important—if depression is caused by forces outside of my control, then how can I possibly have any sort of power over it?

According to that kind of mentality, I can't. I'm powerless. I have no hope of moving forward, because I am a victim of my circumstances.

But then, I heard a talk by Carrie Wrigley. In her talk, she spoke about depression, and offered practical tools for overcoming it. She didn't talk about *"getting by,"* or *mitigating* the symptoms, or learning how to *cope* with it. No, she was offering practical advice on how to **overcome** it.

Think of it: here was an educated therapist, with years of experience working with countless clients. And she was telling the audience—and the world—that there is a way to *overcome* depression.

Her words lit a fire inside of me—a fire borne of *hope*.

I anxiously read everything she had written, and I even interviewed her for a number of different projects. Her words had a profound impact on my life, and have helped me (and many others) to move forward from despair into healing and recovery.

And the most beautiful thing about this book is this: **it gives *you* the power to move forward.** It isn't some knowledge that only a select few people can understand. It isn't a new or expensive drug. It isn't part of a lifetime subscription. *This is real, effective, and practical power that lies within **you**.*

So, if you—or someone you know—is struggling with depression, I invite you to read this book, and put its principles into practice. Because the principles work—if *you* work them.

And *that* is very hopeful indeed!

—Seth Adam Smith

Author of Your Life Isn't For You, and You—Unstuck
sethadamsmith.com

INTRODUCTION

This is not another book about depression. This is a book about RECOVERY from depression, and it is a guidebook for PREVENTING depression in the first place. It is a comprehensive manual brimming with practical, drug-free strategies you can use—starting *today*—to help yourself, or someone you care about.

Here, you will learn the difference between what *feeds* depression, and what *fights* it. You will learn how to intentionally and consistently build a style of life that promotes happiness, wellness, and productivity. You will learn how to depression-proof yourself and those around you, by following simple, practical guidelines that even young children can understand.

This is a book intended to empower and embolden YOU— whether you have struggled with depression for decades, or just mildly felt its early impact in yourself or in others. You may be someone who is responsible for others' care—as a parent, professional healer, teacher, or religious leader—who wants better tools for helping those within your care who struggle. Or, you may be a reasonably happy person who has NEVER wrestled with depression—and you want to keep it that way! Whatever your situation, and whatever your life or family history, you can learn and apply these principles of emotional wellness to help yourself and others.

I have been a counselor for over thirty years, specializing in the treatment of depression, anxiety, abuse, grief, trauma, addiction, relationship issues, and other related problems. I have sat on the front lines of terrible pain with hundreds of struggling people over the years. And I have joyfully watched as they have rebuilt and revitalized their lives, by diligently applying these healing ideas that I have shared with them.

Time after time in this work, I have watched light come back into once-darkened eyes, and vitality pour back into once-shriveled souls. I have seen people powerfully take their lives back, restored to vibrancy and hope. I've seen people regain their sense of purpose, repair old areas of brokenness, and revitalize their cherished relationships, and their personal wellness. I have seen people literally transform their lives in fundamental ways—replacing depression with happiness, health, and vitality.

I know these principles and techniques work, because I have tested them for decades—in my counseling practice, in my family, in my teaching, and in my own personal life. These are ideas I found first to help myself, early in my life, through a series of depressive episodes. I have personally known the crushing weight of depression. I have felt its iron grip, heard its destructively demoralizing voice, and experienced the very physical, as well as emotional, impact of its dark presence. But I have also felt the profound joy and victory of learning to cast off that terrible weight, and intentionally build something better. I have likewise seen that joy and triumph in others I've shared these ideas with. Now, I want that same joy and relief for *YOU*.

So, use this guidebook in whatever ways serve YOU best to meet your needs, both now and in the future. You might want to read it first from beginning to end, to familiarize yourself with the broad range of tools and techniques available to help you. Or, if you have a specific identified need, you might want to go directly to the chapter that is most relevant for you now, and then return to the others later. In the back of the book you will find additional resources, in case you need more intensive research or learning on a given topic.

Use this book to help you GET strong and STAY strong emotionally—and to help others around you to do the same. *Depression need not be permanent, and happiness is an attainable and sustainable condition*—IF you know and consistently apply the principles associated with enduring happiness. Let this be a powerful guidebook for you, in that lifelong adventure of discovery, transformation, and healing.

—Carrie M. Wrigley, LCSW

A QUICK START GUIDE

Overcoming Depression and Building Happiness

L ike the *Quick Start Guide* provided with a new electronic device or piece of software, **Section I** will acquaint you with the most essential ingredients for overcoming depression and strengthening emotional wellness. Each chapter in this section includes **Transformational Tools** that you can start using right away, as Quick Start Strategies, to help you build a solid foundation of happiness and well-being.

Then, **Sections II–IV** will help you to build on that foundation with more detailed instructions. These sections serve as a more *comprehensive owner's manual*, providing guidance, layer by layer, to help you create a healthier brain and a happier lifestyle. These sections draw on a rich variety of **wellness-enhancing strategies**, enabling you to assemble your personalized Happiness Toolkit.

Finally, **Section V** offers *additional resources*, which provide deeper understanding and context, to point you to more information regarding tools that you can strengthen further over time.

CHAPTER ONE

YOUR HAPPINESS TOOLKIT

What It Is, How to Build It, and Why

1–1 What Is *Your* Happiness Toolkit?

The purpose of this book is to teach you how to build *Your* Happiness Toolkit. This is a do-it-yourself resource that is entirely unique to you—an absolutely portable, completely customized toolkit of practical strategies you can use to overcome depression and build a happy, fulfilling life—no matter what challenges you face.

While others can advise you in selecting your particular set of tools, and perhaps help you learn how to more effectively use them—ultimately, the responsibility for building and using *Your Happiness Toolkit* rests entirely with you. This puts you in a position of significant power and control within your own life. It also enables you to affect other lives in powerful positive ways—whether within your own family, or beyond.

Your Happiness Toolkit is a completely portable resource that you can literally take with you everywhere you go, into any circumstance you might face, at any time throughout your life. It is a dependable resource that is always available to you—even in the middle of an unexpected storm, a death in the family, or any other difficult circumstance you might encounter, now or in the future. It increases your resilience, expands your self-confidence, and strengthens your capacity for joy—whether in good times, or in challenging times.

It is a resource that—because you select and build it yourself—is absolutely custom-fit to you personally. It begins with positive strategies that you may have used previously in your life, in times of prior struggle or challenge. It builds on your existing strengths—and then, a layer at a time, adds new skills and capacities.

1–2 How to Build *Your* Happiness Toolkit

Nobody comes into this world with a fully stocked Happiness Toolkit. All of us arrive here as vulnerable, dependent little creatures—unable to feed ourselves, comfort ourselves, or move ourselves around. It is only over the process of time that we learn how to hold up our own little heads, walk on our own little feet, meet our own needs, and soothe our own distresses.

As human beings, we are designed with the lifelong capacity to grow, learn, and change. We draw on that natural capacity, from our earliest days as tiny infants, to our final days as aging adults. We each acquire new insights and skills—a little at a time, over the process of time. Our brains are constantly engaged throughout our lifetimes in the process of neuroplasticity—building new pathways of understanding and capacity, new cellular and neurological structures to support positive new growth.

This is not a process that ends in childhood—or even in adolescence. Literally until the day we die, our brains are capable of learning, changing, and growing. So, it is never too late to "teach an old dog new tricks." Nor is it ever too early to teach a young child practical skills for building and maintaining happiness throughout life.

"A little at a time, over the process of time." It is in this way that you will build *Your* Happiness Toolkit. In fact, happily, it is in this way that you have already built some of the most important elements of your lifetime capacity for happiness—though you may not be aware of it currently.

As you will learn in this book, from the time that you were born—perhaps even before you were born—you were pre-designed and pre-equipped with tools and abilities that can help you to *become* happy and to *stay* happy, no matter what. We will review what some of those tools of happiness are, tools that you already know how to use—though you may have forgotten their existence, or put them aside for a time.

We will also be discussing other happiness tools that you have most likely already learned, in the natural process of growing up. We will identify those tools, dust them off a bit, and expand upon them—building on strengths you've already acquired, and adding to capacities you've already developed—but perhaps never before glimpsed the full power of.

We'll also explore various factors in modern life that may have diverted you away from happiness skills you had once developed. We'll discuss why depression and suicidality are growing so fast in our time—and what *you* can do to stem the tide of depression—in yourself, or in those you care for.

You'll also undergo training in using powerful new happiness tools that you have perhaps *never* heard of before. These new resources will most likely take more time, energy, and effort for you to acquire and master, since you are likely less familiar with them. But, like a complex drill-bit set, or an innovative new power tool, these more complex tools can be amazingly effective—once you know what they are and how to use them. As you begin your acquaintance with these new tools, you can actively remember and make use of those more familiar tools that you have had available since early childhood.

Remember—"a little at a time, over the process of time." In this way, one step at a time, you'll be adding tools—old and new—to *Your* Happiness Toolkit. You'll be doing this mindfully—proactively—incrementally—*gradually*.

So, don't be discouraged if it doesn't happen all at once, if some of the tools seem too challenging to master, or if other people seem further along in the process than you seem to be. This isn't a race, and it isn't a competition. *You start from where you are, and then build from there.* That's how anything of value gets created. And it's how you'll build *Your* Happiness Toolkit —"a little at a time, over the process of time."

1–3 Why *You* Should Build *Your* Happiness Toolkit (The Four "Whys")

There are at least four reasons why *you* should build *Your* Happiness Toolkit—starting today:

1. Because you—and only you—can build it.

2. Because it is more and more needed, in the world we currently live in.

3. Because a happy life is a much more rewarding, satisfying, and productive life.

4. Because your level of happiness greatly impacts those around you (positively or negatively).

Now, let's explore each of these four reasons—these Four "Whys"—in turn:

Why #1: Why You—And Only You—Can Build Your Happiness Toolkit

You, like every other human being on earth, are an absolutely unique, exquisitely distinct individual. No one else has your specific DNA, your life history, your exact personality, your hopes and dreams, your strengths and weaknesses, your sufferings and triumphs—your past, present, or future. You are the only one of you that there ever has been, or that there ever will be.

As a result, your depression and your happiness are also exquisitely unique and personal—and can only be fully understood and fully addressed by *you*. Though others can advise, assist, and support you in your quest, ultimately *you* are the only human being that can truly and entirely get into your own head, and heal your own life, from the inside out. This book will teach you how to do just that.

Why #2: Why *Your* Happiness Toolkit Is More and More Needed, in the World We Currently Live In

A quick scan of the daily headlines is enough to show that the world seems to be getting more and more challenging and undependable—environmentally, politically, sociologically, and personally. Natural disasters of numerous varieties are becoming ever more fierce and commonplace, as environmental pressures strain and drain our embattled planet. Conflicts between nations and political infighting within governments are becoming ever more chronic—and ever more ugly. Traditional connections within families, communities, businesses, and places of worship are eroding—or even shattering—at an unprecedented pace.

In the face of these and other challenges, we may find ourselves feeling overwhelmed, depressed, anxious, and ill-equipped to deal with it all. While understandable, these common reactions ultimately only add to our general distress, and escalate the very problems they are triggered by. In times when everything around us might feel increasingly uncertain, it is ever more important that we have a consistent internal resource that can sustain us through whatever challenge we might face, now or in the future.

A single lit candle can cast light across an entire room. A single bright star in the night sky can be a powerful source of needed hope and steady direction. When we learn to develop internal strength and resilience, when we have a steady resource for building and maintaining happiness that goes with us wherever we go, we can be a significant force for good—first in our own lives, and then in the lives of those around us.

Why #3: Why a Happy Life Is More Rewarding, Satisfying, and Productive

Happiness is a state of being that we universally aspire to. In our personal lives, workplaces, family relationships, and communities, we are most energetic, most resilient, most connected, and most productive when we are *happy*. Unhappiness, in contrast, drains our energy, reduces our effectiveness, strains our relationships, and vastly decreases our productivity—whether at home, at work, or elsewhere.

Learning how to be happy, therefore, is perhaps the single most important life skill we can acquire, and that we can extend to our children and to our loved ones. It is not an automatic state of being—particularly in our twenty-first-century world, where happiness is becoming increasingly counter-cultural. Learning to be happy is learning to be part of the solution, rather than part of the problem. It is a state that must be chosen, a path that must be consistently and consciously selected—not just once, but often—even *daily*.

Learning to choose happiness means—learning to make choices that lead to happy consequences. Throughout this book, we will be exploring various factors that will help you learn how to do that—day by day, and year by year, throughout your lifetime.

Why #4: Why Your Level of Happiness Impacts Those Around You (Positively or Negatively)

Depression is notoriously contagious. It has a draining, discouraging impact—not just on the sufferer, but on those around them as well. Knowing this, some depressed people are tragically tempted to end their own lives—hoping it will end their personal misery, and also believing, *"Everyone will be better off without me."*

Sadly, nothing could be further from the truth. That desperate act of self-elimination tends to fuel more pain and lasting agony in survivors than almost any other human behavior. The answer is not to end *life*. The answer is to end *unhappiness*—and to replace it, actively and intentionally, with something far better.

Psychologist Michael Yapko, in his insightful book *Depression Is Contagious*, notes that it is often assumed that depression is passed down genetically, without our choice or consent; and that automatic transmission of our "bad genes" is something that we can't prevent or control. Certainly research and observation have confirmed that when one family member struggles emotionally, it is more difficult for other family members to resist the negative pull of depression and other emotional challenges.

But, Dr. Yapko also points to new research indicating that it is not just loved ones sharing DNA with the sufferer who might be affected. Individuals with no genetic connection whatsoever—like roommates, coworkers, or fellow students—can be "contaminated" with the impact of someone else's depression, just as easily as a family member can. Depression *is*, in fact, contagious, he writes— whether there is a genetic connection, or not. Depressive thinking, communication, behavior, and relationship patterns can have a profoundly contagious effect on others—with or without shared DNA.

But—happily—it works the other way around too. ***Happiness can also be contagious.*** So, one of the most powerful and important "why's" for building *Your* Happiness Toolkit is this—to help clear the path for your loved ones and others around you to be able to avoid depression, and find happiness themselves.

1–4 People-Pleasing, Perfectionism, and "Productivity"

Let's face it. Depressed people are often tender, sensitive souls— people-pleasers, who often put the needs of others over their own needs. For those deeply caring people, it can sometimes be challenging to justify time spent doing *anything* for themselves. If you are like that, it might feel hard at times to justify the time, effort, and attention it may take to build and maintain *Your* Happiness Toolkit.

Ultimately, however, *you can only give what you have to give*. You cannot share what you do not possess. You cannot truly help others

24

be happy, if you are constantly miserable or depleted yourself. And, strange but true—one of the best ways to promote happiness in those around you is to become and remain happy yourself. So, far from being a selfish act, strengthening *Your* Happiness Toolkit is actually one of the most courageous and powerful things you can do to directly benefit your loved ones and those around you.

On the other hand, some depressed people are highly driven, ambitious, and perfectionistic. These individuals tend to keep themselves busy every second of every day being "productive"—making money or producing other visible results to benefit themselves, their employers, and their families. In this hard-pressed, high-demand, over-crammed schedule, finding time to nourish and sustain themselves can seem next to impossible—and certainly not on the top rung of priority for these driven, perfectionistic individuals.

However, experience has shown that people on this full-tilt schedule of "productivity" will inevitably crash—emotionally, and perhaps also physically—if they continue to neglect their own basic needs. Wise businesses, schools, nations, families, and individuals have, therefore, learned to allocate some regular recovery time for rejuvenation, recreation, and renewal.

Bestselling author Steven R. Covey has masterfully described that reality in his classic book, *The 7 Habits of Highly Effective People*. His research revealed that the most effective and successful people are not those who push themselves and others 24–7 to be "productive." In contrast, Covey found that the "highly effective people" he studied universally engaged in a consistent habit he described as "saw sharpening." Basically, this means—engaging intentionally and consistently in behaviors intended to provide continuous renewal—mentally, physically, spiritually, and socially. To *not* do so, Covey found, produces *ineffectiveness*—as is the case with a saw that never gets sharpened, or a car that never gets an oil change.

Far too often in our busy, pressurized world, we fail to allow this needed time for refreshment and refueling. This, in fact, is one of the most common patterns today that fuels widespread emotional dysfunction in both young and old. Commonly referred to as *"depletion depression,"* this means pushing ourselves long past the time when we've run out of steam—continuing to work when we have nothing left to give to the work. It is a powerful and pervasive form of self-neglect and self-abuse. And it ends up hurting not just those who do it to themselves, but also to those who must absorb the impact when the inevitable crash occurs—resulting from a body and brain that have been pushed too hard, for too long, with too little recovery time.

So, ironically, one of the best things you can do for your boss and coworkers, as well as for your family and loved ones, is to take good care of yourself. This book will teach you how, step by step, and day by day, as you go forth to build and strengthen *Your Happiness Toolkit*.

1–5 Transformational Tool #1: *The Wellness Grid*

As we conclude each chapter in Section I, you will be introduced to a new Transformational Tool that you can begin using immediately, to strengthen your happiness and wellness. The first of these starter tools is called the Wellness Grid. This is a simple tool that allows you to start where you already are, and to begin recovery with what you're already familiar with.

Here's how it works. On a blank piece of paper, first create four boxes of roughly equal size, by making a vertical line down the center of your paper, and then adding a horizontal line across the middle, like this:

Now, within each of those four boxes, add a title, reflecting one of the four basic areas of life:

MENTAL	PHYSICAL
SPIRITUAL	SOCIAL

Next, under each of those four titles, list actions you know could strengthen you in that particular area of life—drawing on what you already have had some experience with. For example:

MENTAL	PHYSICAL
Read a book Listen to a TED Talk Do a puzzle	Eat more fresh vegetables Exercise 15–30 minutes Declutter a room
SPIRITUAL	SOCIAL
Take a walk in nature Attend a church service Read inspiring literature	Call a friend Do something kind Help a family member

Then every day, starting today, make it a point to do at least one or two things listed on your Wellness Grid. You might want to start small, with the items requiring the least effort. Or, you may prefer to tackle first the items that bother you the most.

This one simple strategy has significant power to help keep you happy and well, if you're already in good shape emotionally. And it has remarkable power to begin turning the tide of depression in those who currently struggle. So start with this tool, applying it every day. And then, build upward from there.

CHAPTER TWO

OVERCOMING DEPRESSION:

*What Helps, What Doesn't, and
How to Choose a Healing Course*

➤ **2–1** Overcoming Depression with Positive Action

➤ **2–2** How You *Think* About Depression
Impacts Its Course Over Time

➤ **2–3** Choose an Individualized Approach,
Not a Standardized Approach

➤ **2–4** Pursue Healing from the Inside
Out, Not Just "Treatment"

➤ **2–5** Avoid These Five Ineffective Strategies
for Dealing with Depression

➤ **2–6** Transformational Tool #2: *The Up-or-Down Spiral*

2–1 Overcoming Depression with Positive Action

I'll never forget her—the beautiful young woman who stepped into my office decades ago for her very first counseling appointment. Tears fell softly from her expressive eyes, slipping slowly down her perfectly chiseled cheekbones, as she spoke, "I've gone through some hard things lately. Not … terrible things, but … hard for me. Hard enough that it's really bringing me down. And I'm scared. I've watched my mom struggle my whole life with her depression. I've tried so hard to be understanding and supportive. But the truth is, it's been really hard to spend so many years with her crying alone behind a locked door, or frozen and unresponsive on the couch in front of a TV screen, unable to care for us kids. I've seen her fatigue, her self-doubt, her inability to really do anything she loves. I've seen firsthand what depression is, and what it does to people—even really *good* people.

"And now, I'm starting to see some of those same things in myself. And that really scares me. I'm so worried that I might have those same tendencies—that same DNA—that's made my mom so sick for so many years. Truth is, **I'd rather have cancer than this devastating brain disease.**"

As she spoke, I saw the fear in those big, beautiful eyes. She was young and talented, smart and vibrant, with her whole life ahead of her. But that specter of fear shadowed the vision she had for her future. Her current struggle—a rather normal but disappointing life experience—had understandably left her a little sad, shaken, and disillusioned. But she worried that it was far more than that—evidence of "a devastating brain disease." She worried that she was "broken," just like her mom—that she would never really be happy, that her life was doomed before it ever really even started.

But she *wasn't* doomed, and she wasn't broken. Although she had both the genetic tendency and the negative family history that could have taken root and become a "devastating brain disease"—instead, she learned to take positive, proactive, preventive action to effectively weather her current challenge, and then build the foundation for a happy and fulfilling life.

She didn't stay long in counseling. She didn't need to. She learned what she needed to learn, did what she needed to do, and then moved on—armed and prepared to take on life's future challenges with confidence, capacity, and hope.

Over my thirty-plus years as a counselor, I have worked with hundreds of individuals with similar stories—people that come through the door worried that their struggles are chronic, that their brains are broken, and that their futures are doomed. And over and over again, I see the **unfolding miracle of hope and recovery,** as people first *learn* and then *apply* the principles and practices that build emotional wellness, solid resilience, and lasting joy.

Now, it's *your* turn. You may or may not ever step into my office— or into *any* counselor's office. But whether or not you choose to get professional help, this book can assist you in understanding your particular challenge, launching your particular recovery, and building your particular life of happiness and fulfillment.

You might be like the woman in my office that day—just weathering a short-term struggle, and needing a little direction and encouragement. Or, you might be more like her mom, with a more serious mental health challenge that you've already battled for years. Either way, know that help is available, recovery is possible, and this book can help you find your way to a more fulfilling life—for you personally.

2–2   How You *Think* About Depression Impacts Its Course Over Time

You may have tried to get help for depression before—for yourself or for a loved one. Some of those attempts may not have gone particularly well. Some may even have left you feeling worse—discouraged, reluctant, or scared to try anything else.

But don't give up. **Some approaches are far more effective than others.** So, let's talk about the difference between approaches that promote real and lasting recovery, as opposed to those that may not produce much improvement—or that may even make an existing problem worse, or more chronic.

First and foremost, as the opening story illustrates—the way we *interpret* the symptoms of depression will powerfully impact the outcome of treatment. If we're not careful, we can easily become "depressed about depression" or "anxious about anxiety." We might be tempted to believe the well-funded voices and airbrushed perfection of television ads, full-color pamphlets, and other highly polished advertising materials trumpeting the theory of *"chemical imbalance"* supposedly being the "cause" of depression. You should know that many other explanations and treatment protocols exist—and that these are *far* more effective at producing actual long-term hope, relief, and change. We'll be exploring these other approaches later in this book.

Make no mistake about it: that widespread, heavily marketed "chemical imbalance" theory never had any solid science behind it. But it *did* have a lot of advertising dollars behind it. Many well-researched, insightful books released in recent years reveal the many holes in this well-advertised but ultimately groundless and depressing theory. You can find a listing of those books in the Bibliography section of this book.

For now, in practical terms—if you *believe* that your emotional upsets are evidence of a permanent, disabling brain disease, then you will be far less likely to engage in the necessary actions that can actually help you *heal*. That depressing belief may leave you feeling doomed, discouraged, and defeated—drowning in hopelessness before even *beginning* your healing journey. Such hopelessness is tragically unnecessary—for recovery is truly within your reach—*IF* you learn and implement those strategies known to foster emotional wellness.

The idea that your moods are pre-programmed by your genes or your biochemistry—that there is nothing you can do for it except consume a pharmaceutical product to dull the ache of emotional pain—is a rather bleak and hopeless perspective—one that some authors have described as **"biological determinism."** That destructive belief system, in my experience, *impedes* recovery, rather than promoting it. It tends to keep people stuck *in* their distress, rather than extending a hopeful path forward *out* of their distress.

Happily, however—if you choose, instead, to interpret your symptoms as a valuable warning signal, a needed nudge toward positive change, a crucial call to reparative action—then your symptoms can work *for* you, rather than *against* you. They can provide a helpful barometer of your progress over time, as you learn new skills for dealing with the various conditions and challenges in your life. ***It is this more hopeful view that forms the*** *basis of this book—the belief that as human beings, we have the inborn capacity to truly heal, from the inside out—IF we engage in the actions known to promote and strengthen that healing process.*

A number of years ago, after going through a significantly heartbreaking experience, I fell into a deep emotional black hole that seemed endless, and utterly inescapable. After suffering deeply for several months, I awakened one November morning from a dream that ended with the words, **"Carrie—redesign your life!"**

I didn't know what it meant, or where to even start. But that morning as I rose to my feet to begin the day and looked into my closet for something to wear, I realized that my entire wardrobe at that time was either black, gray, or dark navy blue—reflecting my somber mood, but entirely unhelpful in improving it.

So I drove to the local thrift store with those words *"Redesign your life!"* inscribed on my soul. I was a young mom at the time, and money was tight. But, for a bargain price, I was able to bring home several brightly colored sweaters, bringing warmth and cheer to that cold winter season. I ended up wearing a bright yellow sweater that particular day, a soft pink one the day after that, and a bold red one the day following. The bright colors of those bargain sweaters gave me a much-needed emotional lift, and helped bring a more positive, vibrant energy to my home and to my children—as well as to myself.

Who would have thought that so simple and practical an action as wearing a few colorful sweaters could be the beginning of my recovery from that heartbreaking time? But that simple "redesign" laid the foundation for the next positive change, then the next, and then the one after that.

I see the same thing in my clients every day, as they work to overcome their individual challenges. It is not always the big, well-researched, complex treatment approach that produces the most significant changes. Often it is the simple, unique, and practical things, customized to the needs and preferences of each individual—which brings us to our next point.

2–3 Choose an Individualized Approach, Not a Standardized Approach

Over my years as a counselor, I have worked with many people struggling with various levels of depression, from very mild to very severe. I have found it is crucial to recognize that not all depressions are the same. In fact, they are all exquisitely unique, reflecting each person's individual experience. They can vary in intensity, duration, causal factors, and symptom patterns. They may appear as stand-alone afflictions—or, more commonly, they appear together with other troubling conditions such as *anxiety, self-doubt, grief, addiction, anger, relationship challenges, post-traumatic stress, financial concerns, or physical disease.*

There is no "one-size-fits-all" version of depression. So, of course, there is no "one-size-fits-all" treatment plan that works the same for everyone. In fact, even within the same individual, different depressive episodes can vary significantly—and may, therefore, require different strategies and styles of response to be effective.

Moreover, while becoming depression-free is a worthy and desirable goal, those who achieve it often find that, in and of itself, it falls short of bringing them into the full and happy life they had hoped for. This is because achieving happiness is an entirely different level of human experience. And like depression recovery, it is exquisitely and inescapably unique to each individual. There is no such thing as a happiness pill or a happiness formula that will work perfectly for everyone across the board. Your experience of happiness is unique to *you*. You might share *some* elements in common with other people, but some of the most important elements of *your* enduring happiness will be unique to you alone.

So, a standardized, prefabricated approach to overcoming depression (and pursuing happiness) is unlikely to produce the best result, especially in the long-term. To be effective, treatment must be specifically customized to the individual. Of course, this is unlikely to occur within the standard six-minute interview in a busy doctor's office, following a quick standardized self-test. What *does* work is—a highly individualized assessment and recovery program. This book provides a rich variety of tools to get you started.

2–4   Pursue Healing from the Inside Out, Not Just "Treatment"

Hippocrates, the father of Western medicine, taught that *the human body possesses the innate ability to heal itself, from the inside out.* He taught the physicians of his time that their essential task was to remove obstacles to that healing process—and then, to help set recovery in motion from *within* their patients.

At different points in my life, I have been the grateful recipient of this kind of wise and effective medical care. For example, a few years ago when I got myself much too busy and quite rundown during the Christmas season, I ended up getting very sick, desperately fatigued, and constantly coughing up mucus. My doctor provided resources I could not provide for myself. He carefully listened to my heart and lungs, ordered an X-ray, and made the official diagnosis of pneumonia. He gave me a two-week prescription of antibiotics to help eliminate the infection and set my recovery process in motion.

Thankfully, however, that's not *all* that he did: *he took the time to instruct me as to what I needed to do on a daily basis to facilitate my own recovery.* It wasn't just a matter of taking the prescribed pills. He taught me that I needed to give my body plenty of rest, cleansing fluids, and optimal nutrition—as necessary ingredients for my body to be able to heal itself, from the inside out. He told me that after two weeks on the antibiotic, I should then resume a light exercise program and, thereby, recover my strength and vitality over time.

He warned that I probably would not get my full strength back for several months, and advised me to scale back my commitments and expectations accordingly, to provide the time needed for full healing and recovery. This was *not* welcome news, because at that time I found a significant sense of fulfillment and self-worth from being over-scheduled in too many "positive" directions. But he helped me to see that this lifetime pattern of overwhelming myself was *exactly* what had set me up for sickness in the first place, weakening my immune system, and making me vulnerable for a bacterial takeover. Wisely, he taught me to readjust my lifestyle and thinking, in order to heal my current illness, and prevent similar ailments in the future.

As predicted, it took nearly six months to fully recover my normal strength and vitality. But those long months gave me plenty of time to think about the importance of caring for my body—which had really never been a priority for me before. This illness taught me that my physical body is my most essential instrument, through which I do *everything* else in life. If I neglect or abuse my body, not providing for its basic needs, or pushing it beyond its natural limits, the results of that poor self-management will negatively impact *all* of my other tasks and responsibilities—at work, at home, and in my community.

Now, more than ten years later, as a result of that effective treatment process, I remain fully recovered from that pneumonia, and enjoy better overall physical and mental health. Caring diligently for my own health has made it possible to reach out and care for others, far more consistently and effectively than ever before. I am grateful that this wise doctor did not just hand out a quick prescription, and send me out the door, but that he took the time necessary to help me learn how to care for my body. Now, I rarely have to return to the doctor, because I've learned to consistently provide what my body needs to stay well.

The same principle holds true for depression—and for most other afflictions, both emotional and physical.

People heal most completely—and most permanently—if they are taught how to care for themselves *from the inside out*, to promote genuine healing, and to establish and maintain long-term wellness.

Full healing and recovery consists of four basic stages:

1. **Assessment and Diagnosis**: naming and identifying the affliction in a clear way;

2. **Treatment and Intervention**: finding help to soothe symptoms and provide relief;

3. **Recovery and Rehabilitation**: giving the body what it needs to gradually heal itself; and

4. **Wellness and Relapse Prevention**: caring for the body, over time, to maintain vibrant health.

An effective treatment approach takes you all the way through all four of these stages of healing. So it was with my pneumonia treatment. That wise doctor's approach laid the groundwork for *complete* recovery from that illness—and *complete* prevention of its recurrence. Effective treatment of depression or other ailments follows a similar course, progressing through all four stages, resulting in full and lasting recovery.

However, not all treatment protocols produce this happy and lasting result. Some are more focused on simply providing continuous ongoing "treatment" from the outside, without ever progressing to the Recovery or Wellness stages. Certainly, this is a more profitable approach, as it requires more office visits, long-term prescription plans—and sometimes, more invasive and expensive treatment procedures. However, it is significantly less satisfying for individuals seeking lasting recovery and wellness.

2–5 Avoid These Five Ineffective Strategies for Dealing with Depression

Over the years, I have observed three common forms of treatment that are particularly likely to keep people stuck in a depressive condition, rather than moving effectively through it:

1. **Medication-Only Management**
2. **Assessment-Only Therapy**
3. **Misguided Spirituality**

In addition to these three ineffective treatment approaches, there are two additional responses to depression that should be carefully guarded against. These are even more ineffective and dangerous than the first three, and will inevitably result in the maintenance, or worsening, of the original problem. These are:

1. **Passively Waiting—And Hoping It Goes Away by Itself**
2. **Self-Medicating—To Distract Yourself from the Pain**

Let's discuss each of these in turn:

Ineffective Strategy #1: Medication-Only Management

This has become one of the most widely practiced of treatment strategies—even though research dating from the 1970s revealed that it was the approach most likely to increase depressive relapse over time. The goal of this treatment strategy is to chemically "control" or "manage" symptoms of depression, such as fatigue, low mood, and sleep problems.

The appeal of this approach is that **it appears quick and easy for both the provider and for the patient.** It requires only a minimum amount of time to conduct a quick symptom checklist, and then pull out the prescription pad. Most often, however, *this prescription is not accompanied by information about healing the root causes of the observed symptoms.* Like a Band-Aid or a crutch, it does not actually heal the identified affliction; it simply covers or manages some of the observable symptoms.

About a third of medicated patients do, in fact, report a reduction of distressing symptoms from this approach. However, about a third of the patients get even *worse* symptoms on the medication, and the remaining third notice basically no impact whatsoever, except perhaps side effects—or withdrawal effects, if they decide to discontinue the medication.

But even for those who *do* experience some relief, the psychiatric drugs never really correct (or even help to identify) the underlying pains, habits, conditions, and causes generating and maintaining the depression itself. In addition, if a medication that provides relief is ever discontinued or interrupted, the person's distress recurs—and may markedly increase. Also, the cost of ongoing doctor visits and prescription expenses, as well as dealing with medication side effects, together with the risk of treatment unavailability in the case of natural or human-caused disaster, makes medication-only management inadvisable as an exclusive strategy over the long term.

I generally advise clients as follows: **If you're not already taking psychiatric medication, *don't start*—**there are many effective approaches that can be implemented, and avoiding medication can prevent what might become a potentially difficult withdrawal later. **But, if you are already taking psychiatric medication, for the time being** *do not interrupt it.* Keep your dosage stable, as prescribed, until you have built a solid foundation of other treatment strategies to more permanently and independently manage your moods. Then, under proper medical supervision, you can gradually withdraw from the medications.

If you *do* choose to include medication as part of your treatment, I recommend following the wise advice of psychiatrist Joanna Moncrieff MD, author of *The Myth of the Chemical Cure.* Dr. Moncrieff observes that while medications can ease psychological symptoms in some individuals, they should not interpret these changes as "fixing" a "chemical imbalance." Rather, medications, when used, should only be used short-term (six to eighteen months) to relieve symptoms, while more permanent recovery strategies are applied. Then, gradual medication withdrawal should be undertaken, while continuing to build, over time, on the more sustainable approaches to establish strength, wellness, and resilience—from the inside out.

Ineffective Strategy #2: Assessment-Only Therapy

This is basically a "problem-focused" counseling approach, which typically continually asks *"And what else happened? And then what else happened?"*—encouraging clients to reveal more and more (and focus on) their troubles, past and present, without providing any clear solutions or guidance about how to actually *correct* these conditions. This approach may occur in various forms, including:

Psychoanalysis—wherein the client mostly explores past conditions leading to their present distress. The goal of such counseling is "insight"—and certainly, some insight into past events is needful and helpful. But when past distress is the *primary* focus, often clients come away feeling even more broken, doomed, and discouraged than before. Many new counseling clients tell me, "I swore I'd never go back to therapy, because it just left me feeling even more depressed. I learned to identify all the elements of my family dysfunction, my parents' mistakes, my victimization experiences, and all the other hurts and wounding circumstances throughout my life. So now I can tell you all the things that are *wrong* with me, and with my family, and my life experience. But I have not yet learned any strategies to help me actually deal with *any* of it."

Supportive Counseling—In this approach, clients come in every week and give a running account of their day-to-day hurts and challenges. Counselors are generally kind and supportive, with good listening skills—which can provide some immediate comfort and relief. But again, clients often come away from this type of counseling feeling even more broken—because they focus on the negatives in their lives, without learning any new coping skills to actually resolve or correct the identified challenges.

Support Groups—where the focus is on group members sharing their traumas and negative experiences. Clients often tell me about these groups, "*Now I'm not just upset by my own traumas, but also by the horrific stories shared by other group members!*" Again, while there is some benefit in clients feeling listened to and not having to endure their troubles alone, this approach can overemphasize a focus on *problems* rather than solutions—thus intensifying the negative emotional charge of the events discussed.

Ineffective Strategy #3: Misguided Spirituality

This is an approach that may sometimes be pursued by religious clients. It is the belief that they will only recover if God personally extends His miraculous power to heal them. So they wait for that, they pray for that, they plead for that: *"God, I'm now ready for you to take this burden away from me. OK, I'm ready! Ready, set, go!"* But most of the time, they plead and pray and wait in vain. Their "thorn in their flesh" remains with them; their depression remains unchanged.

Sadly, the longer they pray without relief, the more they may come to doubt themselves and their faith—and to doubt God's willingness to help them at all. This adds even more "fuel to the fire" of their depression, and to their sense of personal worthlessness. It deepens the feeling of futility that so often accompanies serious depression. *"See—even God doesn't want to help me!"*

To be clear, I believe the following:

+ **Appropriate spirituality** can play a massively powerful role in the healing process.

+ **Short-term use of medication** for those disabled by their symptoms can be a helpful *temporary* aid.

+ **Compassion, support, and insight** play a powerful role in the healing process.

But here is what ultimately makes all three of these "ineffective approaches" ineffective. All three involve sufferers putting their major hope and trust in someone or something *outside* of themselves—and in the process, **neglecting to carry out the daily actions that can promote their actual recovery and healing.** Likewise, all three approaches can foster a sense of dependency and neediness, rather than a sense of independence and strength. These approaches tend to focus on brokenness and disability—rather than on building a proactive course of positive, powerful *action* to promote ongoing recovery, from the inside out.

Ineffective Strategy #4: Passively Waiting—And Hoping It Goes Away by Itself

In this approach, people bury themselves in some other focus—activity, work, media—and just wait and hope the condition will go away by itself. Rarely, however, does this approach work. Once the factors generating depression are in place, those conditions tend to escalate and intensify over time. Depression is usually at the root of self-destructive or suicidal behavior—as well as other antisocial or destructive behaviors that cause damage to others. Untreated depression causes untold suffering, both in the depressed individuals, and in those around them. Even the three ineffective treatment strategies mentioned earlier are preferable to this one—because the first three at least build in some support and connection with a helper. But many people all over the world end up choosing this fourth "wait it out" approach—often by default, in the absence of available treatment resources.

Please don't let yourself believe that if you ignore or hide from the problem long enough, that it will somehow, someday, just automatically disappear. If you don't currently have access to treatment resources, then read helpful books like this one—books that can guide you towards knowing how to help yourself and others. ***Knowing what feeds depression, versus what fights it, is the beginning of effective healing and recovery.*** Remember, knowledge is power—and it builds strength and confidence that can greatly contribute to your healing process.

In fact, even if you *do* have access to treatment, you should use these resources to expedite your recovery. Take responsibility to be a partner in your own healing process. Educate yourself by reading self-help books to heal as much as possible *between* your scheduled therapy sessions, so you can experience relief even more quickly and fully. Either way, *do not make the mistake of ignoring the problem!* There are so many simple and powerful things you can do, starting today, to promote your own healing process.

Ineffective Strategy #5: Self-Medicating, To Distract Yourself from the Pain

This approach is perhaps the most ineffective and dangerous of all. It may occur in many forms. Depression sufferers may distract themselves from their emotional pain through illicit drugs, prescription medications, alcohol, sugar, junk food, risk-taking behavior, self-injury, compulsive shopping, gambling, pornography, or (most common in today's world) obsessively disappearing mentally into some media device, like television, video games, Facebook, Netflix binges, etc. Any of these addictive behaviors can only mask pain, and create additional challenges for yourself and others.

Remember: distraction is not healing! Rather, distraction impedes healing, and tends to intensify the very pain that drives you to your particular distraction. Real healing requires awareness, time, and courage. Do not let yourself be drawn into addictive and destructive escape strategies. They can only lead to additional harm and additional pain—which gets in the way of actual, permanent relief.

In vivid contrast to these five ineffective strategies, there are many positive things you can do (starting *today*) to powerfully conquer depression, and to expand happiness in your life, and in the lives of those around you. You will learn about these over the course of this book.

2–6 Transformational Tool #2: Up-or-Down Spiral

You may find it helpful to assess your current emotional condition on this quick rating scale:

-3	-2	-1	0	1	2	3
Severely Depressed	Moderately Depressed	Mildly Depressed	Neither Happy or depressed	Mildly Happy	Moderately Happy	Extremely Happy

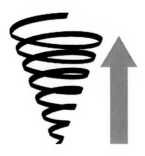

However, your emotional condition does not constantly remain the same. From day to day, hour to hour, and year to year—it tends to fluctuate, much like a barometer - either upward or downward. It can be useful to periodically ask

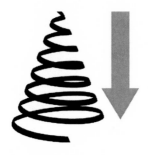

yourself *"What is the direction of my spiral today? Am I on an upward spiral, moving upwards toward more happiness, wellness, and resilience? Or am I on a downward emotional spiral currently, that I need to turn around?"*

The goal, of course, is to be moving consistently in an upward, positive direction. But if you find yourself in a downward spiral at times, ask yourself, ***"What can I do today to start reversing the direction of this spiral?"***

Then, choose a positive activity on your Wellness Grid (Transformational Tool #1) that you find enjoyable or fulfilling, and set it in motion today—even if it's just in a small, unspectacular way.

As you identify and implement positive action, using one or more of these tools, this will help turn the direction of your spiral upward—with one positive factor leading to the next, and to the next, over the process of time. *Small changes lay the groundwork for bigger changes.* Small successes precede bigger successes. So, be patient with yourself as you carry out these changes. You're not going to change the whole pattern at once.

In the remaining sections of this book, you'll be learning more and more skills you can apply to this positive transformation process, thus giving yourself more and more tools you can apply to quickly and powerfully "change the direction of your spiral," even on hard days—adding more power and effectiveness to *Your* Happiness Toolkit.

UNIQUE TO YOU

*Understanding **Your** Depression and **Your** Happiness Toolkit*

➤ **3–1** Integrative Wellness Training, Rather Than Just Symptom Management

➤ **3–2** The Diamond: An Integrative Tool for Individualized Assessment

➤ **3–3** Using the Diamond to Plan *Your* Recovery Strategy (IRA Sequence)

➤ **3–4** From Depression to Happiness— Why Every Recovery Is Unique

➤ **3–5** Transformational Tool #3: *The Diamond*

3–1 Integrative Wellness Training, Rather Than Just Symptom Management

Moving from depression to happiness is a lot like establishing a backyard garden. First, you face and remove the weeds, rocks, tall grass, litter, and other unwanted materials that have been taking up space there. Then, once the ground is clear, you nourish the soil, so that it contains the nutrients necessary to sustain rich new growth. You decide what you want to plant in your newly enriched soil, and then after planting, you continue to water, nourish, and protect your seedlings, so they can continue to grow and flourish over time. Real emotional healing occurs in exactly the same way—*you must first identify and remove the negatives; then you move forward, focusing on and strengthening the positives.*

Over the past thirty years as a counselor, I have learned that people progress most effectively when the focus of their treatment is directed on what they wish to *create*—rather than simply on what they wish to *stop*. If the target of treatment is just to reduce symptoms of a predefined disorder, it's a lot like pulling weeds—but then not moving on to plant an actual garden. The results of such an approach tend to be unsatisfying and incomplete, similar to the ineffective approaches identified in the prior chapter.

A more productive approach is to first identify factors causing distress—which tend to be very specific to the individual—and then to replace those factors with customized elements that produce better results. I call this approach *"Integrative Wellness Training,"* because it draws from a wide variety of treatment strategies, in a balanced and integrated way, training individuals to create and maintain emotional wellness. That is the approach we'll be taking in this book.

3–2 The Diamond: An Integrative Tool for Individualized Assessment

Over the years, I have developed an integrative assessment tool that has proven to be useful in this process of helping people to first identify, and then replace, the factors contributing to their individual distress. Using this tool tends to generate not just powerful insight—but also, profound hope. Because once you clearly see what is *wrong*, then you can immediately go to work to correct it, and make it *right*.

I call this tool "The Diamond," because its four points represent four distinct aspects of human experience—each of which can contribute either to depression, or to happiness. I find it useful with clients to explain the four points of the Diamond, and then have them apply the model to themselves, identifying specific factors on each of the four points that may have contributed to their particular distress. We then strategize on how to replace each of those elements, on each of those four points, with positive factors that promote recovery and wellness over time. At that point, the Diamond becomes not just a helpful assessment tool—but also, a powerful and hope-generating tool for planning and facilitating actual recovery.

I will now explain each of the four points of the Diamond.

Point #1: Relationship Triggers

1. RELATIONSHIPS

Every emotional disruption I have ever encountered, in myself or in a client, began with one or more "trigger experiences," which are specific distressing events that occur, almost always, in the context of a relationship. In the beginning, I thought this insight originated with me. I later learned that this is a core tenet for a well-established and highly effective treatment strategy known as *Interpersonal Therapy* (IPT).

IPT theorizes that depression and other emotional challenges tend to be triggered by one or more of the following types of distressing relationship experiences:

1) Grief, 2) Transition, 3) Conflict, or 4) Lack of Interpersonal Skills.

Let's examine each of those trigger experiences in more detail:

1. **Grief**—This trigger occurs when we lose someone important to us—whether through death, divorce, miscarriage, moving away, graduating, or in some other way becoming separated from a loved one.

2. **Transition**—This trigger is set off when we go through a significant change in our lives. This can even be a happy, positive change we have anticipated for a long time—like a graduation, retirement, or birth of a child. But such changes, even happy ones, can produce sudden uncertainty about the future, and about our own identity, role, or purpose within our new and unfamiliar circumstances.

3. **Conflict**—This trigger can be activated either by *Inter*personal Conflict, in which we experience disagreement or tension with someone important to us; or by *Intra*personal Conflict, where we are painfully conflicted within ourselves over some significant aspect of our lives.

4. **Lack of Interpersonal Skills**—This trigger results from never having learned appropriate social skills in the first place. So, we attempt to engage in relationship after relationship, but keep encountering the same problems over and over—which leads to relationship disruption, disappointment, self-doubt, and depression.

Besides these four triggers identified by IPT researchers, I have observed three others:

5. **Abuse**—This is by far the most destructive of the triggers. It can instantly shatter a person's self-esteem, trust of others, and sense of safety—for years, even decades, after the abuse occurred. It might consist of physical, sexual, verbal, or emotional abuse—or some combination of these. It may even involve violence, trauma, or war. A victim of abuse often has multiple episodes and perpetrators, and multiple layers of abuse, suffering impact from all of these over time.

6. **Loss**—This trigger is similar to grief, but is more general in its range and impact. Whereas grief is defined as losing someone important to you, loss extends to a much broader range of life experiences. You may have lost your health, your figure, your youth, your self-respect, your job, or even your car keys. The severity of this trigger depends on the seriousness of the loss to the individual.

7. **Disappointment**—This common but painful trigger is activated when reality fails to meet with expectations. We might hope or believe something positive will happen—and then become severely disappointed when it doesn't. Again, the impact of this trigger depends on the severity of the specific disappointment to the individual involved.

Some of our trigger experiences may be very fresh and recent. Some might be older, or even buried in the distant past. At times, a more recent trigger experience of a milder nature can trigger impact from an older but more severe trigger experience. Generally, the more severe the depression, the more numerous and severe are the trigger experiences—both recent and past.

Triggers are highly individual in their variety, and in their impact. An experience that may seem relatively insignificant to one person may be entirely devastating to another. A loss or setback that one individual might experience as a mere inconvenience may feel like the end of the world to another individual, for whom the loss has a more potent meaning.

Triggers can vary even within the same individual, experiencing different depressive episodes over time. For example, perhaps someone experienced their first depressive episode in grade school, resulting from bullying or unkindness from classmates (an "Abuse" trigger.) A later episode may have occurred when that individual graduated from junior high, suddenly finding themselves at a large new high school where they felt they had no friends (a "Transition" trigger.) Other depressive episodes may have been launched still later when their significant other broke up with them (a "Grief" trigger,) or when they got in a fight with their best friend (a "Conflict" trigger;) or when marriage ended up being harder than they expected (a "Disappointment" trigger;) or when aging set in, and they lost their youth and vitality (a "Loss" trigger.) If unresolved, these various triggers tend to build on one another, expanding the overall impact over time.

I have seen over many years that identifying these trigger experiences early in the recovery process can help struggling individuals in four ways:

1. **Providing Needed Validation**—that their emotional pain is legitimate and realistic;

2. **Fostering Connection and Support**—as they come to grips with their story and share it with others;

3. **Identifying Treatment Options**—as customized solutions are sought for what specifically hurts;

4. **Building Genuine Hope**—that in facing their core pain, they can finally overcome it, and move on in peace.

Point #2: Thoughts

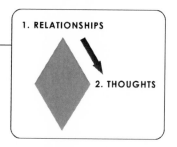

Trigger experiences happen to everyone—in some form or another, over the normal process of life. We all occasionally go through hard times, and have to endure challenging circumstances. *However*—not everyone becomes depressed or anxious after going through a difficult experience.

Ultimately, how we *think* about a given experience predicts its emotional impact, much more directly than just the nature of the experience itself. The ancient Greek philosopher Epictetus wisely observed, *"Men are disturbed not by things, but by the view they take of them."*

When stressful things happen to us, it is very natural to take a negative view of the experience—to think negatively about ourselves, others, or life in general. However, such negative thinking can vastly extend the impact of the trigger experience, and make the negative impact last much longer than the experience itself. For while the trigger event itself may come and go, our *thoughts* can stay with us for years afterward. So a negative experience might be long past—but our thoughts about it can remain intense and powerful, creating new waves of pain and impact with every new recollection of the experience.

Point #3: Behaviors

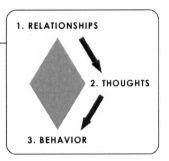

If we adopt and maintain negative beliefs about our trigger experience, this can set us up for the next level of impact. Whatever we have come to *believe* about ourselves, life, and others will become evident in our behavior. We will tend to act out the beliefs that exist within our minds—often fulfilling the very things that we most fear, in a tragic cycle of self-fulfilling prophecy.

Likewise, in our behavior, we may seek to distract ourselves from the pain of our trigger experience. But in so doing, we *decrease* the likelihood of actually solving the problem at hand; and we *increase* the likelihood of setting in motion a whole *new* batch of problems resulting from our escapist actions.

We may turn to mind-numbing substances or behaviors in a desperate effort to avoid pain. Or, we may simply resort to isolative behavior—withdrawing from other people, and from things we used to enjoy. But those behaviors always backfire, strengthening depression even further.

Point #4: Spirituality

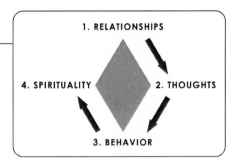

The consequences of our negative thoughts and behaviors often tend to proceed on to a new area of impact. Our spirituality—that deeply held view we have of our own value, our fundamental purpose in life, and our connection to the world and to other human beings—can become significantly disrupted, under the influence of our negative thoughts and behaviors. We may then lose hope—lose our sense of meaning or fundamental purpose of life. This can lead to a terrible sense of despair and utter futility.

Additionally, people who are religious may lose their anchoring faith in God, and find it increasingly difficult to engage in worship practices that may have previously given them a sense of comfort, hope, or purpose. Whether religious or non-religious, the spiritual impact of negative thoughts and behaviors can be significantly damaging, expanding depressive impact even further.

Point #5: Relationship Responses

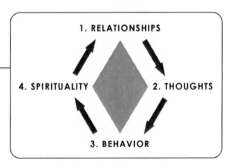

It is at that point that the circle is completed; and depressive impact rolls back around to where it began—to the realm of relationships. This time, at this point in the cycle, it is not so much about *triggers* in relationships; it is more about *responses* to relationships that occur under the influence of negative thoughts, behaviors, and spiritual impact. People in this condition tend to either avoid others, or go into a criticizing "attack mode," seeking to protect themselves from further pain. Or, they might alternate between these patterns of avoidance and attack.

Either way, this pattern is devastating to relationships, which become more fragile in the face of so much negativity. This can then set off a whole new series of relationship triggers—particularly, conflict, grief, transition, disappointment, and loss—not just for the depression sufferer, but also for others in their relationships.

I believe that this cyclic pattern is the real reason for "depression contagion"—within families, and beyond. The negative thoughts, behaviors, spiritual impact, and relationship disruption that accompany and intensify depression can significantly impact many more people than just the sufferer alone.

3–3   Using the Diamond to Plan *Your* Recovery Strategy (IRA Sequence)

Happily, this is a pattern that can be reversed and corrected— once you truly understand what's happening. As you identify the depressive triggers, you can begin applying new strategies to resolve those core issues. Once you identify the negative thoughts that have arisen, you can learn to replace them with beliefs and attitudes that work *for* you, rather than *against* you. Once you have identified behaviors, spiritual impacts, and relationship responses that escalate the problem, you can learn, little by little, to replace these with healthier, happier patterns—bringing comfort and relief into your life, and into the lives of those around you.

I call this corrective process *"The IRA Sequence."* It is composed of three basic steps:

➤ **I–dentify**
➤ **R–eplace**
➤ **A–ssimilate**

Identify—The process begins with *identifying* the factors on all four points of the Diamond that have contributed to the problem. What were the original trigger experiences (both the current triggers, and any unresolved triggers from the past) that might be expanding negative impact? What negative thoughts, behaviors, spiritual impacts, and relationship impacts may have arisen in response to the triggers?

Identifying these various factors can be a little stressful and discouraging at first. But ultimately, this process becomes profoundly liberating. Because once you know what is really wrong in your unique situation, you can then apply customized strategies to set it right.

Replace—After identifying your specific depressive factors, the work of *replacing* them begins. This doesn't happen all at once. You acquire new insights and skills one at a time, over the process of time. The tools in this book are designed to help with that step-by-step process of positive replacement.

Assimilate—Once you have acquired these new skills, you can then *assimilate* them by practicing them over time, until they eventually become the "new normal" for you—and perhaps also for those around you.

3–4   From Depression to Happiness—
Why Every Recovery Is Unique

There is no "one-size-fits-all" approach to depression that works for everyone. Now, it may be easier to understand why this is the case. Trigger experiences are unique to the individuals involved, and patterns of response are also exquisitely unique. So what brings relief to one individual in one situation may be entirely different than what is needed by another individual in another situation.

Likewise, everyone's Happiness Toolkit is entirely unique. What delights one person may be entirely stressful and overwhelming to another person. It's important for you to know what feels good to *you*—because only then can you communicate it to others and implement it in your own behalf. Recovery, after all, consists of "weeding out" the distresses in your life—and then "planting" more of the positives that bring you joy.

3–5   Transformational Tool #3: The Diamond

So now it's your turn to *"Do the Diamond"*—to Identify specific factors contributing to *your* distress, so you can begin finding effective solutions. Here are several worksheets to help you. In the first handout, use the lists provided to identify factors contributing to your current struggle. In the second handout, organize these factors in a "cycle" format, writing them in the blank space around the four areas of the Diamond. Then, work to replace each of these with positive factors to turn the direction of the cycle from negative to positive.

Identifying the Unique Causes of *Your* Depression

This worksheet will provide crucial information in an organized way to help you formulate a comprehensive, effective plan for recovery. **Circle or highlight those items that seem relevant to your most recent depressive episode. Use the empty space to fill in additional or explanatory information. Use additional paper if you need more room.** *Remember—identifying clear causes is the first step to resolving them, and then putting them behind you forever.*

1. **RELATIONSHIP** **TRIGGERS**	**Grief – Transition – Conflict – Lack of Interpersonal Skills – Abuse – Loss – Disappointment** *(Include both recent and past triggers—as the impact of these may accumulate over time)*
2. **DEPRESSIVE** **THOUGHTS**	**Negative Thoughts About:** **Self – Others – The World – The Future – Other**
3. **DEPRESSIVE** **BEHAVIOR**	**Withdrawal – Avoidance – Escapism – Procrastination – Addiction – Self-Harm – Other**
4. **IMPACT ON** **SPIRITUALITY**	**Religious – Meaning – Purpose – Connection – Other**
5. **RELATIONSHIP** **RESPONSES**	**Withdrawal – Attack – Excessive Caretaking – Other**

The Diamond Model:

For Assessment, Treatment, and Prevention of Depression and Other Emotional Disorders

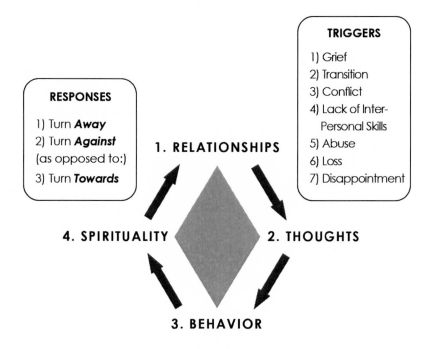

TRIGGERS
1) Grief
2) Transition
3) Conflict
4) Lack of Inter-
   Personal Skills
5) Abuse
6) Loss
7) Disappointment

RESPONSES
1) Turn *Away*
2) Turn *Against*
(as opposed to:)
3) Turn *Towards*

1. RELATIONSHIPS

4. SPIRITUALITY

2. THOUGHTS

3. BEHAVIOR

➤ Identify

➤ Replace

➤ Assimilate

CHAPTER FOUR

21st-CENTURY DEPRESSION

An Expanding, Worldwide Epidemic—
How to Survive and Thrive

➤ **4–1** You're Not Alone—The Increase of
Depression, in the World We Live In

➤ **4–2** To Actually Get Better, You Need
to Actually Fix What's Wrong

➤ **4–3** To Fix What's Wrong, You Need
to First Know What's Wrong

➤ **4–4** What Works, Works—and What
Doesn't Work, Doesn't Work

➤ **4–5** Disease-Promoting Patterns
vs. Health-Promoting Patterns

➤ **4–6** Transformational Tool #4:
The More-or-Less Grid

4–1 You're Not Alone—The Increase of Depression, in the World We Live In

In the previous chapter, we discussed the highly customized factors in our lives that can contribute to depression. Some contributing factors, however, are *not* unique, but tend to affect *all* of us in similar ways. Over the thirty years that I've been a professional counselor, it has been interesting to observe the massive changes that have occurred in our society at large—particularly, those that may have impacted our mental and physical health.

We live in a period of unprecedented prosperity—and unprecedented, break-neck change. In many ways, we are all living together as fellow lab rats in a vast and comprehensive social experiment. Throughout all of human history, human beings have never before lived the way we are currently living. Some of the results of this experiment have been breathtakingly positive. Others have been far more destructive in their impact.

In the thirty years that I have been a counselor, depression has spread like wildfire to ever-expanding epidemic proportions, affecting more and more people throughout the world—not just women and men, but youth and even children as well. In fact, those most at risk currently for serious depression or suicide, strangely enough, are teenagers and young adults, for whom suicide is now the second leading cause of death. Martin Seligman and other researchers have found to their amazement that the younger the research subject, the more likely they are to have suffered a serious depressive episode. On the face of it, that seems entirely illogical.

Older people, by definition, have lived longer—so it would stand to reason that with more time in this world, they would have experienced more depression. But that is just not the case. Young people now suffer from depression and other emotional challenges at a dangerously unprecedented rate.

Over these same thirty years, besides rising depression and suicide rates, a wide variety of other physical and emotional ailments have also become common—and more and more chronic, disabling, and even deadly. These conditions include cancer, heart disease, diabetes, obesity, autoimmune disorders, anxiety, bipolar disorder, ADHD, Alzheimer's, autism, PTSD, drug/alcohol addiction, AIDS, and widespread exposure to combat and terror.

Some of these ailments, including depression, are often blamed on genetics, "chemical imbalance," or just plain bad luck. But **is it reasonable to assume that genetic structure, biochemistry, or luck has gone through that much change in just thirty short years?** *I don't think so.*

Mental health problems have literally become a twenty-first-century epidemic, affecting millions of people all over the world. So if you've ever felt alone in your personal struggle, know that you're not alone. *We are all in this together!*

4–2   To Actually Get Better, You Need to Actually Fix What's Wrong

Some of the conditions that may be impacting your depression, therefore, are not unique to you alone. The world has gone through a massive transformation in recent decades, affecting almost every facet of human life and civilization. Our food is more processed, unnatural, and devoid of nutrients needed for brain and body health. Our air, water, and land are more polluted, saturated with poisonous chemicals and toxins. We get less sunlight, fresh air, physical movement, and restful sleep than any prior generation. These massive changes in our shared **physical environment** can contribute to changes in our bodies and brains that may be entirely inconsistent with physical and mental well-being.

Meanwhile, significant changes have also occurred over recent decades in our shared **social environment**. Stress, busyness, and unrelenting expectations press constantly upon us—in our homes, workplaces, and classrooms. Our families, communities, businesses, and nations have become more unstable, divided, and insecure. Trust, caring, and connection with other human beings has been largely replaced by screens, machines, and artificial programs. Disasters, violence, and terrors worldwide are communicated constantly and instantaneously on our ever-present, ever-broadcasting electronic devices. So all of us—even the youngest of children—are relentlessly exposed to a constant barrage of negativity, anxiety, and stress. It all takes a toll.

This modern lifestyle has become so normal to us that we hardly even consider its impact. Rarely are these factors even considered in a standard assessment for depression or any other illness. When is the last time your doctor or therapist asked you what you ate last night, how long you slept, what you might have watched on TV recently, or what pressures you're dealing with right now at work or at school? But all of these factors, and many more, can affect the delicate chemistry of the brain. All of them can increase our vulnerability to depression, anxiety, and a host of other emotional and physical ailments.

So, as we ponder what might be causing this exploding epidemic of twenty-first-century depression and other disorders, it's unreasonable to blame it all on "genetics." It is highly unlikely that our genetics have changed that much over the past thirty years. But it is abundantly clear that many other things *have* changed over these three short decades, that may have a massively negative impact on our physical and emotional health.

Happily, however, **we can learn to wisely manage the environment of our modern world** in ways that work *for* us, rather than against us. We can learn to shield and nourish ourselves and our vulnerable children in the midst of that unique environment in which we find ourselves, here in the twenty-first-century.

For while the challenges of our time are real, so are the opportunities. Though the direction of our culture may lead toward more stress, illness, and disruption, we can learn to intentionally choose elements in our lives that promote peace, wellness, and joy. We can learn to fix what's broken. Maybe not in the world at large—but within our own brains, bodies, lives, and relationships. And as we find light to illuminate our own darkness, we reflect that light to those around us. *As we transform ourselves, we help remake the world.*

4–3 To Fix What's Wrong, You Need to Know What's Wrong

Though we all face similar environmental challenges, we will each have a unique reaction to that physical and social environment that surrounds us in the modern world. Each of us possesses a biochemistry as unique as our individual thumbprints. Each of us has a lifetime of different experiences, memories, heartbreaks, and triumphs. Each of us experiences the world through the customized lens of our own personality and perspective. So though we might grow up in the same family, live in the same neighborhood, or attend the same school as others around us, these things will affect each of us very differently.

The thoughts and behaviors we adopt in order to deal with the environment around us tend to be unique to us alone. Some of those thoughts and behaviors are adaptive—meaning they work well for us, and produce positive results for us and for those around us. But some of our thoughts and behaviors might be maladaptive, leading to problems for us, or for others.

Again, none of us has the power to fix everything that is wrong in the world. But we *can* learn to identify and repair what is not working well in our own lives. That is the first crucial task of recovery—whether it be from depression, anxiety, grief, abuse, addiction, or even physical illness. In order to recover, in order to truly heal from any of these conditions, we need to first *identify* the factors that made us unwell in the first place. Then, in a clear and intentional way, we need to *correct* those factors, replacing them with elements that can contribute to our happiness and well-being, both now and in the future.

4–4 What Works, Works—And What Doesn't Work, Doesn't Work

I received my formal education in the Social Work program at the University of Utah. There, as a clinical social worker, I was trained to consider each client's *"person-in-environment fit."* In other words, whereas other professionals might focus mostly on the neurobiology, genetics, psychological history, or psychopathology within an *individual,* as a social worker I was trained to also consider the **environmental factors** impacting that person. These might include family dynamics, cultural messages, physical health, economic challenges, etc.

Certainly, we are all affected by our individual "environments"— the families and neighborhoods we grew up in, the messages we are directly exposed to by those around us. But in the modern age, our "environment" has massively grown in its breadth and impact. We are all affected—physically, economically, and emotionally— by the "global village" that we all live in now.

Many researchers have noted that depression and the other "diseases of civilization" have spread widely across the globe, as the habits and lifestyles of "modern" civilization have spread. Nations and cultures that were hardly ever touched in the past by depression, anxiety, diabetes, heart disease, etc., find the rates of those diseases rising exponentially, in proportion to the "modern" lifestyle factors entering those cultures over recent decades. Again, this cannot be attributed to "genetics," which have not markedly changed in the last thirty years. Our high-tech, high-stress, media-intensive, junk-food-saturated modern culture seems to be at war with the core needs of our physical bodies—and of the intricate pathways of our brains and souls.

Modern culture has changed human civilization and lifestyles in many significant ways, including:

- **More sugar and junk food**; less fiber, whole natural foods, and balanced nutrients.

- **More time spent indoors, in artificial environments, with artificial light (day and night)**; less time spent outdoors, in a natural environment, with fresh air, sunshine, and the cycles of natural light.

- **More time sitting, in a sedentary lifestyle**; less time walking and moving, in an active lifestyle.

- **More time spent with screens and machines**; less time spent directly with other human beings.

- **More time alone with electronics for work and recreation;** less time in community with other people.

- **More constant stress and never-ending pressure**; less serenity, relaxation, and rejuvenation.

Is it possible that these lifestyle changes play a role in the development and expansion of our modern diseases, including depression? The evidence seems to point strongly in that direction. Eating denatured, manufactured food, rather than real, living food; focusing on on-screen interactions, rather than real human relationships; drinking chemical-laden beverages, rather than real water—these are among the conditions known to promote vulnerability—not only to depression, but to a wide range of

70

other chronic diseases that have become far more common and widespread over recent decades.

Over the past ten years or so, I have become interested in overall health promotion—not just relating to emotional health, but to physical health as well. I have read many books, watched many documentaries, and followed many programs outlining causes and cures for a wide variety of modern diseases, including cancer, diabetes, and heart disease—programs intended to prevent and reverse these destructive conditions.

It has been remarkable to observe, time after time, the strong similarities between these various programs.

Whether the focus is preventing and healing cancer, diabetes, heart disease, Alzheimer's, autism, obesity, autoimmune disorder, anxiety, or depression—*the prescriptions laid out in the various programs are all virtually identical.* They all amount to reducing or eliminating the artificial, manmade foods in our diet and replacing them with whole, natural foods; reducing stress and increasing sleep and face-to-face interaction with other people; reducing sedentary life in front of a screen, and increasing actual movement and activity.

In observing these similarities, it is clear that *what works, works—and what doesn't work, doesn't work.* Across the board, we promote illness (both emotional and physical) when we engage in substances and lifestyle practices that are not consistent with the needs of our bodies and brains. And we promote wellness (both emotional and physical) when we provide consistently for the needs of our bodies and brains.

The good news about this—indeed, the GREAT news—is that making simple lifestyle changes can help prevent or reverse not only depression, but a vast range of other serious diseases as well. Indeed, it could be said:

The Cure for EVERYTHING is . . .
GET A LIFE!!

A real life,

in the real world,

eating real food,

interacting with real people,

and accomplishing real things—

which can bring real joy,

promote real healing,

and generate real satisfaction.

Building such a life in today's world is certainly not easy. In many ways, in fact, it is utterly counter-cultural—going against the grain of modern life. It doesn't mean we need to go to extremes—completely abandoning our computers, cell phones, or modern conveniences. But it does mean we need to be wiser about how we use these resources, and strive to find balance with the more natural resources that have sustained humans for generations.

4–5 Disease-Promoting Patterns vs. Health-Promoting Patterns

One of my social work professors years ago instructed us that helping a client fundamentally means—discovering both what that person needs *more* of, and also what they need *less* of. I have found this insight to be significantly helpful over many years of counseling. Some of those elements, as discussed in the previous chapter, are highly unique to the individual, emerging from their own unique personality, preferences, life history, etc.

But more and more often in recent years, I find that there are some things that my clients almost universally need *more* of and *less* of in order to recover and retain their mental wellness (and with it, oftentimes, their physical wellness). *In particular, they almost always tend to need:*

MORE	LESS
Whole, natural, high-fiber, high-nutrient FOOD—especially more fresh vegetables, pure water, fresh raw fruit, raw nuts, and dark leafy greens.	**Fake "FOOD" made in a factory, low in nutrients—** Particularly less sugar, less refined carbohydrates, less processed sweetened beverages, and less fried foods.

Physical exercise and ACTIVITY in the real world—regularly exercising large muscle groups and the cardiovascular system, ideally outside, getting fresh air and sunlight during daytime hours.	**MEDIA and sedentary "activity" in a fake world**—watching TV or videos; playing video games; viewing porn; reading trashy novels; browsing social media, especially alone, late at night, by artificial light.
Focus on CREATING something of value, unique to the individual—writing, cooking, sharing a creative talent, building something with their own hands, etc.	**Focus on CONSUMING what others have created**—passively listening to others' music, eating prefabricated "food," buying others' products, etc.
NATURAL "HIGHS" to manage stress and increase well-being—exercise, time in nature, relaxing time with loved ones, quality sleep, etc.	**ADDICTIVE, MOOD-ALTERING SUBSTANCES AND ACTIVITIES**—alcohol, drugs, media, porn, excessive shopping, prescription drugs, etc.
Actual meaningful connection with actual PEOPLE—playing, working, serving, communicating, building community with actual humans, heart-to-heart and face-to-face.	**IMAGINARY OR CYBER-RELATIONSHIPS**—technology-assisted media, fantasy books, novels, gaming, texting, or other electronic communications that crowd out real face-to-face relationships.

Later chapters will address these topics more fully. For now, as you seek to promote the mental and physical health of yourself and your loved ones, you can begin taking simple steps to add *more* of what fosters health and well-being, and *less* of what contributes to disease and dysfunction.

4–6 Transformational Tool #4: The More-or-Less Grid

This next Transformational Tool has two levels. First, simply ask yourself, *"In order to be happier, and enjoy more wellness over time, what do I need MORE of? And what do I need LESS of?"* Record your ideas in a simple graph, like this one:

I NEED MORE:	I NEED LESS:

The second level of the **More-or-Less Grid** blends these elements with the four areas of life referred to in **Transformational Tool #1: The Wellness Grid**. This allows you to plan your healing lifestyle changes in a much more comprehensive fashion. For that, you can use grids like these:

MENTALLY:

I NEED MORE:	I NEED LESS:

PHYSICALLY:

I NEED MORE:	I NEED LESS:

SPIRITUALLY:

I NEED MORE:	I NEED LESS:

SOCIALLY:

I NEED MORE:	I NEED LESS:

As you begin applying these changes, you can learn to live joyfully and healthfully in this twenty-first-century world, drawing on all the rich resources and opportunities that modern life has to offer—all without abandoning those essential conditions that have sustained humanity for generations.

———

CHAPTER FIVE

BUILDING *YOUR* HAPPINESS TOOLKIT
The Ultimate, Lifelong Do-It-Yourself Adventure!

- ➤ **5–1** Happiness Is Not Something to Be Pursued—But Something to Be Built!

- ➤ **5–2** Take Joy in Incremental Growth and Progress, Over Time

- ➤ **5–3** Three Basic Levels of Development and Recovery

- ➤ **5–4** The Sixteen Tools (And Their Opposites)—A Brief Overview

- ➤ **5–5** Transformational Tool #5: *Your* Happiness Toolkit

5–1   Happiness Is Not Something to Be Pursued—But Something to Be Built!

Congratulations! You've made it through the "Quick-Start" section of this book, and are now ready to develop the full power of *Your* Happiness Toolkit.

Hopefully by now, you have learned about and begun to apply "Transformational Tools 1-4." In so doing, you have built a solid foundation for greater happiness and well-being. Now, we're going to build on that foundation, providing additional tools to assist you in your continued progress toward consistent emotional wellness.

Sometimes we believe that happiness is a condition we need to "find" or "pursue." Experience has taught, however, that happiness is actually a condition that must be "built"—a little at a time, over the process of time. No one can give it to you, and no one can take it from you. It is highly unique and personal to you alone. You can learn, level by level, how to build your happiness—and in the process, overcome tendencies toward depression or other challenges, increasing your emotional strength and resilience.

5–2 Take Joy in Incremental Growth and Progress, Over Time

Building anything of value takes time. So, be kind and patient with yourself, as you progress through this learning experience. You're not going to master everything all at once, so proceed at a pace that feels manageable to you. Work steadily as you learn about and implement one strategy at a time.

When a house gets built, there are many stages in its development. First, a hole is dug, and a foundation is laid. Then, a basic framework is established, one beam or girder at a time. The structure of the house is then created on that framework. Plumbing and wiring are added to prepare pathways for light, power, and water. Roof tiles, doors, windows, bricks or stucco, and other materials are added to the exterior. Next, the focus is on the interior, applying or installing paint, carpet, countertops, and appliances. Finally, the house becomes a completed structure when the owners add their own customized furnishings, pictures, and personal items.

So it is with you. Having laid the foundation, you will now add the framework, structure, power, and personal touches to *Your* Happiness Toolkit. Learn to take joy in each step of the journey. Of course, you'll sometimes experience setbacks or challenges. But focus on your successes and accomplishments each day, however small they may seem. Keep going, learning, and moving forward—and bit by bit, you'll achieve your goal.

Remember—*it doesn't happen all at once, and you'll need to be patient with the process.* Don't expect instant happiness or immediate relief. But, if you do the work outlined here, you can expect to experience step-by-step progress, and increased happiness and wellness over time.

5–3   Three Basic Levels of Development and Recovery

The next three sections of this book will acquaint you with these three unique levels of *Your* Happiness Toolkit:

LEVEL 1—*INBORN ABILITIES (TOOLS 1–5)*
Natural powers you were born with— but may have laid aside for a time
LEVEL 2—*LEARNED SKILLS (TOOLS 6–10)*
Skills generally learned at a young age, as a natural part of growing up

LEVEL 3—ADVANCED STRATEGIES (TOOLS 11–16)
Powerful skill sets that must be intentionally and strategically learned

Each of these three Levels contains tools that you can use to strengthen your emotional wellness. The first two Levels consist of tools you probably have already had some experience with. These are the quickest and easiest of the tools to implement (besides the Quick Start Transformational Tools introduced in previous chapters). Continue using these Transformational Tools, as you blend in the new skills you will learn from Levels 1 and 2.

Level 3 tools are more advanced, more complex, and take significantly more time and effort to master. They are literally the "power tools" in your toolkit. As such, you should not start with them. Work up to them, after mastering the other tools. They will bring great strength and insight into *Your* Happiness Toolkit—but you should continue to draw on the strength of the simpler tools, as you become acquainted with the more demanding strategies of Level 3.

5–4   The 16 Tools (And Their Opposites): A Brief Overview

The next few pages consist of handouts you can use for quick reference, as you become acquainted with the new tools presented in the following chapters.

- **Handout #1** contains a full listing of the 16 Tools, including the assigned number, key word, and a brief description of each tool.

- **Handout #2** contrasts these 16 Tools with their opposite patterns, so it can be used as a self-assessment resource, to guide you in identifying current strengths and weaknesses, and knowing where to focus your healing efforts.

- **Handout #3**—*top graph*—This graph assigns each of the 16 Tools to a particular location on the page, for consistency and ease of reference. Like a well-organized physical toolbox, these assigned locations can make it easier for you to remember where to find all 16 Tools, within the three levels of the Toolkit. You'll see that the levels themselves are subdivided, so that similar tools are grouped together, making them easy to locate and remember.

- **Handout #3**—*bottom graph*—This graph summarizes the *opposites* of the 16 Tools. It identifies habits and behaviors that you want to avoid, if your goal is emotional wellness. So, at a glance, you will be able to see which habits will contribute to a "positive spiral" emotionally, and which habits will lead you into a "negative spiral"—so you can choose your course wisely, from day to day.

5–5   Transformational Tool #5: *Your* Happiness Toolkit

So there you have it! Your most powerful Transformational Tool awaits. *Enjoy the journey!*

YOUR HAPPINESS TOOLKIT:

16 Strategies for Happiness, Emotional Wellness, and Healing from the Inside Out

LEVEL 1—*INBORN ABILITIES* (TOOLS 1–5)	
Natural powers you were born with— but may have laid aside for a time	
1. Action	Do what you love—and do what loves you back!
2. Feeling	Feel and express your actual feelings
3. Positivity	Notice and enjoy the good things
4. Learning	Develop new abilities and skills
5. Creativity	Focus on creating rather than consuming

LEVEL 2—*LEARNED SKILLS* (TOOLS 6–10)	
Skills generally learned at a young age, as a natural part of growing up	
6. Identity	Know and value your unique traits and gifts
7. Recording	Write and preserve your life experience
8. Seeking	Reach out for guidance, support, and insight
9. Sociality	Engage in meaningful social connections
10. Service	Joyfully share what you have and are with others

LEVEL 3—ADVANCED STRATEGIES (TOOLS 11–16)

Powerful skill sets that must be intentionally
and strategically learned

11. Health	Care wisely for your body—and your brain
12. Activity	Engage in consistent, health-promoting movement
13. Order	Organize your time, resources, and living space
14. Thinking	Direct your thoughts in positive, productive ways
15. Connection	Communicate and relate well with others
16. Healing	Repair old wounds, and move on with joy!

16 CONTRASTING LIFESTYLE PATTERNS

(Individual, Family, and Cultural)

LIST 1—Patterns Feeding: Depression, Disease, Deterioration, and Disability	LIST 2—Patterns Feeding: Happiness, Wellness, Resilience, and Productivity
1. INACTION: Do Nothing (Or, Only What Others Expect of You)	**1. ACTION:** Do What You Love—And Do What Loves You Back
2. NUMBING: Avoid, Suppress, & Silence Your Actual Feelings	**2. FEELING:** Feel and Express Your Actual Feelings
3. NEGATIVITY: Focus on the Negative (in Self, World, & Others)	**3. POSITIVITY:** Notice and Enjoy the Good Things
4. STAGNATION: Remain Stuck in Old Patterns and Habits	**4. LEARNING:** Develop New Abilities and Skills
5. CONSUMING: Be a Constant Consumer of Others' Products	**5. CREATIVITY:** Focus On Creating Rather Than Consuming

6. COMPARING: Compare Yourself Negatively Against Others	**6. IDENTITY:** Know and Value Your Unique Traits and Gifts
7. REACTIVITY: React Impulsively to Current Experiences	**7. RECORDING:** Write and Preserve Your Life Experience
8. DISTRACTION: Focus Your Attention on Screens and Machines	**8. SEEKING:** Reach Out for Guidance, Support, and Insight
9. AVOIDANCE: Keep to Yourself (Other Than "Social Media")	**9. SOCIALITY:** Engage in Meaningful Social Connections
10. ISOLATION: Stay Focused on Yourself (or, Serve Resentfully)	**10. SERVICE:** Joyfully Share What You Have and Are with Others
11. ILLNESS: Eat Junk; Get Little Sleep, Exercise, and Sunlight	**11. HEALTH:** Care Wisely For Your Body—And Your Brain
12. INACTIVITY: Spend Hours Sitting and Remaining Sedentary	**12. ACTIVITY:** Engage in Consistent, Health-Promoting Movement

13. DISORDER: Live in Chaos, Clutter, and Disorganization	**13. ORDER:** Organize Your Time, Resources, and Living Space
14. TRIGGERING: Believe Negative Thoughts, Get "Triggered"	**14. THINKING:** Direct Your Thoughts in Positive, Productive Ways
15. CONFLICT: Attack or Invalidate Others, in Word and Action	**15. CONNECTION:** Communicate and Relate Well with Others
16. DECAY: Emotionally Deteriorate; Get Stuck in Old Pain	**16. HEALING:** Repair Old Wounds, and Move On With Joy!

-3	-2	-1	0	1	2	3
Strong	*Moderate*	*Mild*	*Neutral*	*Mild*	*Moderate*	*Strong*

(**Option:** *In the margin on either side, rate the level of the trait that more accurately describes your current pattern. This can help assess current strengths and weaknesses, and let you know where to focus your efforts.*)

WHAT IS THE DIRECTION OF *YOUR* SPIRAL TODAY?

Upward Spiral: *Promotes Happiness, Confidence, Resilience, Strong Relationships, and Positive Influence on Others*

INBORN TRAITS

1. Action
2. Feeling
3. Positivity

4. Learning
5. Creativity

LEARNED SKILLS

6. Identity
7. Recording

8. Seeking
9. Sociality
10. Service

ADVANCED

11. Health
12. Activity
13. Order

14. Thinking
15. Connection
16. Healing

WHAT IS THE DIRECTION OF *YOUR* SPIRAL TODAY?

Downward Spiral: *Promotes Depression, Anxiety, Addiction, Broken Relationships, and Negative Impact on Others*

INBORN TRAITS

1. Inaction
2. Numbing
3. Negativity

4. Stagnation
5. Consuming

LEARNED SKILLS

6. Comparing
7. Reactivity

8. Distraction
9. Avoidance
10. Isolation

ADVANCED

11. Illness
12. Disorder
13. Triggering

14. Accusation
15. Conflict
16. Decay

A Final Note: You may find, as you review these handouts, that your current patterns fall more in the "Downward Spiral" range; and that your current lifestyle contains more items from the depression-feeding "List 1," than items from the more positive "List 2." If so, resist the temptation to feel discouraged or overwhelmed. This book lays out a clear path for you to follow, to strategically build more happiness, productivity, and resilience than you've ever experienced before.

Remember—the 16 Tools were crafted precisely to overcome the 16 "Downward Spiral" patterns that feed depression and other challenges. So, if you've identified a few weak spots—or even a lot of them—rejoice! You're about to embark on a life-changing, transformative adventure! First, *here's a Section I summary:*

5 TRANSFORMATIONAL TOOLS:

1. WELLNESS GRID	Physical, Mental, Spiritual, Emotional
2. UP-OR-DOWN SPIRAL	Upward Direction or Downward Direction?
3. DIAMOND	Triggers, Thoughts, Behaviors, Spirituality, Relationships
4. MORE-OR-LESS GRID	"I Need More . . . / I Need Less . . ." in the Four Areas
5. *YOUR HAPPINESS TOOLKIT*	16 Strategies, Levels 1–3

	What Do I Need MORE of?	What Do I Need LESS of?
PHYSICALLY:		
MENTALLY:		
SPIRITUALLY:		
SOCIALLY:		

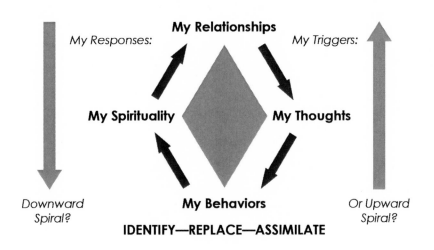

IDENTIFY—REPLACE—ASSIMILATE

YOUR HAPPINESS TOOLKIT, LEVEL 1

Inborn Traits

INBORN TRAITS

1. Action
2. Feeling
3. Positivity

4. Learning
5. Creativity

LEARNED SKILLS

6. Identity
7. Recording

8. Seeking
9. Sociality
10. Service

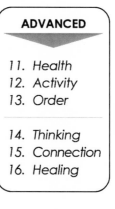

ADVANCED

11. Health
12. Activity
13. Order

14. Thinking
15. Connection
16. Healing

S ome of the most powerful tools you can use to overcome depression and build joy have literally been with you since your infancy. These are inborn abilities that contribute greatly to the resilience of young children—and that likewise can strengthen your resilience now, as you put them to current effective use.

These inborn tools may have gotten a little dusty over the years. You may have been taught long ago to squelch or ignore these important Inborn Traits. But as you learn about them, recover them, dust them off, and adapt them for use in your current circumstances, they can contribute greatly to your joy and fulfillment.

Besides the **Quick Start Strategies** described in Section I, **these five tools are the easiest of the sixteen for most people to master,** because nearly all of us have had at least some experience with them previously. These are universal human gifts that happy people of all ages tend to use consistently (and need to continue to use, to remain happy and well); and that depressed people of all ages can learn to recover and use, in order to improve their mental health, and greatly enhance their well-being.

———

ACTION:

Do What You Love—And Do What Loves You Back!

- ➤ **1–1** Positive Action—The Foundation of Wellness and Happiness

- ➤ **1–2** Why Do We Stop Doing What We Love?

- ➤ **1–3** Positive, Proactive, and Productive—Choosing Actions That Love You Back

- ➤ **1–4** Don't Wait Until You "Feel Like It"—Implementing the "As If" Principle

- ➤ **1–5** Finding a Balance: Doing What You Love, and Doing What is Required

INBORN TRAITS

1. Action
2. Feeling
3. Positivity

4. Learning
5. Creativity

LEARNED SKILLS

6. Identity
7. Recording

8. Seeking
9. Sociality
10. Service

ADVANCED

11. Health
12. Activity
13. Order

14. Thinking
15. Connection
16. Healing

1–1 Positive Action—The Foundation of Happiness and Wellness

Tool #1 in *Your* Happiness Toolkit is—the ACTION Tool. This is literally the foundation of all that follows. It is like the hammer in a standard toolbox. It has hundreds of uses, and no toolbox is complete without it. It is generally the first tool acquired— the entry point for all the others that will be added over time.

In many ways, **you are already familiar with this tool, and have been using for years.** Human life, from some of its earliest stages, is characterized by *action*. Even pre-born infants in the womb can be observed to carry out simple behaviors, such as sucking their thumbs, grasping their toes, stretching out their arms or legs, or shifting their positions. Once born into the world, infants expand their repertoire of actions to include breathing, crying, cooing, taking in nourishment; and then later smiling, laughing, exploring, crawling, playing, feeding themselves, and interacting with those around them. Likewise, your entrance into the world was most likely accompanied by these normal, almost universal actions.

As a child grows, the Action Tool grows with them. Learning to stand, learning to walk, learning to master more complex games and toys, and learning to think, write, spell, read, create, sing, dance, tie shoes, brush teeth, ride a bike—so many simple actions are part of the normal process of growing up. As we get older, we tend to customize our action plans more and more to fit our own unique interests and talents, in addition to these more basic actions we all generally start with.

Here's a quick survey to help you identify some of your unique interests (organized by the four areas on the Wellness Grid.) Feel free to write in others not included on the list.

Recreational Survey

Please circle your interests, and/or rate your interest in the following activities:

MENTAL—ARTISTIC
Acting / Musical Instrument / Singing / Drawing / Painting / Photography / Sculpting / Videography

MENTAL—INTELLECTUAL
Attending a Lecture / Reading Fiction / Reading Non-Fiction / Researching / Studying / Writing

MENTAL—OTHER

Board Games / Checkers / Chess / Coin Collecting / Puzzles / Sudoku

PHYSICAL—EXERCISE

Biking / Dancing / Jogging / Karate / Roller Skating / Running / Swimming / Walking / Weight Lifting / Yoga

PHYSICAL—HANDIWORK

Auto Detailing / Crafts / Embroidery / Knitting / Metal Work / Model Building / Quilting / Woodworking

PHYSICAL—RECREATION

Boating / Camping / Climbing / Canoeing / Fishing / Hiking / Horseback Riding / Mountain Biking / Skiing

PHYSICAL—SPORTS

Badminton / Baseball / Basketball / Football / Golf / Hockey / Racquetball / Soccer / Tennis / Volleyball

PHYSICAL—OTHER

Bowling / Croquet / Cooking / Cleaning / Gardening / Home Organization / Interior Design / Yard Work

SPIRITUAL—PUBLIC

Attending Church / Public Speaking /
Serving in Church / Volunteering

SPIRITUAL—PRIVATE

Being in Nature / Bible Study / Goal Setting /
Praying / Reading Inspirational Literature

SOCIAL—VISITING PUBLIC PLACES

Concert / Museum / Opera / Park /
Shopping / Sight Seeing / Theatre

SOCIAL—VISITING, PRIVATE

Lunch with a Friend / Talking One-On-
One / Visiting a Family Member

-3	-2	-1	0	1	2	3
Strong Dislike	Moderate Dislike	Mild Dislike	Neutral	Mild Enjoyment	Moderate Enjoyment	Strong Enjoyment

Your mix will be different than anyone else's—because _you_ are different than anyone else. Behaviors that make you happy (or unhappy) will differ from what works for other people. Some things, of course, we all tend to have in common. All of us do better when we eat healthy food, get some exercise, go to bed early enough to enjoy quality sleep, etc.

Other things are very different from person to person. For example—I personally love public speaking, acting on stage and film, or singing for an audience. I am never happier than when I get to do those things. They're an essential part of *my* Happiness Toolkit. When I don't get to do them, I miss them, and I'm just not happy.

But for some other people, those same Actions would strike absolute terror (or boredom!) into their hearts. Their customized happiness-promotion behaviors might include: playing basketball, doing extreme sports, attending big social events, or listening to loud music—all of which I find overwhelming. So we're very individual in what feeds our happiness. Doing what we love to do is an essential part of living a happy life—from infancy into old age. *But we don't always do that.*

1–2 Why Do We Stop Doing What We Love?

Though Action is so natural to us, we may have stopped doing the things we love, the things that bring *us* joy. The reasons for this are as individual as we are. We might have been shamed for doing what we love—and told to do something different. We might have been told that what we love is silly, impractical, unimportant, or even selfish. Very often, the people telling us these things want us to do what *they* want us to do—instead of what *we* want to do. These messages can come from parents, teachers, church, friends, family members, employers, spouses, or even the media or surrounding culture.

Besides such *outside* pressure to stop doing what we love, we sometimes face *internal* pressures that can stop positive action.

Depression is one of those internal pressures. When we are depressed, one of the most common symptoms is a loss of energy, motivation, and desire to do things—even things we once enjoyed. Depression, as discussed in Section I, is typically set off initially by some kind of trigger experience. These might include:

1. **Grief:** When we lose someone important to us, we may miss them so terribly that it drains all the enjoyment out of behaviors we used to love. We may even feel guilty engaging in an enjoyable behavior—because our loved one is no longer able to be there to share it with us.

2. **Transition:** When life changes, our roles change, and things we used to enjoy may no longer seem desirable, relevant, or even possible. This is may result from changed circumstances, health conditions, environment, or other factors. Losing the opportunity or ability to do what we love is part of what can make transitions so difficult.

3. **Conflict:** We may experience *interpersonal* conflict with someone important to us, who wants us to stop doing something we love, and do what they want us to do instead. We may even experience *intrapersonal* conflict— part of us wanting to do what we love, and another part of us fighting against that.

4. **Abuse:** Abuse can feel so traumatic and shattering that, at least for a time, it may obliterate our ability to enjoy *anything*. We may have even been abused or guilted for engaging in our preferred behavior—which can make it even more difficult later to resume that behavior.

When we stop doing what we love in response to our triggers, it tends to add fuel to the fire of depression—resulting in even more loss, pain, and disappointment. *It is important to turn this destructive pattern around!*

The five Transformational Tools introduced in Section I are designed to start you in this process. They can help you identify actions that increase happiness for *you*—whether these are behaviors you've done in the past, or new behaviors you establish now, to deal with emerging circumstances in the present. As a review:

- **The Wellness Grid** in Chapter 1 encouraged you to identify, implement, and re-ignite positive behaviors you're already familiar with in four key areas of life—Mental, Physical, Spiritual, and Social.

- **The Spiral** in Chapter 2 urged you to consider if your choices are leading you in an "upward spiral," or in a "downward spiral"—and to adjust behavior, if necessary, to change the direction of that spiral.

- **The Diamond** in Chapter 3 revealed how negative behavior tends to follow depressive triggers and thoughts, in developing the negative cycle of depression. It discussed how replacing those negative thoughts and behaviors with positive ones can help transform that negative cycle into a positive cycle.

- **The More-or-Less Grid** in Chapter 4 encouraged you to identify things you need to do *more* of, versus things you need to do *less* of, in order to promote recovery and enduring wellness.

- **The Happiness Toolkit** introduced in Chapter 5 exposed you to all of the 16 Tools you'll learn more about in Sections 2-4; the many things you can do, in a positive, intentional ways, to banish depression, and build the foundation for a joyful, fulfilling life.

Each of these five Transformational Tools reflects a treatment strategy known as *Behavioral Activation (BA)*, which is very powerful in promoting depression recovery. These tools work best when you choose wisely which behaviors to increase, and which to decrease.

1–3   Positive, Proactive, and Productive— Choosing Actions That Love You Back

Action is something you've been doing in some form all along— literally for all the years or decades of your life. Some of those Actions work for you better than others, bringing more lasting joy, and more enduring and positive consequences. Those are the Actions you want to strengthen, in order to banish depression, and build long-term happiness and fulfillment.

But not all action is good for you. Some actions increase the very problem you're trying to correct. Learning to tell the difference between behaviors that work *for* you, and behaviors that work *against* you, is an important part of recovery and wellness.

Action that strengthens wellness tends to be:

1. **Positive**—contributing to happiness and creating positive results for you, and for those you care about.

2. **Proactive**—something you intentionally choose, in accordance with your personal goals and values.

3. **Productive**—producing something of value that you can find satisfaction in - both now, and in the future.

In contrast, some actions you love may not "love you back." Eating too much sugar or junk food. Spending too much money. Skipping school. Yelling at family members. Procrastinating on important tasks. Shooting up heroin. Looking at pornography. Cutting on yourself. Sitting around watching TV all day. Playing video games for hours at a time, neglecting other responsibilities. These and similar behaviors might temporarily bring some relief or satisfaction—but ultimately, they tend to generate negative results. Choose actions that bring satisfaction now, *and* that will bring positive results long-term—for yourself, and for those you love.

Also, as mentioned previously, depression often leads to **Inaction.** Under the influence of depression, people may cease to find enjoyment in things they used to love doing. So they stop doing what they love—setting themselves up for even more loss, and deeper depression.

Three common patterns associated with Inaction are:

1. **Rumination**—Sitting alone, thinking deep depressing thoughts, staring at a wall—and doing nothing else.

2. **Distraction**—Trying to escape your depressing feelings with some engrossing media device.

3. **Compliance**—Doing what others expect of you— but not doing what personally brings *you* joy.

I have been amazed, time and time again, to observe how quickly mood and energy can improve, when people increase time spent doing positive, proactive, productive things that they personally love to do. Likewise, it is remarkable how intensely mood and energy can plummet, when people stop doing what they love, and fall instead into inaction, negative action, or submissive compliance.

Rate your current pattern on the scale below:

LIST 1—Patterns Feeding:	LIST 2—Patterns Feeding:
Depression, Disease, Deterioration, and Disability	Happiness, Wellness, Resilience, and Productivity
1. INACTION: Do Nothing (Or, Only What Others Expect of You)	**1. ACTION:** Do What You Love—And Do What Loves You Back

-3	-2	-1	0	1	2	3
Strong	Moderate	Mild	Neutral	Mild	Moderate	Strong

If your current pattern falls on the negative side, the strategies discussed here can help reverse that pattern. If you're already on the positive side, these strategies can help you maintain and strengthen your happy lifestyle even further over time.

1–4 Don't Wait Until You "Feel Like It"— Implementing the "As If" Principle

So, what do you do if you *know* what you should be doing, but… you just can't bring yourself to *do* it? This is one of the most perplexing challenges in depression recovery. But it is one of the most important issues to resolve, since Action truly is the foundational tool upon which everything else rests.

Depression can be a self-perpetuating cycle. The more severe it is, the more it makes you want to do things that *feed* it—and the less it makes you want to do things that help *overcome* it. So, under the influence of depression, it is not uncommon for people to avoid sunlight; eat only junk (or nothing at all); stay sedentary; avoid interaction with others; sit in a dark room alone and ruminate; stop doing what they love; let their living space get messy; and even avoid basic personal hygiene, such as taking a shower. Depression whispers that it's all "just too hard." And it can be very difficult to fight those heavy, depressing impulses.

But the more you obey that dark voice, the stronger it gets— and the more pain and regret that tends to generate—leading to increased feelings of worthlessness, despair, and futility. *One of the very WORST things you can do is—get a medical prescription, and then just passively sit, and "wait for the medication to kick in,"* to supposedly "resolve" your depressive feelings and symptoms.

Even if you *do* choose to take medication, as part of your treatment regimen, be sure to pair it with positive lifestyle change and behavioral intervention. Otherwise, the passivity of simply "waiting" without positive change or action can add even further to the progressive downward spiral of depression. Medication can take weeks to start kicking in. In contrast, *positive behavior can start bringing you relief almost immediately.* So, here are some tips that can help you get "unstuck," and begin moving forward again with positive action:

1. **Name the Discouraging Voice**—Distinguish *yourself* from the *depression*. When you find yourself not wanting to do something you know you should do, don't say, "*I'm broken, I'm depressed, so I can't do it.*" Instead, say "*The depression is saying to me, 'You don't want to do it.' But I'm stronger than that. I'm not going to let depression win.*" And then, take positive action—even if it's a very small step.

2. **Turn Off the TV and Other Media**—TV, video games, social media apps, and other media are designed to be addictive—to keep you consuming the product as long as possible. This increases profits for the manufacturer. But it doesn't provide benefit to *you*. I have learned that when a client tells me, "Nothing happened this week," or "I didn't do anything this week," it almost always translates into "I was passively consuming media the entire week." Turn it off. Remove the distraction. Refocus your energy into some kind of positive activity.

3. **Act "As If"**—This strategy is the tried-and-true "old stand-by" of behavior modification for depression. It basically means, "Act *AS IF*" you weren't depressed. Engage in activities you would carry out if you weren't depressed. Don't expect to "want to" do it. And don't wait to "want to." Just DO IT. Once you get going, it's much easier to *keep* going—reaping the positive results of positive action, making ongoing progress easier.

4. **Do *Something*—Not Everything or Nothing**—Depression often gets you thinking in extremes, like *"If it's not worth doing well, it's not worth doing at all."* This thinking keeps you stuck. Don't try to do "everything"—and especially, don't try to do everything "perfectly." This is a guaranteed way to keep yourself stuck, because when you expect perfection, you tend to wait until you feel like doing it "perfectly"—which is very unlikely to occur. Don't do "nothing." Don't try to do "everything." Just "do *something*."

5. **Start Small**—As you make behavioral changes, start small, in tiny, manageable increments. Today, you may not be ready for a marathon—but you could walk to your mailbox and back. Today, you won't clean the entire house—but you could start dejunking your kitchen drawer. Start small, and then work up, as you get stronger.

6. **Keep Track of Your Successes**—As you start positive new behavior, keep track of your achievements, however small. Write your successes into a calendar or on a list. Even give yourself points, stars, or stickers if you have to. Make it fun! Remember—*starting* a behavior is hard, but *continuing* it is much easier.

7. **Find Ways to Reward Yourself**—As you do this hard work of establishing positive behavior, find ways to reward yourself for your good efforts. Eventually, the behavior and its positive results will become its own reward. But for today, an extra outside reward can help motivate you, as you make that hard initial change.

1–5 Finding a Balance: Doing What You Love, and Doing What Is Required

As mentioned earlier, we all come into this world with the inborn ability to engage in ACTION—to do what we love. It would be nice if we could only "do what we love" continuously, without interruption throughout our lives. But the reality is—growing up requires that we take on tasks that we don't particularly enjoy—but which are required to carry out important responsibilities at home, school, or work.

How can we find a balance—fulfilling these needed tasks and responsibilities, but also continuing to "do what we love"? These suggestions may help:

1. **Pace Yourself**—Be steady, not excessive, as you carry out needed tasks. Take things at a manageable pace—and if it starts feeling like too much, then be sure to slow down, and catch your breath. *Depletion depression* is one of the most common forms of depression in our busy, frenetic, demanding world. Be like the wise marathon runner who doesn't take off in a sprint during the first mile—but rather paces himself continuously over the full course of the marathon, so he'll have energy enough to finish and win the race.

2. **Take Breaks**—As you carry out needed tasks, be sure to take some periods for rest and refueling. Otherwise, you'll burn out quickly, become overwhelmed, and be less effective in your assigned task. Tony Schwartz, a best-selling author, wrote a particularly insightful book called *The Way We're Working Isn't Working*. There, he documents the destructive impact of constant, unrelenting work pressure—whether in adults, or in students. He contrasts that with a more manageable work schedule that includes "breaks"—periods of less intensity, and even of regeneration and enjoyment. He found that people are far more productive on a schedule that includes these interspersed break periods.

3. **Remember to "Sharpen Your Saw"**—Steve Covey's book *The 7 Habits of Highly Effective People* reports that *"Habit 7— Sharpen the Saw"* is vital for maintaining effectiveness. For a saw to work efficiently, it sometimes needs to stop sawing, and become newly re-sharpened. Likewise, for a car to keep running effectively, it needs to sometimes be refueled, re-oiled, and have the tires rotated. In a similar fashion, we remain the most productive if we provide regular periods of renewal and regeneration, rather than remain constantly in a frenetic push to stay "productive" at all times. "Highly effective people" take time to regenerate and renew themselves. This is a habit we would all be wise to emulate.

4. **Alternate Demanding "Work" Tasks with More Enjoyable Activities**—An ancient proverb observes:

   "All work and no play makes Jack a dull boy.
   But all play and no work makes Jack a useless boy."

I have found, in myself and in others, that productivity is highest—and life is sweetest—when neither work nor play are allowed to crowd out the other. When used together, they actually support and facilitate each other. Work is sweeter and more sustainable, when you have something fun to look forward to at the end of the task. Play is more fully enjoyed, when you know you've already taken care of essential responsibilities.

5. **Maintain a Mix: Hard Work, Pleasant Work, Fun**—In structuring your day, it is wise to factor in all of these three types of activities. *"Hard Work" is* the work you dread—tasks that take a lot of energy, effort, and focus—but that absolutely need to be done. *"Pleasant Work"* is still work-related, but it doesn't involve as much direct effort or stress as "hard work." *"Fun" is* non-work-related—things you do to recover and rest from your work tasks. It is wise to maintain a balanced mix of these three kinds of activities, in order to build a fulfilling, happy, and productive life.

By engaging consistently in positive, proactive, productive Action, you lay the groundwork for depression recovery, and for enduring wellness. Let's continue now with **Tool #2: FEELING.**

FEELING:

Feel and Express Your Actual Feelings

INBORN TRAITS

1. Action
2. Feeling
3. Positivity

4. Learning
5. Creativity

LEARNED SKILLS

6. Identity
7. Recording

8. Seeking
9. Sociality
10. Service

ADVANCED

11. Health
12. Activity
13. Order

14. Thinking
15. Connection
16. Healing

2–1   Expressing Genuine Feelings—
An Inborn Ability

Tool #2 in *Your* Happiness Toolkit is—the FEELING Tool. Like Tool #1, it is an ability we are almost universally born with. We tend to arrive in this world already equipped with the crucial ability to cry in distress, to gaze with contentment, to scream in fear or frustration, to cling to our caregivers for safety and nurturance. No one has to teach us how to do these things. Indeed, these are instinctual abilities, essential for our survival as vulnerable, powerless little humans. None of us are born with the ability to feed ourselves, clothe ourselves, or move ourselves around to other locations. In order to even survive in this world, we must communicate our infant needs to someone more powerful than we are. Feeling and expressing our feelings helps us do so.

Generally, by the time we become toddlers, we have already attained the ability to feel and express an even broader range of feelings—frustration, anger, sadness, contentment, anxiety, love, etc. And over the years, as we progress through life, our capacity to feel expands with us, as our brains develop, and our life experiences accumulate. As with Tool #1, you are already familiar with Tool #2, and have been using it for years.

However, though the Feeling Tool is so natural and instinctual, over the process of growing up, we often learn to numb, avoid, hide, submerge, or even suppress our true feelings. There are many reasons for this—but the result is—unexpressed feelings often contribute to the development of depression, low self-esteem, trauma issues, behavioral problems, and even physical health challenges. Recovering the ability that we were born with—to feel and express our feelings—is a crucial ingredient for emotional recovery and enduring wellness.

2–2 Why Do We Stop Expressing Our Actual Feelings?

Over the process of growing up, we may get the message that our feelings don't matter to those around us. Our needs may be experienced by others as trivial, inconvenient, unimportant, or even infuriating. Our true, raw feelings may sometimes trigger uncomfortable or unwanted feelings within these individuals themselves. So, in direct and indirect ways, we may be given the message as we grow up that our feelings should be kept to ourselves, or eliminated altogether—that we should not be feeling what we are, in fact, feeling.

These messages may come to us *directly*, through expressions such as:

- *"Stop crying—or I'll give you something to cry about!"*
- *"Children are to be seen, and not heard."*
- *"What are you getting so upset for?"*
- *"That's ridiculous—you're not making any sense!"*
- *"Stop being so selfish."*
- *"Don't be such a baby."*
- *"Boys don't cry."*
- *"I'm just trying to toughen you up."*

Or those messages can come *indirectly*—through an exasperated sigh, a closed door, a roll of the eyes, or the neglect or long postponement of our expressed need. We can quickly learn in such an environment that our feelings are "wrong," unwanted, that they just get us into trouble, or that they seem too much for others to handle. So we learn to push them down, to avoid conflict with those around us. We learn to squelch and suppress our feelings—sometimes so effectively that even we ourselves forget that they exist. *But that which is suppressed or hidden doesn't cease to be real. And it doesn't cease to create a real and lasting impact.*

I have learned over the years that depression almost *always* includes this element of hiding feelings from ourselves or others. Those squashed feelings become toxic and intensified. Sometimes they are even converted into physical problems, on a cellular level. Most often, however, those displaced, discounted feelings turn into emotional problems, sometimes accompanied also by behavioral problems.

To a certain extent, of course, *bridling* our feelings is a needed and necessary ability we develop over time—a virtually universal development associated with normal life experiences like—going to school, learning to do chores, complying with social norms like putting on clothes, or following basic traffic rules. A person who continues throughout life exclusively following their own instincts, feelings, or desires could likely end up incarcerated. But a person who goes through life not just bridling but *suppressing* their feelings is likely to end up with significant emotional challenges.

Rate your current pattern on the scale below, circling the number that best reflects your current status:

LIST 1—*Patterns Feeding:*	LIST 2—*Patterns Feeding:*
Depression, Disease, Deterioration, and Disability	Happiness, Wellness, Resilience, and Productivity
2. NUMBING: Avoid, Suppress, & Silence Your Actual Feelings	**2. FEELING:** Feel and Express Your Actual Feelings

-3	-2	-1	0	1	2	3
Strong	Moderate	Mild	Neutral	Mild	Moderate	Strong

Certainly, **the most extreme forms of feeling suppression occur in the tragic context of abuse.** Abuse basically says to a victim, *"My needs and feelings matter—and yours don't. You need to comply with what I want, even if it is in direct opposition to what you want.*

You exist to serve me. What I say goes. What you say goes out the window. What I believe is important, IS what is important. What I say needs to be done, IS what needs to be done."

Abuse is most the destructive and emotionally toxic when it is inflicted on a young, impressionable child, who is just beginning to learn how to experience themselves and others in this world. But it can do significant emotional harm to an individual at any point in the life cycle, from early infancy to old age. Almost always, that harm includes—learning to deny, suppress, and avoid genuine feelings.

Or, we might learn to express feelings *selectively*—for example, expressing our frustration, anger, or rage—but not the more tender and vulnerable feelings underneath it, such as hurt, fear, disappointment, or regret. When our angry feelings are expressed, but the more tender feelings underneath remain hidden, it can produce new layers of harm, or even of abuse, in those around us—which can then produce new ripples of the depression cycle in us and in others. A person who only expresses chronic anger may say to those around them, **"Well, I'm just telling you how I FEEL!"** However, they're not sharing *all* of what they feel. They're often using the shield of anger as yet another way to hide from and suppress the more vulnerable feelings behind the anger. This is ultimately just another variety of feeling suppression—one that in many families generates a persistent, multi-generational cycle of abuse and depression.

Whether learned from abuse, social conditioning, or other factors, feeling suppression can become a persistent habit, making us vulnerable to other emotional and physical problems. Feeling suppression is often at the heart of not just depression, but also of behavior problems, including 1) acting out and 2) addiction. We may turn to these behaviors to distract or numb ourselves away from legitimate pain—not wanting to feel what we actually feel. **Acting-out behaviors may include**: self-injury, violence, aggression, yelling, or even suicide attempts. **Addictions may develop for** alcohol, illicit drugs, prescription drugs, smoking, sugar, video games, shopping, pornography, or the most common addiction of all in our time: addiction to our cell phones and other media devices.

When pain is at the heart of these patterns, as is generally the case, the behavior will not stop simply by punishing or criminalizing it. Stopping the "War On Drugs," for example, will never be successful simply through increasing the rigor of prison sentences for drug use. Likewise, no pornography addiction is ever resolved fully by just "white knuckling" it away. Rather, to resolve a problem behavior, it is essential to identify and resolve the foundations of it. You need to discover precisely what is hurting, and then find practical ways to resolve that problem.

2–3 Building Self-Awareness: What Are You Feeling Today?

You can't express feelings to anyone else, until you can face and express them to yourself. You can't share with your spouse, your therapist, your doctor, or anyone else what you are feeling, if you remain unaware yourself of what you are feeling. Most importantly, you cannot fix or resolve a difficult feeling, the problem behavior it generates, or the negative impact it passes on to those you love—without first identifying, and then resolving, the broad range of feelings that lie at the foundation of it all. So here is an exercise that may be useful to you, to increase awareness of what you are feeling:

MOOD LOG #1

———

This exercise is the earliest building block for a powerful depression treatment strategy known as "Cognitive Therapy," which you will learn more about in a later chapter. For now, here is the formula for the mood log that I assign to my own clients, often at the end of a first therapy session:

WHEN YOU ARE UPSET (sad, angry, frustrated, scared, etc.)

Grab a cheap notebook, and jot down the following:

1—SITUATION:

What is going on around you when you notice feeling upset? Include day, date, time, and place. Also, if relevant, a specific trigger event preceding the upset.

2—FEELINGS:

Name the feeling or feelings you are experiencing. Then **rate the intensity level** of each feeling on a scale from 1–10. (*1= low intensity, 10= high intensity*)

3—THOUGHTS:

Identify the thoughts going through your head as you're experiencing these feelings.

In a later chapter, you'll learn to replace these thoughts and feelings with more positive ones. For now, it is enough to simply increase awareness of them by recording them.

Example:

1. SITUATION:	Thursday, July 17, 7 pm, in my bedroom—boyfriend was 2 hours late picking me up for a date.
2. FEELINGS:	Sadness (8); worry (7); anger (4); worthlessness (9).
3. THOUGHTS:	*"Guess I'm just not that important to him." "He's probably with someone else and just hasn't told me yet." "Guys never really like me for very long." "I hope he's not dead on the freeway somewhere. Where is he?" "He has no right to treat me this way, over and over. He's such a jerk!" "Why am I even with him? He does this to me all the time." "No one really cares about me or wants to spend time with me." "I'm such a loser."*

Once you see your situations, feelings, and thoughts on paper, you can start seeing patterns and intervening productively to resolve those patterns, to improve your situation over time.

2–4 Developing an Expanded Vocabulary for Expressing Feelings

As you start keeping track of your moods, it may be useful for you to reference a list of possible feeling words to draw from, to make it easier to find just the right word to express what you are feeling.

120

The next two pages contain listings of a wide range of feelings. Scan these to locate words to identify and express what you are feeling:

FEELINGS SURVEY

What are you feeling today? How intensely are you feeling it?

1	2	3	4	5	6	7	8	9	10
	Mild			Moderate			Strong		

THE BASIC FOUR:

Sad / Mad / Scared / Happy

SAD:	
MILD:	blue, bummed, disappointed, discontented, disheartened, let down, melancholy, sorrowful
MODERATE:	dejected, demoralized, depressed, discouraged, dismal, gloomy, grumpy, pessimistic
STRONG:	anguished, crushed, destroyed, grieving, grief-stricken, heartbroken, helpless, hopeless

MAD:	
MILD:	aggravated, annoyed, bothered, disturbed, frustrated, irritated, offended, disturbed
MODERATE:	agitated, angry, disgusted, exasperated, peeved, provoked, spiteful, turbulent
STRONG:	contemptuous, enraged, furious, hateful, hostile, incensed, infuriated, outraged, vengeful

SCARED:	
MILD:	concerned, edgy, nervous, preoccupied, uncomfortable, wary, worried
MODERATE:	afraid, alarmed, anxious, apprehensive, distressed, fearful
STRONG:	frantic, panicked, paralyzed, petrified, terrified

HAPPY:	
MILD:	calm, centered, content, encouraged, hopeful, optimistic, peaceful, pleased, relaxed
MODERATE:	amused, cheerful, delighted, enthusiastic, excited, fulfilled, joyful, relieved, satisfied
STRONG:	ecstatic, elated, exhilarated, fantastic, jubilant, overjoyed, thrilled

HURT:	
MILD:	belittled, inadequate, inferior, insignificant, insulted, rejected, small, squashed, stifled
MODERATE:	abused, betrayed, bitter, cheated, deceived, mistreated, robbed, scorned, wounded
STRONG:	broken, degraded, devastated, persecuted, tormented, tortured, traumatized

LONELY:	
MILD:	adrift, alone, disconnected, empty, forgotten, invisible, unappreciated, unneeded
MODERATE:	alienated, discarded, disliked, excluded, ignored, isolated, neglected, unaccepted
STRONG:	abandoned, deserted, left out, useless, rejected, worthless

RESENTFUL:	
MILD:	judged, shortchanged, repressed, taken advantage of, taken for granted
MODERATE:	controlled, manipulated, owned, powerless, trapped
STRONG:	exploited, intimidated, used, victimized, violated

OVERWHELMED:

MILD:	amazed, astonished, dazed, disbelieving, helpless, incredulous, powerless
MODERATE:	alarmed, awestruck, defeated, dismayed, overcome, shocked, stunned, surprised
STRONG:	ambushed, appalled, horrified, smothered, suffocated, trapped

ACCUSED:

attacked, berated, blamed, condemned, cornered, disgraced, humiliated, shamed

CAUTIOUS:

guarded, hesitant, insecure, leery, pensive, self-conscious, shy, suspicious, unsure

CONFUSED:

baffled, bewildered, clueless, lost, mixed up, mystified, perplexed, puzzled, stumped

GUILTY:

apologetic, aghast, ashamed, embarrassed, exposed, regretful, sheepish, sorry

TIRED:

burned out, defeated, drained, exhausted, fatigued, lifeless, overloaded, stretched, weary

UNFEELING:

bored, disillusioned, indifferent, in shock, numb, paralyzed, unfeeling, uninterested

MISC.:

envious, jealous, ambivalent, torn, antsy, restless

CARING:

affectionate, appreciative, compassionate, concerned, cuddly, fond, intimate, kindly, tender

CONFIDENT:

bold, brave, comfortable, eager, safe, secure, self-assured

INTERESTED:

absorbed, curious, inspired, intrigued

LOVED:

adored, cherished, needed, pampered,
spoiled, treasured, trusting

PASSIONATE:

amorous, aroused, infatuated, playful,
romantic, seductive, sexy, stimulated

UNDERSTOOD:

accepted, complete, listened to,
recognized, supported, validated

IMPORTANT QUESTIONS TO ASK:

1. **What** am I feeling today?

2. **How intensely** am I feeling it?

3. **How long** have I felt it?

4. **When and where** do I feel this most strongly?

2–5 Expressing Your Actual Feelings to Others

Once you have increased awareness of your own feelings, it becomes possible to express those feelings to others around you—whether that is your therapist, teacher, friend, priest, family member, or significant other. This will produce the best results if you express those feelings in a safe, positive, and productive way, in which you express what you are feeling about a given situation. To express feelings productively, you can follow a well-known format known as the "**I Message.**" This consists of the following structure:

I FEEL:	
ABOUT:	
BECAUSE:	

Or, another format that may be useful, if you are responding to someone else's behavior, might be:

WHEN YOU:	
I FEEL:	
BECAUSE:	

Example:

"I feel worried and stressed, when you show up late for our dates, because I wonder if you got hurt, or if you don't care about our relationship anymore."

Or....

"When you show up late for our dates, I feel worried and stressed, because I wonder if you got hurt, or if you don't care about our relationship anymore."

You can also use this simple "I Message" format to share positive, upbeat messages, such as:

"I felt safe, happy, and loved today, when you played with our son after work because I love seeing our son so happy."

Or

"When you played with our son today after work I felt safe, happy, and loved because I love seeing our son so happy."

Learning to become aware of our true feelings, and then expressing them to others in a safe, positive way, can contribute powerfully to a sense of emotional well-being. Generally, **the more specific and precise the message, the more effective it is, and the more positive the impact can be, on ourselves and others.**

POSITIVITY:

Notice and Enjoy the Good Things

INBORN TRAITS

1. Action
2. Feeling
3. Positivity

4. Learning
5. Creativity

LEARNED SKILLS

6. Identity
7. Recording

8. Seeking
9. Sociality
10. Service

ADVANCED

11. Health
12. Activity
13. Order

14. Thinking
15. Connection
16. Healing

3–1 Noticing and Enjoying the Positive—A Simple But Powerful Skill

Tool #3 in *YOUR* Happiness Toolkit is—the POSITIVITY tool. This is the cheeriest and most upbeat of all the tools. It is also one of the simplest to use—but is one of the most powerful and life-changing. It requires no cost, and little or no training to launch or reactivate this significant, mood-elevating tool in your own behalf.

Like Tools #1 and #2, this third tool is an inborn trait that you have most likely already had some familiarity with. Even the youngest of babies seem to enter this world with large eyes, fascinated by their surroundings. Watching a young baby or child discover the simple beauties of this world is a powerful way to remember, all over again, how truly wondrous this world can be. Young children seem to innately engage in intense observation—noticing intently the people and things around them, and experiencing extraordinary joy and satisfaction over ordinary things—a meal, a tree, a dog, a toy, the return of a loved caregiver, etc.

We all at some point experienced that early state of being newly introduced into this world. Over the years, we may sometimes come to forget or stop noticing the positive elements of our life experience, and start focusing more on the harsher elements. This condition is particularly common with depression, which almost universally turns our focus to the negative elements in ourselves, our loved ones, and the world around us. Recovering our innate capacity to notice and enjoy the positive is a simple but powerful dimension of depression recovery—and of long-term wellness and enjoyment of life, throughout our lifetimes.

3–2   Building Positive Awareness— What Do You Appreciate Today?

An exercise that I almost always assign early to new counseling clients is—The Gratitude Journal. This written record is distinct from the Daily Mood Log discussed previously. Instructions for beginning a Gratitude Journal are simple, but powerful:

Exercise 1: Keeping a Gratitude Journal

Every day, beginning today, write down at least three positive things that you notice. These entries don't need to be long—they can literally be quick phrases or bullet points. They can address general characteristics in yourself, or in someone you know. They can be achievements you're proud of in yourself or someone close to you. They can be elements of your unique life experience, or they can be elements of the life we all share as fellow inhabitants of planet Earth. Jot at least three of these entries into your written record every day. More is better—but three a day is sufficient to begin reactivating that innate trait of positivity that can help you overcome gloominess and depression.

Here's a sample of the kind of items you might want to include in your daily Gratitude Journal:

Tuesday: *Today, I am grateful:*

- For my health—especially since many others in my school were out sick this week.

- For my friend Sarah—her kindness when I was feeling down after math class today.

- That even though I got a C on my test, it's early in the semester, and I can still do some extra credit to bring up my grade.

Wednesday: *Today I am grateful:*

- That my hair finally flipped in the right direction when I curled it.

- For a particularly bright and sunny day.

- For a funny story someone told over lunch that cheered me up and made me laugh.

- That I was able to get to the gym and exercise today.

You can customize your list to best meet your current needs. For example, if you're struggling with self-worth, make sure at least one item on the list identifies a positive trait in yourself. If you're frustrated with your spouse, record at least one positive thing a day about that person. If you're going through a particularly hard time, record what specific things got you through each day—or even through each hour. By customizing your list, you can more quickly turn the negatives of your life into positives.

Exercise 2: Expressing Gratitude to Someone Else

If you want to get extra benefit out of your gratitude list, to help yourself feel better even more quickly, then blend in this additional element. *Every day, express gratitude to at least one person in your life.* It can be about big things or small things. It can be directed at a friend who was kind to you, a teacher who helped you, a family member who cared about you, or anyone else who impacted you in some positive way.

Expressing gratitude out loud gives the positives in your life even more presence and power. If you're a religious person, you may want to include gratitude phrases in your communications with God; for example, "Dear God, thank you for helping me find the gloves I lost earlier this morning," or "Thank you for giving me such a kind and caring husband." Expressing gratitude increases your own joy and satisfaction, as you recognize the positives in your life. It also brings a lift to the person you express thanks to, bringing double benefit from the same small action.

Exercise 3: Expressing Gratitude Even in Hard Times

If you are going through a difficult time, it can be hard to find *anything* positive to write about. But the gratitude exercise is *particularly* needed and valuable on those hard days—because as you actively look for positive things to record in your Gratitude Journal, it balances out your perspective. You remember that though your difficulties are real, so are the positives that help you get through them from day to day.

3–3 Gratitude or Resentment—You Decide Which Perspective to Adopt

I once heard a speaker observe that *every* experience in life can be met either with gratitude, or with resentment. Some individuals respond to even positive experiences with resentment, distrust, or negativity— making positive situations feel negative, and hard situations feel unbearable. In contrast, other individuals meet even difficult experiences with gratitude. This response helps them weather the challenge at hand, and get through it more efficiently and effectively.

Rate your current pattern on the scale below:

LIST 1—Patterns Feeding:	LIST 2—Patterns Feeding:
Depression, Disease, Deterioration, and Disability	Happiness, Wellness, Resilience, and Productivity
3. NEGATIVITY: Focus on the Negative (in Self, World, & Others)	**3. POSITIVITY:** Notice and Enjoy the Good Things

-3	-2	-1	0	1	2	3
Strong	Moderate	Mild	Neutral	Mild	Moderate	Strong

Happily, even if we have spent decades stuck in negative response, we can learn to shift our perspective back to a more positive outlook. A powerful guide in this process is the book *Learned Optimism* (1990), by psychologist Martin Seligman. In it, Dr. Seligman observes that while people may have natural tendencies toward either optimism or pessimism, based on their core personality, family history, or life experience, they can at any time learn to choose an alternate response. In most cases, Dr. Seligman writes, an optimistic response will bring the most productive consequences.

Intentionally looking for and appreciating the positive is one of simplest but most powerful things you can do each day, in order to keep your perspective and mood moving in a positive direction. If you are already doing that, *keep it up!* It is a habit that will serve you well throughout your life. If you tend, instead, to focus on the negative, then start today to shift that habit by keeping a Gratitude Journal, and expressing gratitude daily. It may be challenging at first, but will feel more and more natural as you gain more experience in doing it. It won't be long before you start to reap the positive consequences of a more positive perspective. Life will feel sweeter, people will seem kinder, and your own satisfaction in your own efforts will be greatly expanded.

3–4 Mindfulness—A Path to Expanded Appreciation and Enjoyment

In recent years, an ancient Buddhist practice has gained more and more respect in modern Western circles. This practice is referred to as *"mindfulness."* It basically means—*being where you are while you are there*—being in your body, in your breath, in this moment in time, in this particular location, under these particular circumstances. Mindfulness is powerful, because being fully engaged in the present moment is a potent antidote to 1) depression's tendency to trap you in dark ruminations or regrets of the past, or 2) anxiety's tendency to propel you into dark fears and fantasies of possible catastrophes in the future.

Being fully here, fully in the present, fully engaged in what is happening around you right now, gives you maximum power to enjoy life, and appreciate its daily gifts to you. It is a powerful ally in your wrestle against depression, and in your quest to experience satisfaction and joy throughout your life.

To get started with mindfulness, **first tune into your breath**— that constant flowing resource that sustains life and nourishes every cell of your body and brain. Take a slow deep breath in, closing your eyes if you like. Then breathe out fully, slowly releasing the stress of the day. Repeat this process several times. Be aware of where you might be carrying stress in your body. Breathe consciously into those muscle systems, and then breathe out any tension you might find there. Focusing on your breathing grounds you within yourself, provides needed oxygen to your brain and body, and has a significantly calming impact.

Next, tune fully into your surroundings, through your five senses. What sounds are part of this space and moment? What does the temperature feel like on your skin? What are the smells, textures, and elements that make this time and space unique? Just notice what you notice. And keep breathing deeply through the process. Enjoy being exactly where you are, exactly when you are there. Practice this first while you are alone, when you can give full focus to the experience.

Later, when you feel ready, begin to explore what it means to be "fully here" with other people. Listen to them without interrupting. Look into their eyes, their faces, their hearts. Observe them without judging. Interact with them peacefully, and with respect. It will be easier to do that if you remain centered yourself. Be where you are, and be where *they* are. Don't let yourself disappear into the cyber world of manufactured image and fantasy, through your phone, video game, or immersive novel. Be here *now*. It may take some courage at first. But over the process of time, as you fully engage with life and people in the present tense, you will find that your life takes on a richness and enjoyment you may never before have thought possible.

If you'd like to learn more about mindfulness and its application to depression recovery, you might enjoy an insightful book entitled *The Mindful Way Through Depression*. Or, engage mindfully in physical exercise, including yoga, tai chi, weightlifting, or Pilates, all of which draw deeply on the power of breath, and help you become accustomed to full engagement in the present moment—right here, right now.

3–5 Positive Psychology—Opening New Doors for a New Millennium

Since about the year 2000, a new psychological approach has emerged that is gaining ever more of a following among healing professionals and others. This discipline is referred to as "Positive Psychology." Launched by Dr. Martin Seligman while he was serving as president of the American Psychological Association, Positive Psychology focuses on strengthening wellness, more than on simply managing illness. Dr. Seligman described this new approach in his excellent books *Authentic Happiness* and *Flourish*.

Dr. Seligman observed that over the 1900s, psychological professionals became very aware of mental illnesses and syndromes, and focused on efforts to manage symptoms of those distressing conditions. But he extended a challenge to his twenty-first-century colleagues and others to begin looking higher than just focusing on "mental illness." He is now one of many researchers and healing professionals who are directly **studying and strengthening mental *wellness* as a primary focus**— exploring the conditions contributing to emotional wellness, and implementing those directly, rather than focusing primarily on negative symptoms.

This promising new approach identifies and strengthens positives in an individual, rather than just focusing and rooting out negatives. It is a cheerful approach to the healing process that many find refreshing and hopeful, and that we will be drawing on substantially in the chapters that follow.

TOOL FOUR

———

LEARNING:

Develop New Abilities and Skills

- ➤ **4–1** The Joy of Lifelong Learning and Development

- ➤ **4–2** Neuroplasticity—The Brain's Lifelong Ability to Change Itself

- ➤ **4–3** How We Get Stuck, and Why We Might Remain Stuck

- ➤ **4–4** Your Learning Style—Visual, Auditory, or Kinesthetic?

- ➤ **4–5** Learning in a Balanced and Manageable Way

INBORN TRAITS

1. Action
2. Feeling
3. Positivity

4. Learning
5. Creativity

LEARNED SKILLS

6. Identity
7. Recording

8. Seeking
9. Sociality
10. Service

ADVANCED

11. Health
12. Activity
13. Order

14. Thinking
15. Connection
16. Healing

4–1   The Joy of Lifelong Learning and Development

Tool #4 in *Your* Happiness Toolkit is—the LEARNING tool. Like the others in Level 1, this tool is inborn and instinctual. Even from our earliest weeks in this world, we possess the ability to absorb new information, develop new capacities, and take on new challenges. We gather information continuously—from our surroundings, from our life experiences, and from observing others around us. As our abilities grow through our continued learning process, we enjoy greater capacity, freedom, confidence, and joy.

Through our earliest years, we learn to hold up our own little heads, stand on our own little feet, and tie our own shoes. We learn how to read and how to write; how to form numbers and letters. We learn how to ride a bike, throw a ball, color a picture, record our thoughts on a page, build a friendship. We learn and grow in all four of the basic dimensions of life—physical, mental, spiritual, and social. Each skill we learn brings a sense of victory and achievement; each new lesson lays groundwork for lessons still to come.

We do not cease to learn when we reach maturity. Continued learning can bring freshness to our thoughts, and renewed purpose and vitality to our lives. And in the rich environment of a twenty-first-century world, we can enjoy unprecedented access to a vast range of powerful learning experiences throughout life. Our modern technologies bring the wisdom of the ages literally to our fingertips, accessible within seconds. Lifelong learning can be a rich source of enjoyment, fulfillment, and personal growth, from infancy to old age.

4–2   Neuroplasticity—The Brain's Lifelong Ability to Change Itself

Through most of human history, it was believed that the brain stopped learning after a certain age—that "it's hard to teach an old dog new tricks." More recent research, however, has revealed that, like the rest of the body, the human brain is capable of generating healthy new cells *throughout* life—*if* it is provided with the materials and processes needed to do so. The term "neuroplasticity" describes this lifetime capacity the brain ("neuro") possesses to grow, develop, and change over time ("plasticity")—a process documented by psychiatrist Dr. Norman Doidge, in his groundbreaking book, *The Brain That Changes Itself* (2007).

Particularly in our time, when the world and the demands of the workplace are changing at an unprecedented rate, **learning how** *to effectively learn* is perhaps one of the most essential skills we can acquire and maintain throughout our lives—one that grows with us as we encounter a variety of new challenges over the years. This growth-producing trait we were all born with—the capacity to learn—can continually add to our abilities, expand our opportunities, and multiply our enjoyments, from our earliest years to our final hours in this world. *It is never too late to learn.*

Our ability to learn also has powerful antidepressant qualities. The act of learning brings a sense of fulfillment, achievement, and increased confidence that does much to help overpower depression. Learning also helps regenerate *hope*—hope that things can be better, as we learn and apply new insights and skills. We can literally reshape our lives, any time we chose to do so, by first learning and then putting into practice life-changing strategies, such as those shared in this book.

4–3   How We Get Stuck, and Why We Might Remain Stuck

Though opportunities for learning are ever-present, we may, over time, settle into habits that remain with us for years—whether or not they work for us. Some of us follow patterns observed in childhood—even if those patterns caused us pain originally. Some work in jobs requiring repetitive, mind-numbing action. Some of us simply get used to carrying out the same repetitive daily routine—doing things the same way we've always done them, thinking in the same ways we've always thought—even if these ways are not in our best interest.

It may feel easier to do so—particularly if we're feeling down or depressed. Depression can make any activity, even learning, feel difficult. But if we're not activating new circuits of the brain, we are unlikely to experience healing growth and neuroplasticity— the development of healthy new brain cells. The more "stuck in a rut" we get, the more we literally feed depression. And the more depressed we feel, the less likely we are to engage in positive learning and activity. It's a self-perpetuating cycle—a destructive cycle that must be interrupted if we are to ever break the crushing grasp of depression on our minds, hearts, and lives.

Rate your current pattern on the scale below:

LIST 1—Patterns Feeding: Depression, Disease, Deterioration, and Disability	LIST 2—Patterns Feeding: Happiness, Wellness, Resilience, and Productivity
4. STAGNATION: Remain Stuck in Old Patterns and Habits	**4. LEARNING:** Develop New Abilities and Skills

-3	-2	-1	0	1	2	3
Strong	Moderate	Mild	Neutral	Mild	Moderate	Strong

4–4   Your Learning Style—Visual, Auditory, or Kinesthetic?

Fortunately, the stagnation pattern can be broken, and positive brain health can be activated by even small increments of learning and development. It is not necessary—or even desirable—to try to learn everything all at once, or in the same way that someone else might learn. We are very unique in our learning styles, and different learning approaches work better for different people, at different times in their individual lives. *To promote brain health, fight depression, and maintain emotional wellness, try to learn something new and positive, each and every day.*

There are many ways in which you can do this. Three major learning styles to be aware of in this process are:

1. **VISUAL**—learning through the eyes by *seeing* something.

2. **AUDITORY**—learning through the ears by *hearing* something.

3. **KINESTHETIC**—learning through action by *doing* something.

Of course, we can learn in all three ways, and can benefit from all three approaches. But some approaches may feel more natural to us than others—or more helpful or doable in learning various skills at various times. For example, when learning a new computer program, step-by-step video instruction *(visual)* may be a more effective learning approach than simply hearing someone explain the task. When learning a new cooking skill, or a new exercise move, or how to play a musical instrument, hands-on practical instruction (*kinesthetic*) will generally be the most effective approach. In contrast, if our hands are already busy with mindless tasks, *auditory* learning can be a great way to infuse our minds with powerful new ideas—for example, by listening to an insightful audiobook while washing the dishes, sweeping the floor, raking leaves, or putting on makeup.

Some of the most effective learning experiences include all three of these learning styles. Wise teachers intentionally include material for all three kinds of students. They:

- **explain and describe** (*auditory*),

- **show and demonstrate** (*visual*), and

- **provide opportunity for practical implementation** (*kinesthetic*).

In this way, the learning process is the most clear, complete, and satisfying for the majority of students, bringing the most effective and enduring results.

You can customize your learning process to fit your current preference, needs, and energy level. If your energy is low, due to illness, depression, or general overwhelm, you may find auditory learning to be the most fitting and least demanding of the learning styles. If you're a high-energy person, you may find the kinesthetic style to be the most practical and engaging. Visual learners tend to be the fastest learners, taking in information quickly through their eyes, including by reading.

You can mix and match these styles to meet the need at hand, and to match your current energy level. But again, even if you're having a particularly depressing or low-energy day, try to do *something* that can help you learn something positive. Don't let the stagnation cycle hold you hostage for one day longer. *Every day, learn something new.*

There are many ways in which you can engage in effective learning. These include:

1. **Learning from Insightful Books (or Audiobooks):** This approach tends to be powerful and time-efficient, allowing you to learn quickly from authors who took the time necessary to record insights that may have taken them decades to gather. The pre-digested form of a book allows you to learn helpful information at your own pace—a chapter at a time, or even a paragraph or sentence at a time, as your time and energy allow.

2. **Reviewing or Browsing Books You've Already Read:** This approach allows you to gain additional benefit from a book you've already been through at least once. You will notice new ideas each time you return to a book. Because you will be in a different place in your life each time you return, you'll notice different things, and gain different benefits from the information. Jotting down notes or highlighting book pages can be helpful ways to harvest, remember, and personalize the insights you gain from your reading.

Note: on particularly stressful, busy, or depressing days, reading or reviewing a book can take a minimum of time and energy, but can produce powerful benefits to help you overcome your daily challenges—even if you just read or reread a few lines, or a paragraph or two each day.

3. **Learning from Electronic Resources:** In our modern age, we have instant access to a vast sea of videos, websites, articles, and online learning resources—all accessible within a few seconds of an internet search. These resources can help us learn visually, and deliver to us direct sights and sounds that even a king's ransom couldn't have bought previously. We are the most fortunate of individuals, if we use this vast resource wisely. It is a highly visual resource; and, in the case of video, also blends in strong auditory information.

   However, there are some possible *downsides to electronic learning*. If we're not careful, we can easily get lost or adrift in it, if we're not clear and proactive in our objectives. We can become very reactive online, simply flitting impulsively from image to image, or website to website, without a clear sense of purpose. We can easily get distracted from our original goal by other content we encounter online. If we use this resource unwisely, it can actually *contribute* to our depression and our distraction, and even to our destruction if we veer off into pornographic or other negative content, or get hooked into time-wasting drivel.

So electronic resources can be significantly powerful sources of learning—but must be handled with utmost care and self-control in order to be effective.

4. **Learning from Other People:** Whether from a real-life teacher, a book, a video, or just everyday life, other people can be hugely valuable sources of learning. We can draw on others' wisdom, experience, and skill as we develop our own, so that we don't have to learn everything from scratch.

   Anthony Robbins, in his books *Unlimited Power* and *Awaken the Giant Within*, wisely suggests finding mentors who already excel at the things you want to become good at. He suggests studying not only what these mentors *do*, but also what they *think*, in order to achieve success. Once you know their strategy—what they *think* and what they *do* in order to create a certain result—you can follow their example, thinking and doing the same things that worked for them, in order to achieve success more quickly and effectively yourself.

5. **Learning from Our Own Experience:** This is the traditional and fundamental way of learning—within our own skin, and in the context of our own lives. However, it is also the slowest method of learning—sometimes known as "learning the hard way" or "learning from the school of hard knocks." Some of this, of course, is essential—but we can save ourselves time and trouble by not relying exclusively on this style of learning. Our own success and learning processes can be greatly expedited by drawing on insights from others.

4–5   Learning in a Balanced and Manageable Way

It is important, of course, for us to pace ourselves in the learning process. Some people become overwhelmed by trying to learn too much, too soon, or for too long. We learn best when we are learning gradually—when we give ourselves some time to test, implement, and get comfortable using one new skill or insight, before moving on to the next one. A non-stop onslaught of new things to learn can quickly become overwhelming, discouraging, or even depressing.

So it is crucial to **balance learning** with regenerative activity, physical exercise, enjoyable social interaction, and rest, in order to be effective. That is true for adults in their learning process. It is even more true for youth, and especially for children. We must always beware of policies and procedures that, in their push for expanded learning and productivity, instead, increase the likelihood of burnout and discouragement.

Providing time for personal renewal between learning experiences is a crucial element in the learning process. The more demanding the learning material is, the more important it is to allow mind and body to rest between learning experiences—even if it's just for a short period. Going on a walk, taking a bubble bath, eating a nutritious meal, talking to a friend, playing with a child, or even tidying a room are activities that can help break up the learning process into more manageable chunks. So, while learning is an important part of our mental health over time, *pacing* that learning process is equally important, so the information we learn can truly stick, and so we can derive full and lasting benefit out of the things we are working so hard to learn.

Likewise, it is helpful to **diversify our learning experiences**, just as we might diversify our financial resources. Years ago, while receiving my formal education as a counselor, I was trained in a model known as *"Systematic Eclecticism."* This means—drawing insights, perspectives, and healing strategies from a wide variety of sources; then blending them all together in a balanced, systematic way. This was perhaps the most valuable part of my education—learning to gather many different techniques from many different sources, and then pulling them together into a cohesive strategy that could be customized to help a wide variety of individuals. *This is the philosophy and process that I used to create this book—* pulling from many wellness-enhancing strategies that individuals can customize, to address the need at hand.

In a similar way, systematic eclecticism can help *you* to gather and blend together different elements of information that can help you meet the specific, changing needs of yourself and others. Different elements will be needed at different times, to meet changing circumstances in your life.

As we have discussed, learning can be achieved in many ways; and it can be helpful to seek learning in a variety of styles, from a variety of sources, to meet a wide variety of needs. We'll continue to explore many of these potentially useful strategies to help you and those you love, in the chapters that follow.

CREATIVITY:

Focus on Creating Rather Than Consuming

➤ **5-1** Creativity—Why It Is So Important for Emotional Health

➤ **5-2** Consuming and Passive Entertainment—A Modern Scourge

➤ **5-3** Creative Expression—A Path of Discovery, A Road Through Pain

➤ **5-4** Your Worst Nightmare Can Become Your Greatest Inspiration

➤ **5-5** Mobilizing Your Inborn Traits for Recovery and Wellness

INBORN TRAITS

1. Action
2. Feeling
3. Positivity

4. Learning
5. Creativity

LEARNED SKILLS

6. Identity
7. Recording

8. Seeking
9. Sociality
10. Service

ADVANCED

11. Health
12. Activity
13. Order

14. Thinking
15. Connection
16. Healing

5–1 Creativity—Why It Is So Important for Emotional Health

T ool #5 in *Your* Happiness Toolkit is the CREATIVITY tool. This the last of the Level 1 tools in your toolkit. Like the four tools previously discussed, it is an inborn trait that no one needs to teach you. In fact, of all the sixteen tools, it is the most individual—because it is fundamentally the expression of your unique contribution and voice in this world— something no one else can duplicate.

Tools #1–4 relate to your *response* to this world—how you act in it, feel about it, interpret it, and learn about it. Creativity is different. It relates to what you give *back* to this world, what you *express* from your inner self. Creativity is a core part of who we are as human beings. **We are not merely capable of reacting** to what's going on *around* us. We are also capable of sharing what's going on *inside* of us—a gift to the world that is unique in each and every person.

Creativity in young childhood is expressed in a myriad of ways. It's the picture you drew of yourself and your family on the first day of school. It's the paint colors and theme you chose for your art project. It's the song you sang while you were falling asleep at night. It's the particular tower of blocks you built when you were four years old; or the particular creation you assembled from your Lego collection; or the puppet show, pretend game, or Barbie scene you played out with your toys. Creativity is part of the natural inheritance of childhood—as natural to us as breathing. No one has to teach you how to use it. No one *can* teach you how to use it. It is a natural, inborn, defining trait of being human.

Creativity brings with it a special kind of joy and satisfaction— something inside us that says, "I *did* this. I *made* this. I *created* this." It's nice, of course, to learn from other people's insights, and to enjoy their creations. It's wonderful to tune in to the beauties of the earth, and to all the good things around us that life has to offer. But there is something uniquely fulfilling about creating something *yourself*—an expression of *you*, of that unique *something* that exists in you alone.

Likewise, there is a special and unique joy that comes from creating something *together*. As various people combine their individual talents, voices, and perspectives, marvelous things happen that don't occur in any other way. Whether in a play, a choir, a band, a video, a science project, or a business, creating something together develops deep and lasting bonds, as co-creators share their unique ideas with one another, developing a product that no individual person could ever create alone. There is a level of fulfillment and connection in that experience, that can never be duplicated by simply regurgitating established data.

Even our communities benefit when creativity is shared, as a broad community experience. Traditionally, communities sang together, danced together, built things together. They watched live theatre being performed on live stages by live performers—laughing and crying together as a community, sharing a catharsis experience, as the story unfolded before their united gaze.

These creativity episodes—as individuals, in small groups, or as communities—can truly be some of the peak experiences of human life. Where they exist, life can feel rich, fulfilling, and connected. Where they are lacking, life can feel empty, purposeless, and without fresh vision or meaningful connection.

5–2   Consuming and Passive Entertainment—A Modern Scourge

In our day and age, the experience of creativity is becoming more and more rare—in individuals, small groups, and communities. We no longer gather and sing together, using our unique talents. Instead, we tend to sit alone with our headphones, silently consuming the pre-recorded, electronically delivered sounds on our individualized playlists. We no longer gather and dance together as communities, or sit together in large theaters to experience a shared catharsis. Instead, we tend to sit alone with our cell phone, computer, or electronic notepad, scrolling through endless options for pre-formatted passive entertainment. We no longer build things together, and then treasure the things we build. Instead, we individually go shopping for the perfect, pre-manufactured item to meet our current desire—until a new product catches our eye, displacing the prior purchase.

In short, **we have largely ceased to live as creators and co-creators. Instead, we tend to exist more and more as constant "consumers,"** whose job it is to keep the national economy afloat, through an endless stream of impulse purchases. Where we used to grow, harvest, and cook our own food, we now pull up to the drive-in window, and make our order. Where we once sang, we now listen to others sing; where we once danced, we now watch well-trained, scantily clad experts do the job for us. Passive entertainment and constant consumption—these are characteristics, more and more, that occupy and define our modern lives.

Even in the lives of our young children, these changes are evident. The sound of children running, laughing, and playing outside together has been largely replaced by the electronic beeps and blips of the video game played nightly for hours, alone in the basement. The schools that once rang with the sound of school choirs, bands, and theatre productions are now relatively silent, as students sit alone at their desks, studying quietly for yet another standardized test. The "let's pretend" games of past generations of children have now been almost entirely replaced with the innumerable fantasy movies, novels, games, and videos that permeate the lives of modern youth and children. Toy stores have all but disappeared, crowded out by electronics.

Rate your current pattern on the scale below:

LIST 1—Patterns Feeding:	LIST 2—Patterns Feeding:
Depression, Disease, Deterioration, and Disability	Happiness, Wellness, Resilience, and Productivity
5. CONSUMING: Be a Constant Consumer of Others' Products	**5. CREATIVITY:** Focus On Creating Rather Than Consuming

-3	-2	-1	0	1	2	3
Strong	Moderate	Mild	Neutral	Mild	Moderate	Strong

Ours is an age of rampant addiction—including in our young—addiction to illicit drugs, alcohol, smoking, sugar, junk food, prescription drugs, compulsive shopping, and even pornography. But there is one addiction that currently is more pervasive than all the others combined. It is—an *addiction to media*—the need to constantly be occupied with one's phone or another electronic device.

We might be checking our social media apps, texting our acquaintances, catching another round of Candy Crush, or browsing YouTube for another entertaining but meaningless video. We may each choose different apps on our phone, watch different videos on YouTube, or select different songs on Pandora. The *content* of our media obsession may vary markedly from person to person. But **what we are almost all doing is consuming other people's creations—rather than developing creations of our own.** This is a habit that squashes joy, and feeds depression. However, *it is not an inevitable pattern*, even in the times we live in.

In *A Tale of Two Cities*, one of his most famous novels, Charles Dickens observed:

> *It was the best of times, it was the worst of times,*
>
> *it was the age of wisdom, it was the age of foolishness,*
>
> *it was the epoch of belief, it was the epoch of incredulity,*
>
> *it was the season of Light, it was the season of Darkness,*
>
> *it was the spring of hope, it was the winter of despair,*
>
> *we had everything before us, we had nothing before us.*

As Dickens wrote of this time period, so it is with us. The conditions and patterns that characterize our time can either work *for* us or *against* us—depending on how we respond to them. The technologies and devices that permeate our modern world can drown out our inner voice, numb our creative impulses, and reduce us to little more than passive consumers of other people's ideas, products, and creations.

Or . . . used wisely, modern technology can greatly facilitate our creative process. From the comfort of our own homes, we can now use technology to compose and record music, shoot and edit video, write and publish books, learn new musical and creative skills, develop images and animations, and send our unique creations all over the world, instantly, at the touch of a button. The same devices that can obscure our vision and crush our creativity can, when used wisely, allow us to develop and share our creations at a level and a breadth never imagined possible by the greatest artists and visionaries of the past. We are fortunate indeed to have access to these powerful technological tools—*if* we use them proactively and wisely—to create, and not just to consume.

5–3   Creative Expression—A Path of Discovery, A Road Through Pain

Finding a way to express ourselves creatively can truly be a window into our deepest, truest, most joyous self. As we begin to see what comes *out* of us, we learn more about what is *inside* of us. And that discovery brings profound satisfaction and self-awareness, as well as a rich new means of connecting with others.

You may think to yourself, *"But I'm just not that creative. I just don't have any artistic talents or interests."* There are many options to explore to find and release your creative inner self, to express your inner heart. These options include:

ARTISTIC:

Visual Art:
doodling, drawing, sketching, painting, sculpting, designing

Music:
singing alone, singing with a group, playing
an instrument, writing a song

Theatre:
acting on stage, acting on film, directing, skits, psychodrama

Dancing:
line dancing, formal dance (ballet, tap, jazz, modern), Zumba, country dance

Photography:
still photography, videography, photo editing, video editing

Writing:
poetry, free verse, fiction, non-fiction, blog, memoirs

PRACTICAL:

Housework:
home organization, interior design, gardening, baking, planning and cooking meals

Handiwork:
leatherwork, carpentry, embroidery, knitting, crocheting, sewing, jewelry making, crafts

Personal Grooming:
wardrobe planning, hair and makeup design

Because the creative process is so powerful for revealing the inner self, it is often used by therapists and other healing professionals to help make the unconscious conscious, and to expose feelings and issues requiring relief and healing. You don't have to be a professional artist to benefit from these healing activities.

CREATIVITY-ORIENTED THERAPIES INCLUDE:

Play Therapy:
with young children, using toys to represent
and resolve inner conflicts

Music, Dance, or Art Therapy:
giving people tools to express themselves, work through trauma, etc.

Psychodrama, Family Sculpture, Role Playing:
acting out conflicts, to practice resolving them

Creative expression can play a powerful role not just in expressing the inner self, but also in identifying and resolving deep pain, grief, trauma, and conflict. Creative work, particularly acting and music, has been my personal healing path through many of the steepest challenges and heartbreaks of my life. It has had a similar impact on others I have known over the years, whether they receive formal counseling or not. Veterans of war, survivors of abuse, witnesses of crime and natural disasters, and others facing overwhelming sorrow and grief are among those who can benefit greatly from having a safe outlet to express and share what they have endured—and what they have learned from enduring it.

5–4   Your Worst Nightmare Can Become Your Greatest Inspiration

I have had the privilege over the years of working with a number of top-quality musicians, actors, and other artists, who credit the intensity and passion of their best work to their worst, most heart-wrenching life experiences. I have seen them time and again transform their agonizing pain into spectacularly honest, beautiful artistic masterpieces. I have heard them express their enduring gratitude for even the most difficult experiences of their lives, and the role those difficulties played in helping them to craft that insightful lyric, that heartfelt moment captured on film, that stirring symphonic expression of victory over adversity. These are the actors that are able to cry on cue, drawing from the richness and intensity of their own life experience. These are the singers and musicians that tug at the heartstrings, expressing vulnerability we all feel at times, but rarely dare express. These are the screenwriters, playwrights, authors, and composers who tell stories and share feelings, through their creative work, that we can all relate to on a visceral level. The inner demons they fight and overcome are what drive, motivate, inspire, and facilitate their very best work.

Inspiration often flows freest when we are at our lowest. Creativity often rises to its greatest heights in the midst of the most exquisite pain. No experience is ever wasted, for from great pain can come great insight.

Over the years, I have also become acquainted with therapists and other healers whose compassionate work was largely motivated by their own pain, and their own recovery. Having come through the fire themselves, having walked a thorny path and gotten successfully through to the other side, they now come boldly to assist in the rescue of others. Because they know how it feels to hurt, they are able to help others in pain—far more deeply and with far more understanding than people who never experienced any major sorrows in life. These people are truly my heroes—the "wounded healers" who reach out in compassion to others.

Finally, over my years as a counselor, I have met literally hundreds of people, from every walk of life, who having endured the pain of depression, abuse, grief, addiction, divorce, or other hardships, move through their own recovery process, and then proceed onward to help support and guide others going through similar challenges. The determination to help others is sometimes what gets these struggling individuals through their own pain. In the ultimate act of resplendent creativity, these courageous people work to reshape their own lives into something beautiful and productive—and then, courageously assist others in doing the same.

You don't have to be a professional performing artist or healer to turn your pain into a force for good in the world. **You simply have to be willing to feel what you feel, heal what you must heal, learn what you must learn, and then be willing to share those hard-won lessons with others.**

Of all the creations that human beings are capable of, this is perhaps the most powerful and significant of all—to take the raw materials of a rough and difficult life experience, and transform it all into a well-lived, happy, and fulfilling life, full of service, kindness, and compassion.

5–5 Mobilizing Your Inborn Traits for Recovery and Wellness

Congratulations! In completing Section 2 of this book, you are now acquainted with the first five tools in *Your* Happiness Toolkit. These are the Level 1 "Inborn Traits" that can be reactivated and infused with new power to help you overcome depression, and build a joyful, fulfilling life. As a review, these five tools are:

Tool 1—ACTION:
Do What You Love—And Do What Loves You Back!

Tool 2—FEELING:
Feel and Express Your Actual Feelings

Tool 3—POSITIVITY:
Notice and Enjoy the Good Things

Tool 4—LEARNING:
Develop New Abilities and Skills

Tool 5—CREATIVITY:
Focus on Creating, Rather Than Consuming

Together with the Transformational Tools introduced in Section I, these Level 1 tools can help you daily to craft a positive lifestyle that promotes emotional recovery and enduring wellness. Now, before introducing the Level 2 tools in the following section, here is a worksheet to help summarize all you've learned so far:

THE LEVEL 1 TOOLS, AND THE 5 TRANSFORMATIONAL TOOLS:

LEVEL 1 TOOLS (INBORN TRAITS):	
Tool 1—ACTION:	Do what you love—and do what loves you back!
Tool 2—FEELING:	Feel and Express Your Actual Feelings
Tool 3—POSITIVITY:	Notice and Enjoy the Good Things
Tool 4—LEARNING:	Develop New Abilities and Skills
Tool 5—CREATIVITY:	Focus on Creating Rather Than Consuming

5 TRANSFORMATIONAL TOOLS:

1. WELLNESS GRID	Physical, Mental, Spiritual, Emotional
2. UP-OR-DOWN SPIRAL	Upward Direction or Downward Direction?
3. DIAMOND	Triggers, Thoughts, Behaviors, Spirituality, Relationships
4. MORE-OR-LESS GRID	"I Need More . . . / I Need Less . . ." in the Four Areas
5. YOUR HAPPINESS TOOLKIT	16 Strategies, Levels 1–3

	What Do I Need MORE of?	What Do I Need LESS of?
PHYSICALLY:		
MENTALLY:		
SPIRITUALLY:		
EMOTIONALLY:		

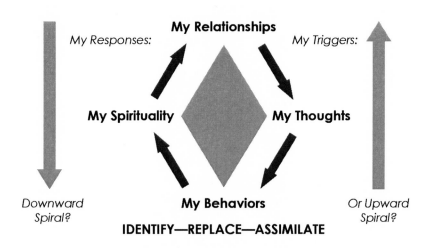

YOUR HAPPINESS TOOLKIT, LEVEL 2

Learned Skills

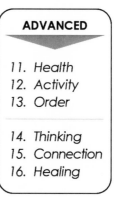

INBORN TRAITS

1. Action
2. Feeling
3. Positivity

4. Learning
5. Creativity

LEARNED SKILLS

6. Identity
7. Recording

8. Seeking
9. Sociality
10. Service

ADVANCED

11. Health
12. Activity
13. Order

14. Thinking
15. Connection
16. Healing

I n this section, we will be adding tools that you have most likely been exposed to naturally over the process of growing up. Most people are introduced to these skills as children, and are well practiced at using them by the time they're about eight years old. These tools add richness and balance to the human personality.

However, like the Inborn Traits introduced in the previous section, these Learned Skills can be suppressed or even silenced by a negative environment. In more severe cases, an environment may have been sufficiently negative to even prevent the development of these skills in the first place. In any case, learning to put them effectively to use in your life now can be a powerful, positive addition to *Your* Happiness Toolkit.

These skills are more demanding than those outlined in the Quick Start Guide, or in Level 1 of the Toolkit. If you have been fortunate to learn and use them in your life before, they will be easier for you to put to use now, building on your prior experience. If these skills are relatively new to you, they may require a more intense learning curve upfront—but can bring fresh, new energy and hope into your life, as you learn to implement them. Either way, using these tools can greatly add to your resilience, productivity, and overall happiness.

IDENTITY:

Know and Value Your Unique Traits and Gifts

➤ **6–1** "Who Am I?"—Mobilizing the Power of Self-Awareness

➤ **6–2** Comparative Worth vs. Innate Worth

➤ **6–3** Personality Typing, to Understand and Value Yourself and Others

➤ **6–4** Temperament—Why We Are All Needed, Just As We Are

➤ **6–5** Type Development—How We Change and Grow Over Time

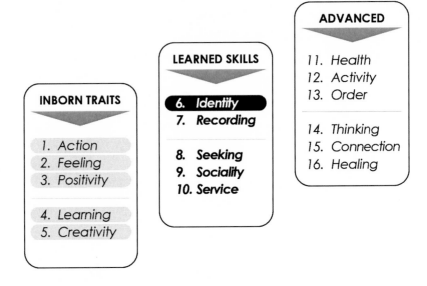

6–1 "Who Am I?"—Mobilizing the Power of Self-Awareness

Tool #6 in YOUR Happiness Toolkit is—the IDENTITY tool. This is a tool you were most likely exposed to in childhood. One of its earliest expressions may have been on that first day in elementary school when your teacher passed out a handout entitled "Who Am I?" Perhaps you were asked to fill it out with information including your name, a hand-drawn self-portrait, your favorite color, food, TV show, and so forth. You may have even been asked what you wanted to be when you grew up.

Even at that early stage, your response—like that of each of the other students—was different from the rest. Your unique identity, personality, likes and dislikes, strengths and weaknesses, talents and gifts had already begun to emerge. And over the years since, you have continued to grow into the person that you uniquely are.

Before we truly learn who we *are* in this world, we tend to learn who we *aren't*. That can sometimes be a painful and disappointing process—finding out what we're *not* good at, where we *don't* fit in. But finding out who we are and who we aren't, where we fit and where we don't, what we're good at and what we're not, is an essential part of our growing-up experience.

In the process, we learn that we're naturally better at some things than other people—and that they're naturally better at some things than we are. We learn about ourselves from observing what classes we do well or poorly in, what friends we attract, and what other people say about us.

It is helpful for us to know who we are, particularly as we pursue emotional healing and wellness. It helps us select strategies that can be most useful for *us* personally—that can bring us the most joy and satisfaction. Just as importantly, it can help us determine which facets of our lives may currently be contributing to our distress, anxiety, or conflict—so that we can effectively identify these factors, and then resolve them.

The items in *Your* Happiness Toolkit that will be of most worth to you might be vastly different than things that would be useful to someone else. So it is helpful early in the healing process to determine your unique personality, talents, and gifts—so that your healing process can be carefully customized to meet *your* needs.

6–2 Comparative Worth vs. Innate Worth

If we don't truly know who we are, and what we are uniquely good at, we can easily be drawn into a painful lifestyle characterized by comparing and competition. It is as if we are constantly measuring ourselves against others, to see how we measure up—at home, at school, in the workplace, at church, or anywhere else. Our "measuring sticks" might be based on grades, income, the number of children we have, the size of our houses, the brand of our cars, the cut of our jeans, or even the weights or measurements of our various body parts.

This mental habit of comparing ourselves against others is very common in people struggling with depression, anxiety, and low self-esteem. It can make our self-esteem very unstable, if our sense of personal worth is based on which measuring stick we're using at the moment, and who we're measuring ourselves against.

In some situations, we might judge ourselves to be *better* than the person standing next to us—and, therefore, feel temporarily superior. Just as easily, however, we might compare ourselves to someone who is stronger than us in some identified area— and then, we are likely to feel inferior, or even worthless, in comparison. This is a very common pattern in those struggling with depression and other emotional challenges. Happily, it is a pattern that once identified, can be broken, and replaced with something far better.

Rate your current pattern on the scale below:

LIST 1—Patterns Feeding:	LIST 2—Patterns Feeding:
Depression, Disease, Deterioration, and Disability	Happiness, Wellness, Resilience, and Productivity
6. COMPARING: Compare Yourself Negatively Against Others	**6. IDENTITY:** Know and Value Your Unique Traits and Gifts

-3	-2	-1	0	1	2	3
Strong	Moderate	Mild	Neutral	Mild	Moderate	Strong

Constantly comparing ourselves against others tends to be exhausting and discouraging. It's as if we're in constant competition with each other, for basic worth and validation. Under this system, if someone else excels or wins, we may feel as if we have lost. This can make it very difficult for us to appreciate or support others—because their gain seems to be our loss. Their success seems to constitute our failure. Their triumph seems to declare our defeat.

But . . . *what if* there was enough worth to go around—if there was an infinite supply, enough for everyone? When you know your own traits and gifts, and how those vary from the traits and gifts of others, *you can rest confident in your own value—even as you celebrate someone else's victory.* Your sense of self-worth can remain stable and consistent, regardless of what is going on around you. It's a truly beautiful way to live.

6–3   Personality Typing, to Understand and Value Yourself and Others

When I was nineteen years old, I was given a great gift by a professor who taught at the university I attended. He was a theatre professor, but also had a background in psychology. He gave me a book by David Keirsey and Marilyn Bates called *Please Understand Me*. The book's title rang poignantly true to me at the time. I was a young theatre student during those years, literally competing against my classmates for roles and opportunities, and often experiencing the rejection and disappointment of someone else being chosen for a desired role, instead of me. I often felt frustrated, discouraged, and at times, even deeply depressed— severely doubting my own worth, and wondering if there would *ever* be a place for me—not just in an onstage performance, but in the great unfolding drama of life.

As I read the pages of *Please Understand Me*, I began to slowly comprehend why I so often felt different from almost everybody else I knew. I learned from the book that there are essentially sixteen different types of people, who are motivated by different things, possess different strengths and weaknesses, connect in different ways, and enjoy different types of experiences. I learned that my type was one of the rarest of the sixteen, which explained why I so rarely felt understood by others at the time. I also learned about the unique *strengths* of my type—and the known *weaknesses*.

Perhaps even more importantly, I learned about the *other* fifteen types of people mentioned in the book. It was as if I was given a magical telescope—a way to glimpse fifteen other perspectives different than mine—to be able to see through other eyes. As I began to understand where other people were coming from, they began to feel far less intimidating and hurtful to me. I began to see how my gifts and characteristics could blend *with* theirs, in a powerful synthesis that produced better results than any of us alone could produce.

That book lifted me out of a severe depression, and set my feet on a happier course over the many decades since that time. I learned that the book was based on a personality test crafted in the 1940s by an insightful mother-daughter team, Katherine Cook Briggs and Isabel Briggs Myers. The test, known as the *Myers-Briggs Type Indicator (MBTI)*, has inspired many spin-off books and tests, including the book I was given. Many versions of the test are now available online, including my current favorite, a free version which can be found at *16personalities.com.*

I now routinely have counseling clients, family members, friends, and others take the test. For them, as for me, the understanding of self and others generated by the test has proved truly life-changing, and has a vast range of positive and practical uses, including:

1. **Basic self-understanding:** helping people identify their natural characteristics, strengths, and weaknesses.

2. **Treatment planning:** customizing treatment approaches to the specific needs of the individual.

3. **Career and education counseling:** identifying an optimal career path for an individual of a particular type.

4. **Pre-marital counseling:** assessing compatibility or likely conflicts between possible life partners.

5. **Marriage and family therapy:** building understanding and mutual respect between family members.

6. **Parenting:** helping parents customize their parenting approach to the needs of their various children.

7. **Education:** helping teachers customize their teaching style to the needs of their various students.

8. **Human resources:** helping businesses attract the right employees, and assigning them the right tasks.

Many resources are now available that apply the MBTI to various practical uses. Besides *Please Understand Me* and *16personalities. com*, some of my favorites are: *Do What You Are* (career/ education); *Nurture by Nature* (parenting); *Just Your Type* (premarital/marital relationships), all by Paul Tieger and Barbara Barron-Tieger; and *Gifts Differing* by Isabel Briggs Myers (one of the originators of the MBTI.)

In introducing the MBTI, the following exercise can be helpful:

Introductory Exercise:

(Please do the exercise one step at a time, without reading ahead)

STEP 1:

Pull out a pen, and a fresh piece of paper.

STEP 2:

Print your name at the top of the page;
then sign your name under it.

STEP 3:

Now—do the same thing—but do it with your other hand.

STEP 4:

Notice any differences you feel
between step 2 and step 3.

When I have clients do this exercise in my office, they often race right through steps 1 and 2 with confidence, exclaiming "Oh, this is easy!" Then, in step 3, when I instruct them to carry out the exercise with their other hand, they often giggle with uncertainty, saying things like, "Oh, I don't think I can do that!"

Every time, they surprise themselves by accomplishing the task—but it takes considerably more effort, attention, and concentration—and their step 3 result never looks as polished or confident as step 2.

I start with this exercise to illustrate an important point: **We really can do almost anything we set our minds to. But we won't necessarily do everything *well*.** Can a right-handed person write with their left hand? Certainly. But they'll never do it as well as an actual left-handed person. Typically, it looks like the awkward scrawl of a very young child. The same applies to a left-handed person trying to write with their right hand.

This exercise illustrates one of the major points of the MBTI. As human beings, we possess different characteristics—and some are more natural to us than others. We can force ourselves to do what is not natural to us—but we'll never be as fluid or skilled at it as someone who naturally possesses that skill. *We will always do our best, most satisfying, and happiest work when we draw on our natural strengths.* We will always feel most stressed, awkward, and anxious when we are pressed to do something that is a natural weakness for us.

Each of the sixteen types has natural strengths and weaknesses. In the MBTI, these sixteen types are derived from comparing four sets of opposite traits—and determining which traits are the most natural and comfortable for the individual being tested. Each of the traits is assigned a name and a letter, as follows:

AN INDIVIDUAL MIGHT BE MORE:	OR MORE:
E—Extroverted	I—Introverted
S—Sensory	N—Intuitive
T—Thinking	F—Feeling
J—Judging	P—Perceiving

Here is a graph summarizing the comparative strengths of each of these traits. More information is in the books and websites referenced, but this quick summary provided here can give you a good start.

For each pair of opposite traits (side by side), **consider which side sounds more like you—your natural "comfort zone:"**

STRENGTHS OF PERSONALITY PREFERENCES:

E—Extroverted *(55% of people)*	I—Introverted *(45% of people)*
Breadth of ideas and relationships	Depth of ideas and relationships
Variety/outreach; broad awareness	Precision/focus; specific awareness
Many friends with brief contact	Fewer friends with longer contact
Talking; thinking out loud; diving right in	Listening; processing internally before diving in
Energized by being with other people	Need time alone, or with just a few others
Outer world	Inner world
Initiate contact	Wait their turn
Easy to approach; sociable	More reserved and serious
Enjoy crowds, bustling activity	Enjoy solitude/closeness with a few they trust

S—Sensory *(65% of people)*	N—Intuitive *(35% of people)*
Aware of details, logistics ("the trees")	See the big picture ("the forest")
Access the world through the five senses	World experienced through inner eye
Awareness of people and things	Awareness of ideas and concepts
Practical and concrete; tune in to facts	Visionary and abstract; appreciate theories
Realism—see actualities	Idealism—see possibilities
Prefer hands-on, usable information	Enjoy symbolism and metaphors
Utilize and care for what is here now	Envision and invent what is not here now
Common sense and prior experience	Fantasy and imagination
Prefer doing things the usual way	Like doing things in new and unique ways

T—Thinking	F—Feeling
(50% of people; 65% of men)	*(50% of people; 65% of women)*
Direct with others, "to the point"	Considerate of others; personal and warm
Firm; not afraid of conflict	Gentle; avoid conflict
Cool headed; enjoy competition/debate	Warm hearted; enjoy cooperation/harmony
Make decisions by logic, reason	Make decisions by feelings; effect on people
Thick skin; value honesty, frankness	Sensitivity, diplomacy; value kindness, tact
Strength of will	Strength of compassion
Focus on laws, principles, standards	Aware of circumstances, considerations
Justice and fairness	Mercy and tenderness
Determine consequences	Exercise compassion

J—Judging	P—Perceiving
(60% of people)	*(40% of people)*
Making decisions	Exploring options
Careful prior planning	Spontaneity
Scheduling; very aware of time	Adaptability; responsive to emerging needs
Orderliness and structure; disturbed by disorder	Tolerance; ability to be comfortable in chaos
Organization	Flexibility
Determining "one right way"	Seeing the value of various alternatives
Getting the job done	Enjoying the process
Directing life	Letting life happen
Coming to closure	Remaining open

For each of these pairs of opposites, as outlined here—which side describes you more?

WOULD YOU SAY YOU ARE MORE:	OR MORE:
E—Extroverted	I—Introverted
S—Sensory	N—Intuitive
T—Thinking	F—Feeling
J—Judging	P—Perceiving

For each of the pairs, circle the letter that sounds more like you. This gives you the four letters representing your personality type.

The 16 MBTI types are abbreviated as follows:

ESTJ—ISTJ—ESFJ—ISFJ	ESTP—ISTP—ESFP—ISFP
ENTJ—INTJ—ENTP—INTP	ENFP—INFP—ENFJ—INFJ

Out of these 16 options, circle the type corresponding to the four letters you circled above. This is your type.

Once you know your type, you can access various books or websites to learn more about it. Of course, you could also take some version of the test itself. But this kind of informed self-evaluation tends to generate a fairly accurate type assessment, that in most cases matches test results, and with more awareness of what is actually being evaluated.

With the graph below, estimate *to what extent* you relate to one side or the other on a continuum. Mark your degree of preference for each of the four traits:

VS—Very Strong   *S—Strong*   *Mod—Moderate*   *Mild*

E	VS	S	Mod	Mild	Blend	Mild	Mod	S	VS	I
S	VS	S	Mod	Mild	Blend	Mild	Mod	S	VS	N
T	VS	S	Mod	Mild	Blend	Mild	Mod	S	VS	F
J	VS	S	Mod	Mild	Blend	Mild	Mod	S	VS	P

This gives you a visual picture of your specific type. Then, once you are familiar with these eight traits and how they come together to create the sixteen types, you can make a solid educated guess on the personality types of family members, friends, dating partners, work associates, and others that you know well. With couples and families, it is useful to use the table above to graph each person's preferences, to create a clear visual picture of similarities and differences. *Using a different color to represent each individual, graph each person's level of preference for each of the traits.* The resulting graph will allow you to see at a glance how similar or different you are, and where your most potent areas for conflict or connection are likely to be.

6–4   Temperament—Why We Are All Needed, Just As We Are

One other useful dimension of the MBTI is determining *temperament*. The 16 types are organized into 4 temperaments—4 types within each temperament, as follows:

SP's (Fun-Lovers) *ESTP – ISTP – ESFP – ISFP*	
Motivated by:	Fun, Action, Pleasure, Excitement
Professions:	Entertainers, comedians Race car drivers, athletes, dancers Mechanics, construction workers Soldiers, firemen, police, marksmen Beauticians, craftsmen, technical artists
Strengths:	Fun, enjoyment, using physical tools, craftsmanship, physicality, spontaneity
Weaknesses:	Seriousness, studiousness (often labeled ADHD), following directions
Type of Love Relationship Desired:	Playmate

SJ's (Stabilizers)
ESTJ—ISTJ—ESFJ—ISFJ

Motivated by:	Duty, Task Completion, Doing Things Right
Professions:	Administrators, managers Bankers, business people, accountants Teachers, secretaries, librarians Homemakers, nurses, caregivers
Strengths:	Stabilization; passing on values and traditions; task fulfillment; responsibility
Weaknesses:	Adaptability, spontaneity, dealing with new ideas or differences in others
Type of Love Relationship Desired:	Helpmeet

NT's (Inventors)
ENTJ—INTJ—ENTP—INTP

Motivated by:	Competence, Excellence, Achievement
Professions:	Scientists, researchers Inventors, computer gurus, university professors Executives, military commanders Architects, engineers, system developers

Strengths:	Independence, logical thinking, careful objective analysis, intense study, inventiveness
Weaknesses:	Tolerance, emotional sensitivity, having fun
Type of Love Relationship Desired:	Mindmate

NF's (Questers)
ENFP – INFP – ENFJ – INFJ

Motivated by:	Helping people to become the best they can be Creating ideas that make a better society
Professions:	Counselors, psychologists
Strengths:	Broad vision, imagination, awareness of possibilities, sense of mission
Weaknesses:	Realism, dealing with details, tolerating repetition
Type of Love Relationship Desired:	Soulmate

Because Temperament is a broader characterization, it may be easier to assess than Type. It is important to assess, because people of different temperaments are motivated by fundamentally different things, and may define a successful relationship in fundamentally different ways. It is easier to bridge the gap, if you know what you're dealing with - and why others may not be motivated by the same things that excite you.

People with "S" temperaments outnumber people of "N" temperaments by about three to one. That's probably an optimal ratio—three people maintaining what is already established, for each one person focused on developing new ideas. People of all sixteen types and all four temperaments are needed, to maintain a balanced, effective society. By definition, we all possess different gifts, strengths, and weaknesses.

While we tend to have a primary temperament, we may also have elements of the others as well. I have found it useful to not just allocate people to one single temperament box, but rather to carry out a practice I've called *temperament scaling:*

Steps for Temperament Scaling

1. Decide which of the four temperaments is the most like you (your primary temperament—your **#1**)

2. Decide which of the temperaments is the second most like you (your secondary temperament—your **#2**)

3. Decide which of the temperaments is the LEAST like you, that you relate to the least (your **#4**)

4. Add the remaining temperament
   between #2 and #4 (your **#3**)

5. Graph these temperaments, from the most
   preferred to the least preferred, as follows:

1	2	3	4
Most preferred			Least preferred

For example—let's consider a married couple, Hank and Angie. Here's their temperament scaling:

Hank *(a quiet INTJ software engineer):*

1	2	3	4
NT	SJ	SP	NF

Angie *(a vivacious ESFP kindergarten teacher):*

1	2	3	4
SP	SJ	NF	NT

Their types are opposite, and are unlikely to connect on his #1 (NT), as it's her #4. They'll experience the easiest interaction on their shared #2, SJ—doing tasks and completing assignments together. Their second easiest connection will occur on her #1, SP—doing fun things in the real world—which is his #3.

Hence, with temperament scaling, you can find commonalities and connection strategies even for people very different from one another—or even opposite, according to personality typing. Ultimately, that's what it's all about with this work—finding ways to *first validate and respect yourself and others*; and then to *connect and meaningfully synergize with others*—even people you don't naturally share much in common with.

6–5   Type Development: How We Change and Grow Over Time

In learning about this work, people often ask, "Does personality change over time?" The answer is—both yes and no. The core personality you were born with will always be your core personality—the natural center where you will always do your best work, and experience your most meaningful connections. However, personality *does* change over time. This can occur in two different ways. One way is healthy; the other is unhealthy. It is very important to understand the difference between the two:

1. **Type Development**—This type of change is HEALTHY. The individual knows, values, and retains their original strengths, recognizing that these will always be their core strengths. But then, over time, they add in "good enough" elements of the opposite trait, to balance and expand their original set of strengths.

For example, let's say that an INFP starts with her core preferences:

I (Introversion); **N** (Intuition); **F** (Feeling); and **P** (Perception.)

Over time, to meet the needs of situations and people around her, she gradually blends in elements of:

E (Extroversion); **S** (Sensation); **T** (Thinking); and **J** (Judgment.)

This development process is HEALTHY because it keeps the core self solid and the core strengths strong. It is like starting to fill a toolbox with a hammer, some pliers, a flathead screwdriver, and a Phillips screwdriver—and then later adding other tools—perhaps a drill, a saw, a wrench, and a ruler. The later set of tools is used together with the first set—creating a rich variety of capabilities to address different needs over time.

2. **Type Falsification**—This type of change is UNHEALTHY. The individual feels shamed over their natural traits, and tries to get rid of them, and trade them in for the opposite traits. For example, the introvert may try to abandon their introversion, and act extroverted; the male Feeler (relatively rare in his gender) may seek to toughen up his tender heart, and act more like a bold Thinker, to fit more comfortably into the world of traditional men.

This type of change is like tossing out the hammer, pliers, and screwdrivers of the original toolbox, and trying to function, instead, on the second set of tools. However, these are never as strong or natural for that individual as their original set. This type of change is UNHEALTHY, because it crushes the core self and its core strengths, replacing them with traits that will never be as strong, comfortable, or natural.

Type Falsification is a very common contributor to depression, anxiety, and low self-esteem. It is like the right-handed person trying to write constantly with their left hand—frustrating, exhausting, and ultimately unproductive. I find that it is something that must be identified and corrected, in order to heal these ailments.

Taylor Hartman, author of another system of personality typing, described in his book *The Color Code*, similarly observed that your core personality will always be your core personality. In his system, represented by colors, a "Red" is bold and competitive; a "White" is peaceful and conflict-avoiding; a "Yellow" is fun and adventure-seeking; and a "Blue" is sensitive and contemplative.

Hartman writes that, for example, while a "Blue" will always remain a "Blue"—over time, like a butterfly, they might grow wings with patches of White, Red, and Yellow, added to the Blue, to help them fly even higher, and accomplish even more. It is a lovely analogy that can be applied very effectively to all of the MBTI types and temperaments. We will always be what we naturally are—but if we prize and protect that core, we can add other strengths and abilities over time, to balance and complement our core personality.

The best way to add in these other strengths is to learn from people who naturally possess them—again, not to *replace* our own core strengths, but to *add* to them over time. This allows people to learn from each other, with mutual respect and validation—rather than arguing about whose way is "right." Isabel Myers Briggs' seminal book *Gifts Differing* was inspired by a Bible phrase from Romans 12:4–6 that reads:

> *For as we have many members in one body, So we,*
> *being many, are one body . . . and every one members*
> *one of another . . . Having then **gifts differing***
> *according to the grace that is given to us.*

In other words, the human body is composed of many different parts, each doing a different job. We function best when we respect each part, allowing each to do its unique work cooperatively with all the others.

Another Bible phrase from 1 Corinthians 12:20–21 observes:

> *But now are they many members, yet but one body. And*
> ***the eye cannot say unto the hand, I have no need of thee:***
> *nor again the head to the feet, I have no need of you.*

This is not just true of the Christian community. It is also true of our general world community. We are *all* needed and important. We *all* add different pieces to the puzzle, different talents to the project at hand, different perspectives to the situation. We see best when we see *together*. We think best when we *think together*, blending our diverse observations into one united, inclusive whole.

Before we understand this, we all have a tendency to engage in what might be called *"Psychological Bigotry."* In other words, we believe that what we think is right, *IS* right; and that the way we do it, *IS* the way it should be done. We feel the need to "set others straight," so they can embrace the "truth" by seeing and doing things *our* way—and giving up the unique way *they* see or do things. Psychological bigotry *always* sets us up for conflict (one of the depressive triggers), as each person goes to battle to defend their own point of view.

But if we are smart, we'll stop arguing about who is "right" or what is "true." Instead, we'll start blending in the views of other people, alongside our own—creating a much more complete and balanced picture, reflecting a more complete understanding of the situation. We'll trade in the natural "telescope" of our own bias, for a set of "binoculars" that allows us to see others' perspectives, in addition to our own—resulting in a broader and more enlightening view.

Becoming more aware of our own identity can also be a powerful springboard into compassion, validation, and genuine respect for others—even others who are significantly different from ourselves. When we understand what makes us tick, what motivates us, and what we're naturally good at, it is easier to grasp how others differ from us—and how each of our perspectives and skill sets can be useful in creating a more balanced and productive world.

Conflicts evaporate, self-esteem blossoms, and depression and anxiety fade, as we stop trying to be what we're not, stop trying to get others to be what they're not, and simply learn to truly love and appreciate ourselves and others—just the way we are—protecting and cherishing our inborn **IDENTITY.**

RECORDING:

Write and Preserve Your Life Experience

➤ **7–1** Building Positive Awareness,
by Recording Your Life Experience

➤ **7–2** The Dangers of Reactivity,
The Fragmentation of Experience

➤ **7–3** Varieties of Techniques for
Recording Life Experience

➤ **7–4** Using Writing to Soothe
and Channel Strong Emotions

➤ **7–5** Preserving Your Personal
Legacy, for Yourself and Others

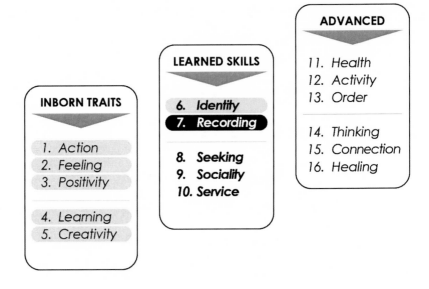

7–1 Building Positive Awareness, by Recording Your Life Experience

Tool #7 in *Your* Happiness Toolkit is—the RECORDING tool. This is another of the tools we are typically introduced to in our early years at school—but may neglect to use later in our lives, in the midst of various competing demands. When used consistently, this tool can greatly increase our awareness, appreciation, and joy. It is a powerful tool that can be effectively used to fight the ravages of depression, and then to help maintain a happy and peaceful emotional climate throughout our lives.

Recording life experience was a common feature for many prior generations. Keeping a daily diary, captain's log, or personal journal was an engrained habit for many individuals. Writing long letters to loved ones serving on military campaigns, missionary journeys, or far away on other adventures was an important way to share news of important events, as well as to maintain emotional connection—even across oceans or distant continents. Even now, the journals and personal letters of significant people in our cultural history, or our family tree, remain treasures of inestimable worth, in preserving the memories and lessons of the past.

Later, when photography became a widespread resource, many households began to preserve photos and other memorabilia in scrapbooks, baby books, and photo albums. Being able to thumb through the physical pages of these precious, memory-preserving resources safeguards our shared legacy, and carries on our connection to past generations, and to their lessons for our future.

Record-keeping preserves our memories, expands our awareness, and extends our hard-won life lessons to benefit us and others, long beyond the occurrence of the original recorded events. What we learned the hard way in an earlier season of life, once recorded, can continue to warn and inspire us and others at a later time.

George Santayana penned the insightful words, *"Those who cannot learn from history are doomed to repeat it."* In contrast, those who *do* learn from past lessons are prepared to build insightful new life experiences, sidestepping the dangers exposed and preserved in recorded history.

7–2   The Dangers of Reactivity, The Fragmentation of Experience

Remembering and recording our life experience, beyond the limits of today's short-lived tweet or social media post, is quickly becoming a lost art. Likewise, the benefits of remembered life experience are becoming lost or forgotten resources. We live daily in a rush of daily headlines, sound bites, tweets, blips, ads, and images. Over time, it can all become a monstrous, meaningless sea of useless information. We react instinctively to the impulse and heat of the moment, overwhelmed with the distractions and deadlines of our current everyday experience. Caught perpetually in this "reaction mode," we lose perspective, a sense of meaning, and the ability to learn from our own experience, and from the experiences of others.

We live in fragments and broken shards of human experience—in the midst of momentary and ever-changing "notifications" of hourly events, breaking news stories, social media updates, video uploads, and other ultimately irrelevant occurrences. Under the onslaught, we can easily forget to piece together the meaning and purpose of our overall life experience. We can needlessly get caught anew in old traps that previously ensnared us or others—so distracted and overwhelmed, so much of the time, that we have no presence of mind left to give to things that matter most. Day by day, these conditions literally *fuel* depression and anxiety.

Happily, however, these are all completely reversible patterns, once we become aware of them. Even in the swirling environment of modern life, we can find perspective and meaning—*if* we know where to look.

Rate your current pattern on the scale below:

LIST 1—Patterns Feeding:	LIST 2—Patterns Feeding:
Depression, Disease, Deterioration, and Disability	Happiness, Wellness, Resilience, and Productivity
7. REACTIVITY: React Impulsively to Current Experiences	**7. RECORDING:** Write and Preserve Your Life Experience

-3	-2	-1	0	1	2	3
Strong	Moderate	Mild	Neutral	Mild	Moderate	Strong

Once in a while, we would be wise to stop the clock, turn off the notifications, silence the distractions, and listen deeply to the voice of our own heart and spirit. In a quiet morning hour, before anyone else is awake; on top of a silent mountain wilderness; or alone in the car for a few minutes after a long busy workday—we can each find a few quiet moments to pull out a pen and notebook, and gather our own private thoughts.

Rather than repeatedly responding and reacting, we can sometimes engage in reflecting and recording. Rather than just hurtling mindlessly from moment to moment, pressure to pressure, and stress to stress, we can press the pause button—even if it's just for a few quiet minutes—to think about why we're doing what we're doing, and whether or not we're doing the things that matter most—to us, and to those we care about.

In those moments, we can for a time silence the noise of the newscasters, the ever-present soundtrack of distant musicians, and the endless voices of TV or video personalities. In that quiet, soulful time, we can think deeply about what actually matters to us—what we're trying to achieve, what obstacles we've been facing, what heartbreaks we've been enduring, what lessons we've been learning, and what life events we've been enjoying. We can think about where we've been, where we are now, and where we are headed—both in the short term, and in the long term.

Socrates observed, many centuries ago, *"The unexamined life is not worth living."* In contrast, the life that we purposefully ponder and plan, that we consciously craft and create—that is the intentional life, the proactive and meaningful life—that can bring lasting joy and fulfillment into our everyday life experience.

7–3 Varieties of Techniques for Recording Life Experience

There are many techniques you can use to record your individual life experience. Some of these we have already mentioned in prior chapters. These include the **Daily Mood Log** in the FEELINGS chapter, the **Gratitude Journal** in the POSITIVITY chapter, and the **Transformational Tools** described throughout Section I.

In addition, here are some methods you can use to gather your private thoughts and record your personal life experiences:

1. **Daily diary**—You can purchase an old-style diary, or even just a standard notebook; and then every day spend a few minutes jotting down briefly the basic events of that day.

2. **Narrative journal**—This is a more formal record, where you write (or type) in more detail about significant life experiences, what they meant to you, and what you learned from experiencing them.

3. **Workbook notes**—These are notes you keep as you work through a self-help book or workbook that asks you to participate in writing exercises, to help overcome depression or other emotional challenges.

4. **Brainstorm notebook**—This is a cheap notebook you keep by your bed, so you can capture waking thoughts and brainstorms as they occur. Later, if you wish, you can go back and turn these scribbled notes into more formal and well-organized writing.

5. **Letter writing**—You can write a formal letter or email to someone important to you, capturing your thoughts or feelings, or describing significant life experiences. You could also make an extra copy, and include it in your personal journal, as part of your life history.

6. **Expanded day-planner**—Many of us use some kind of planners to record scheduled events, deadlines, etc. Planners can also be a helpful place to think about our broader goals—such as relationship goals, and personal values and aspirations. Two excellent resources to assist you in implementing this strategy are *The 7 Habits of Highly*

Effective People by Steven R. Covey, and *Lifebalance* by Linda and Richard Eyre.

7. **Life history**—At some point, it is helpful to write your life story, pulling together all the strands of important events, lessons, and legacy items, to help you communicate to others what your life's purpose is and has been.

8. **Scrapbooks, blogs, vlogs, photo albums, etc.**—Be creative in recording your life experience. It need not be simply in written words alone. It can be as individual as you are, including a variety of different elements. The HEALING chapter (Tool #16) near the end of the book will provide some additional writing tools to help you process some of your steeper life challenges. For now, however, practice on the above methods, and try to do a little recording every day. You'll be amazed how quickly it expands your perspective, relieves your stress, lifts your depression, enlivens your mood, broadens your awareness, and increases your overall self-confidence.

7–4 Using Writing to Soothe and Channel Strong Emotions

Many people find that the simple act of writing, in and of itself, has a calming and centering effect, when they are overwhelmed with strong emotions. It is a good idea, when you are feeling highly emotional, to find a quiet space, and pour your feelings out onto paper, using any of the methods mentioned in the above list.

Physically writing with a pen and paper seems to have the most immediate and powerful calming effect. This is largely because the very act of holding a pen, and forming the symbols representing the words, requires activation of the left side of the brain—the more logical, analytical side. The overcharged emotional brain is given some relief and focus by that steadier, more rational part of the brain, even in that simple act of physically forming letters and words.

Also, when you feel the need to "get something out of your system," having those feelings flow out from your brain, through your pen, onto your paper, can provide tremendous emotional relief. Because now the *paper* is holding those poisonous feelings—so *you* don't have to any longer.

Even if you burn, shred, or toss out your emotional writing as soon as you're done with it, it can be helpful for you to produce it, in order to increase clarity for yourself about what exactly is bothering you, and to activate your logical brain in evaluating options for resolving your identified concerns.

7–5 Preserving Your Personal Legacy, for Yourself and Others

You will soon find that the act of consistently recording your personal thoughts helps you draw together the normally fragmented, overwhelmed pieces of yourself into a safe and protected space. The daily experience of gathering and recording your thoughts, feelings, experiences, triumphs, failures, hopes, and dreams, over time, will produce a record that you can refer back to, time and time again. Such a record can also provide perspective, keep happy memories alive, set disturbing memories to rest, and preserve the benefit of your hard-won learning experiences for the long haul. In such a way, you can treasure up for yourself a personal legacy that you can draw on for deep strength and valuable perspective, over many years to come.

Likewise, **if you choose to do so, you can create a legacy record for others to benefit from.** You can summarize your experiences and things you have learned in a book, a memoir, a journal, a blog, a website, a scrapbook, or some other kind of creative project. Passing your life lessons on to benefit others is a profoundly joyful and healing experience. No experience is ever wasted, and even the most challenging of life experiences, once recorded, can ease the path of others passing through similar circumstances.

Having now explored the **IDENTITY** and **RECORDING** Tools to increase your self-awareness and self- understanding, we'll now discuss three tools that can help you to build more satisfying relationships with others. Positive relationships are some of the most powerful tools to prevent and heal depression, and to bring joy and well-being into your daily life. We'll explore three elements of relationship-building: **SEEKING, SOCIALITY,** and **SERVICE.** Like the legs of a three-legged stool, these three elements balance and support each other, as you learn to build and maintain effective, satisfying relationships—an important dimension of a fulfilling life.

TOOL EIGHT

———

SEEKING:

Reach Out for Guidance, Support, and Insight

➤ **8–1** Seeking for Help—A Crucial,
Life-Sustaining Skill

➤ **8–2** What Goes Wrong—How
We Learn *Not* to Seek Help

➤ **8–3** The Tendency to Turn to
Screens and Machines

➤ **8–4** Three Styles of Attachment,
and Their Lifelong Impact

➤ **8–5** Building the Capacity to
Reach Out in Times of Need

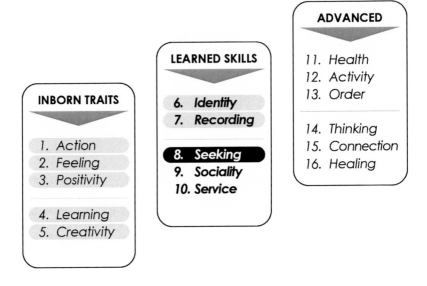

8–1   Seeking for Help—A Crucial, Life-Sustaining Skill

Tool #8 in *Your* Happiness Toolkit is—the SEEKING tool. This tool is one we use literally from our very first moments of life. As human beings, none of us can survive even our infancy without significant outside support. Someone out there needs to feed us, clothe us, comfort us, and move us around, since we arrive here unable to do *any* of these things for ourselves. So typically, our very first independent act, after being born into this world, is to take in a deep breath of oxygen, open our mouths, and loudly *cry* for help.

It is a skill we use often in those first few days, weeks, and years of life. We cry when we're hungry. We cry when we're cold. We cry when our diaper needs changing. We cry when we're lonely, when we're bored, when we're in pain, when we're angry, when we're scared. It's all we can do at that early stage to call for our caregivers. Our cry is a signal that we need something that we can't provide for ourselves. A wise caregiver learns to interpret our various cries, and how they reflect our changing needs.

Over the years, we continue to use this tool to turn to others stronger, smarter, and more capable than ourselves. Each successful experience seeking and receiving needed help builds confidence that others will be available for us. We ask for and receive guiding support from parents, teachers, coaches, ministers, siblings, extended family members, and others. Over time, we gain more confidence and strength within ourselves, so that we can take care of our own needs, and then, help provide care for others. At least—that is the way it is *supposed* to work. But . . . things don't always work out the way they are *supposed* to.

Erik Erikson, a twentieth-century psychologist who studied children, defined eight stages that human beings typically go through in the normal process of development. The first and most foundational of these stages he called **Trust vs. Mistrust.** He observed that from birth to eighteen months, a young child ideally learns that they can trust that their needs will be provided for, that needed care will consistently be given.

Those early experiences provide an emotional foundation of trust, of feeling safe in the world, allowing children to develop with the deep assurance that they're not alone, that their needs matter, and that someone will be there to help. However, Erikson observed, if those needs for nurturance are *not* met during that early stage, it tends instead to build the emotional foundation of *mistrust*—

which can then persist throughout life, making it difficult to ask for or receive needed help from others.

8-2 What Goes Wrong—How We Learn *Not* to Seek Help

There are many things that can interrupt or displace this normal and healthy process of learning to seek help when we need it. These factors may include:

1. Parental Unavailability

When parents are physically or even emotionally unavailable, it can interrupt this normal process of seeking needed help. When a cry for help comes, it may essentially fall on deaf or distracted ears. It doesn't take long for a young child to learn to stop issuing the call, if it consistently results in little or no relief.

Parental unavailability may result from other competing responsibilities (work tasks, other children's needs); their own depression or overwhelm; media distractions; or even addiction. Or, it might be influenced by misguided parent training, such as the common instruction decades ago to let infants "cry it out," so they can learn to "self soothe." Instead, what children tend to learn from this response pattern is that they're not safe in the world, that no one will be there for them, and that it is pointless for them to try to express their needs.

2. Child Abuse

A more severe and destructive factor is *any* kind of abuse—physical, verbal, emotional, or sexual. Abuse teaches a child that their personal needs and desires don't matter, that only their abuser's needs matter, and that their supposed "job" is simply to comply with the abuser's demands. This pattern can deeply harm one's ability to trust others, and can generate lasting feelings of worthlessness and despair.

3. Parentification

Sometimes at an early age, a child is required to take on more responsibility in the family than is appropriate for their age or family role. This is particularly common in oldest children, who may be expected to care for or police younger children in the family; or in marital conflict or divorce, when distressed parents might engage a child as an ally, or even as a "pseudo spouse"—confiding in them, crying to them, leaning on them for support.

A parentified child is one whose own dependency needs are displaced, to service the dependency needs of others, including their own parents. This pattern often results in a lifetime tendency for people to obsessively seek self-worth by taking excessive and inappropriate responsibility for others—often at the expense of their own legitimate needs. This pattern is referred to as "codependence." Conversely, some other "parentified children" rebel against this pattern, "protecting" themselves by thinking only of themselves, and avoiding responsibility for others. Both of these responses prevent positive and healthy attachments over time.

4. Later Abuse, Trauma, Betrayal, or Violence

Children are not the only ones who experience life disruptions resulting in a reluctance to reach out for help. *Trauma, betrayal, violence, or abuse can occur at any point in the life cycle,* to people of any age, from babyhood to old age. Whenever such an event occurs, it can shatter the sense of trust and safety in the world, and motivate its victims to turn inward, to avoid being hurt, disappointed, or devastated again.

8–3   The Tendency to Turn to Screens and Machines

When human beings are unavailable or feel unsafe to turn to, it is not unusual for people to seek a substitute. Some individuals end up turning to alcohol, drugs, sugar, pornography, or other addictive processes to drown out discomfort, and provide at least temporary (though ultimately counter-productive) relief.

Even more common is the increasingly rampant tendency to turn to electronic media. Media has become an ever-present emotional sedative, used to silence pain and alienation by providing the counterfeit relief of directing attention elsewhere for a time.

From the "built-in babysitter" that conveniently occupies the attention of a young child; to the newly divorced single parent who flicks on the radio or Pandora, so they "won't have to feel alone;" to the ever-flickering blue screen of the lonely retiree staring aimlessly all day at the TV—media screens and machines have become an increasingly common, almost universal, people substitute.

Sadly, even in homes where access to other people *is* available, often household members are still staring into some screen, rather than interacting directly with one another. They might be checking their social media feed or message center (again); playing yet another computer game; watching (or even binge-watching) videos; aimlessly browsing the internet; disappearing into an immersive virtual reality (VR) experience; clicking through channels on a TV or cable system; or enjoying a personal music playlist through the isolation of headphones—even while in the presence of other people.

Ultimately, all of these devices contribute to an environment of increasing emotional unavailability. We turn to each other less and less, as we reach for our electronic devices more and more.

Rate your current pattern on the scale below:

LIST 1—Patterns Feeding:	LIST 2—Patterns Feeding:
Depression, Disease, Deterioration, and Disability	Happiness, Wellness, Resilience, and Productivity
8. DISTRACTION: Focus Your Attention on Screens and Machines	**8. SEEKING:** Reach Out for Guidance, Support, and Insight

-3	-2	-1	0	1	2	3
Strong	Moderate	Mild	Neutral	Mild	Moderate	Strong

It is easy to understand why media devices are so powerful a distraction or substitution for actual person-to-person contact. Unlike people, media devices are always available to us, day or night. They never disappoint us, let us down, abuse us, or criticize us. They are entirely within our control, taking us exactly where we want to go, showing us exactly what we want to see, literally within the click of a button. They are intoxicatingly powerful. *The more highly developed a device is, the more immersive of a distraction it can be.*

But media devices, powerful as they may be, can never truly substitute for human attachment. Emotionally, spiritually, chemically, and even physically, meaningful interaction with other real human beings is essential for our health—and especially for our mental health. The strength of our human attachments affects our lifetime resilience, mood, confidence, and grit. So ultimately, real person-to-person attachment is a crucial experience, for which there is no effective substitute.

8–4   Three Styles of Attachment, and Their Lifelong Impact

The way that people learn to attach (or *not* attach) to others in childhood becomes the natural template for how they tend to interact with others throughout life. This pattern may be positive—or it may be disruptive.

The twentieth-century psychologist John Bowlby studied attachment between young babies and their mothers. Bowlby described three different attachment styles, visible first in that early parent-child bonding:

1. **Secure Attachment**—In this attachment style, the parent is *consistently available* to the child, physically and emotionally, and is consistently responsive to their needs and feelings. The child knows that the parent is steady and dependable. Trust, confidence, and joy flourish in this kind of highly connected relationship.

2. **Insecure Attachment**—In this style, the parent is *sometimes available* to the child, emotionally and physically, but is also *frequently unavailable*. So the child never knows which version of the parent they're going to get—the kindly available version, or the detached unavailable version.

   The child, therefore, resorts to tantrums, protests, and dramatic outbursts, in a desperate effort to sway or cajole the parent back into meaningful interaction. This may result in a high-conflict relationship between parent and child, which can be frustrating and discouraging on both sides. The child never knows what to expect—and the parent can't figure out why their child so often misbehaves, and seems so out of control.

3. **Avoidant Attachment**—In this style, the parent is rarely available emotionally, and may or may not provide essential physical care. The child learns from this pattern that it is pointless to even try to engage the parent in meaningful interaction. So the child learns instead to turn mostly inward for need fulfillment.

This is the attachment style most likely to generate excessive reliance on screens and machines. Not only do the electronics produce the illusion that "someone" is "there;" they also drown out the pain of unsatisfying or neglected real relationships.

The attachment style experienced in early childhood typically becomes the natural default for relationships occurring later in life, with friends, dating partners, work associates, a spouse, and even one's own children. Those who had the good fortune of enjoying secure attachment with parents enter later relationships already equipped with productive habits, mindsets, and skills that help facilitate secure attachment elsewhere. However, for those who experienced insecure or avoidant attachment with parents, these negative habits will likewise tend to persist into later relationships. Insecure attachments continue to foster conflict, drama, and tension, while avoidant attachments continue to generate alienation, distance, and detachment.

This seems to be a situation that is vastly escalating over time. In an age of rampant divorce, demanding single parenthood, high-stress working parents, pornography, ever-present media, and general relationship avoidance, fewer and fewer children experience the warm and consistent support of secure attachment. This is a cycle that feeds on itself, because *the fewer people there are that experienced secure attachment, the less likely they are to be able to extend secure attachment to their own children and others.*

Lacking the skills to form and maintain effective, satisfying relationships can be a significant and recurring trigger for depression and other emotional challenges throughout life. The most natural thing in the world, for those who have experienced the pain of insecure or avoidant attachment, is to carry those same patterns into new circumstances with new people, in a self-protective way. But this understandable tendency can often sabotage new relationships—sometimes before they even start—expanding the pain and loss already experienced previously, thereby launching *yet* another rotation through the depressive cycle.

Fortunately, however, this is not an inevitable or unchangeable pattern. As educator and author Neal A. Maxwell observed:

> *Yesterday need not hold tomorrow hostage.*

As we become aware of our own accustomed attachment style, we can assess whether it is strengthening our relationship capacity—or not. And then, we can decide to keep that accustomed style—or not.

8–5   Building the Capacity to Reach Out in Times of Need

As we recognize the limitations of insecure or avoidant attachment styles, we can then choose intentionally to trade them in for a more secure and rewarding style that fosters genuine connection, meaningful interaction, and mutual satisfaction.

There are three modes of human interaction that we'll be discussing over the next few chapters. They are:

1. SEEKING:	reaching out for help from someone more experienced and powerful than we are.
2. SOCIALITY:	reaching out to peers in friendship and equality, mutually supporting each other.
3. SERVICE:	reaching out to others less fortunate than ourselves to offer needed help and support.

We'll cover the **Sociality Tool** and **Service Tool** in the next two chapters. For now, here are some suggestions to help you begin applying the **Seeking Tool**:

10 PRACTICAL STRATEGIES FOR "SEEKING"

Reaching Out for Guidance, Support, and Insight:

1. Unplug—Turn Off Distracting Media

This is the first and perhaps most important step. *As long as you remain numbed and distracted within an imaginary world, you will be unlikely to seek meaningful change or connection in the real one.*

So—set clear limits for yourself regarding media use. Don't engage in passive media use (TV, videos, computer games, social media, etc.) for more than an hour or two a day. *Have a clear media curfew,* turning off all screens and machines for at least one hour before bedtime. This will improve your sleep, and provide you some daily quiet time to assess your goals, hear your own guiding inner voice, and make specific action plans.

Similarly, limit any "reading for entertainment" to an hour or two per day. Fantasy books, like electronic entertainment, can spin you away into an imaginary world that can distract you from important necessities of your actual life, and from your actual relationships with real people. Distraction, avoidance, and escapism go hand in hand in disrupting the normal establishment and maintenance of meaningful human connection. To create healthier patterns, you *must* create some time and space for actual bonding with other humans.

2. *Choose Actual Connection*—**Decide to Stop Hiding**

Again, the most natural and understandable reaction, after you've felt hurt or neglected, is to isolate yourself from others, turn inward, and avoid human interaction. You might turn your eyes downward, avoid eye contact with others, and remain focused on some media device, book, or simply on your own feet.

However, such behavior is a significant part of how you may have gotten stuck in the first place—and it is a pattern that is likely to *keep* you stuck. It communicates submissiveness and insecurity. Though you may *think* it makes you safe or invisible, it can actually make you more vulnerable—often inviting further bullying, ridicule, or isolation. It is not a behavior that serves you; rather, it gets in your way—perhaps for years, or even for decades. It is a pattern that feeds alienation and depression. *It's time to let it go.*

3. *Go Where the People Are*—Focus on **Real-World Relationships**

This is an important though challenging step, as Susan Jeffers observes in her insightful books *Feel the Fear—And Do it Anyway!* and *Dare to Connect!* Keep your head up, your posture erect, and your eyes open, directly meeting the eyes of others. Find the inner courage to pursue something that can bring you better results, though it may feel unfamiliar. *Change requires change; transformation requires transformation.*

Dare to choose change—to do what you haven't done before. Remember, "If you keep doing what you're doing, you'll keep getting what you're getting!" If you don't want to keep getting what you're getting, you need to stop doing what you're doing—and courageously choose something better for yourself.

4. *Assess Your Needs*—**Clearly Identify
Your Needs and Desires**

You can only find effective help if you know what you're
looking for. You can only reach a goal if you've established
one in the first place. You can only communicate your
needs and desires to someone else, if you clearly know
yourself what they are.

So, think carefully about what you want, what you
need, and what outside support might be necessary
to help you meet your most important goals. In this
way, you will be best prepared to seek out and identify
the individuals who can best help you to meet your
personal objectives.

5. *Evaluate Your Option*—**Who Can
Help You Meet Your Needs?**

Once you know what your needs are, you can seek out
specific resource people to help you. Want to learn to
play a new musical instrument? Seek out an effective
teacher. Want help to overcome depression? Find a
skilled counselor. Want help to put your finances in
order? Locate an experienced financial advisor. Want to
enjoy a more meaningful spiritual connection? Turn to
a reputable spiritual leader—or better yet, turn directly
to the ultimate source of wisdom and serenity—to God
Himself.

6. *Ask For Help*—Be Willing to Make Direct Requests

Once you find what you're looking for, ask for it directly. If you don't ask directly, it significantly decreases the likelihood that you'll find or receive what you need. Even the most skilled human helper can't read your mind or discern your needs without you communicating them out loud. Save yourself valuable time by directly expressing your needs and the specific ways in which you need help to meet your personal goals.

7. *Receive Graciously*—Be Willing to Accept Help When It Is Extended

When others offer you help to meet a current need, accept it graciously. Some people are reluctant to accept help from others, thinking it means they are weak or incapable. Don't make that mistake. Giving and receiving are both important elements of healthy, balanced relationships. Don't be afraid to receive in your time of need. Receiving graciously is an essential part of every healthy relationship.

8. *Allocate Resources*—Be Willing to Pay for Help When Needed

Sometimes, the help you need is only available on a paid basis. If so, don't hesitate to hire someone who can effectively provide the help that you need. Ultimately it will save you time and make you more productive, to hire competent help. Of course, to get the most out of your investment, be sure to consistently carry out tasks your advisors assign to you, so you can progress as efficiently and effectively as possible.

9. *Strengthen Spirituality*—Seek Help
   from a Higher Power

It is worth noting here that when attachment gets disrupted with significant human relationships, it can also have a profoundly negative impact on spirituality. *If you experienced unavailability, criticism, or rejection from parents or others, it can be easy to assume that God is likewise unavailable, critical, or rejecting.* People often build their image of God on the basis of what they experienced from significant others. The attachment style they experienced in childhood (secure, insecure, or avoidant) often becomes their default response not only in their relationships with other people, but also in their personal relationship with God.

Happily, this is a pattern that can be turned around, once you recognize it. For many people, healing the relationship with God is a powerful stepping stone for improving relationships with others, and can provide a "Higher Power" that facilitates profound healing and transformation.

10. *Stay Balanced*—Balance "Seeking" with Self-Care, Sociality, and Service

Remember to care well for yourself in all the ways that you can—physically, mentally, emotionally, and spiritually. Do all you can to help and educate yourself—and then reach out for additional assistance in the areas you can't address alone. Be sure also to tune in to the needs of others, and be a support to them. *If you regularly seek support from others without giving back, you may unwittingly be pushing people away.*

So, engage in **SEEKING**—but also in **SOCIALITY** and **SERVICE.** The balance between those dimensions of human connection is essential for establishing and maintaining healthy relationships. The next two chapters will teach you more about how to do just that, as an essential part of *Your* Happiness Toolkit.

SOCIALITY:

Engage in Meaningful Social Connections

9–1 Peer Relationships in Home, Play, School, Dating, and Work Environments

Tool #9 in *Your* Happiness Toolkit is—the SOCIALITY Tool. This is a tool we typically begin using early in life, as we become exposed to peer relationships. For many people, this begins in the *home* at a young age.

Often our siblings are the first peers we are exposed to. We might already have brothers or sisters when we arrive in this world, or they might join the family soon after we do. As we grow up together, we learn to share resources—our toys, our opportunities, our parents' time and attention. Over time, we learn to carve out our own place and identity within our families, and in the world beyond.

Sibling relationships may be some of the most heartfelt and enduring of peer relationships throughout our lives. Most of us will outlive our parents; friends and neighbors move away; work associates and romantic attachments change over the years. But our family connections with our siblings can persist, in many cases, throughout our lifetimes. In ideal cases, our siblings may be some of our best and most trusted friends.

Play environments are often the next place providing exposure to peer relationships. This might occur in our homes, churches, daycares, neighborhoods, or schools. Child's play can help us develop important skills for social engagement, including awareness, curiosity, interest, sharing, compassion, and cooperation. We learn that there are things that we can build more completely, and experiences we can enjoy more fully, when we engage directly with others.

Entering *school* generally provides a whole new context for peer connection. In school, we learn together, play together, build community, and begin to compete with one another. We find out what we're good at and what we're not so good at; who we connect with and who we don't. As we spend whole days together, we often find our "tribe"—a group of people who share our interests and expand our awareness. We use the social skills developed at school throughout our lives.

As we enter our teens, we move into the new social environment of *dating*. We find special people that we are attracted to, and have shared interests with. We develop a more intimate and exclusive style of relating, as we pair up with dating partners and eventually progress toward mate selection and marriage. Finding a spouse to share life with is generally the most enduring and significant of our peer connections.

Finally, the world of **work** provides yet another context for peer connection. The more highly developed our work skills, the greater the likelihood that our work will resonate with our deepest selves, and lead us to people possessing many of the same talents, interests, and abilities that we do. Collegial relationships with work peers can bring richness and enjoyment into our work lives, and provide important networking opportunities that can expand our opportunities and successes throughout our lives.

In each of these five environments for peer connection—*home, play, school, dating, and work*—we can have experiences that significantly shape our personality, habits, and interests. Many of these experiences are helpful, increasing our confidence and capacity over time. Some, however, may not be so positive.

9–2 What Gets in the Way of Meaningful Social Connections?

Rarely does anyone go through a lifetime in which every peer contact is helpful and supportive. We are all under continuous development, with built-in weaknesses, blind spots, vulnerabilities, and weak moments. So undoubtedly, as we encounter more and more people, we will have ever-increasing exposure to other people's faults and imperfections.

Sometimes, we may even become the target of those weaknesses, as others may treat us with insensitivity, unkindness, or even cruelty. We might experience bullying, social rejection, violence, or abuse at the hands of our peers—whether those peers be our siblings, fellow students, dating partners, or coworkers.

When faced with these kinds of harmful experiences, we might form a protective emotional "bubble" around ourselves, or go into a private emotional "box," hoping to avoid additional pain. As noted previously, we may begin using excessive media as a way to escape or avoid human contact that could feel hurtful or frightening. We might avoid peer contact altogether—other than perhaps the minimal exposure and connection provided at a safe distance by social media. Hiding and avoidance may feel safer than connection and exposure.

Rate your current pattern on the scale below:

LIST 1—Patterns Feeding:	LIST 2—Patterns Feeding:
Depression, Disease, Deterioration, and Disability	Happiness, Wellness, Resilience, and Productivity
9. AVOIDANCE: Keep to Yourself (Other Than "Social Media")	**9. SOCIALITY:** Engage in Meaningful Social Connections

-3	-2	-1	0	1	2	3
Strong	Moderate	Mild	Neutral	Mild	Moderate	Strong

Ultimately, our ability (or inability) to connect effectively with peers will affect us in the most significant dimensions of our lives. Freud observed that **mental health is characterized by two fundamental abilities—***to love and to work.* Both "love" and "work" are greatly facilitated by good social skills and social confidence. However, both "love" and "work" can be compromised, made less effective, or even rendered impossible by deficits in our social skills—especially if we "stay in the box" or "in the bubble," in a condition of constant hiding, avoidance, or media distraction—habits that inevitably feed depression and loneliness.

Peer relationships require a certain amount of personal courage, grit, and endurance. But these very qualities are part of what make us effective in meeting the demands of love and of work. They are fundamental characteristics that help us overcome whatever challenge we may meet in life. Even the heartbreaks, humiliations, and social setbacks we might experience in our peer relationships can educate and strengthen us, as we continue our growth and development over time.

9–3 Personality, Attachment Styles, and Birth Order—Impact on Sociality

Besides our prior life experience, our style of relating to peers may be affected by a number of factors, including:

1. **Personality**—As discussed previously in the Identity chapter, some individuals are more naturally extroverted, curious, and sociable, enjoying the presence of many other people. Other individuals are more naturally introverted,

private, and selective, preferring the presence a few carefully screened people, and needing more alone time. Extroverts tend to make friends more easily and naturally, while introverts tend to keep their distance longer, and are generally more cautious about who they initially approach.

Both extroverts and introverts can have rich and fulfilling social lives—but extroverts tend to attract a wide variety of friends with brief contact, while introverts tends to prefer deeper, more focused relationships—a few friends with long-term contact. Both styles can be fulfilling and healthy for the individuals involved.

2. **Attachment Styles**—As discussed in the previous chapter, a person's approach to relationships can also be impacted by attachment styles launched in early childhood—either secure, insecure, or avoidant attachment. Those who enjoyed secure attachment with their parents in early childhood generally have an easier time developing later relationships than those who experienced insecure or avoidant attachment as children.

3. **Birth Order**—Kevin Leman's observations in *The Birth Order Book* reveal some intriguing patterns common in oldest, middle, and youngest children—and how their position in the family tends to affect their social patterns throughout life.

Oldest children are typically responsible, organized, and determined individuals. They are accustomed to relationships with adults, since adults were the only ones present when they first arrived in the world. Firstborns are often given responsibilities within the family for the care and supervision of younger siblings—so they are often the ones blamed if a younger child makes a mess, starts a conflict, or creates a problem.

This lifetime experience tends to make firstborns natural leaders. They are used to being in charge; are often accustomed to exercising power and control over others; and may dislike being seen on an equal footing with other children. Peer relationships may be a greater challenge for firstborns, as they can be naturally inclined to boss others around, and expect to stay squarely in the spotlight, or at the head of the pack—a tendency that may not go over well with others who might not enjoy being dominated in this way. Firstborns may feel a little lost socially if they don't have a position of clear authority or dominance within the group.

Youngest children are by the definition the babies of the family. Depending on the particular dynamics of the family, they may be coddled, adored, or bossed around—both by their parents, and by their older siblings. Significantly younger children may sometimes feel like second-class citizens within the family, with few voting privileges and little decision-making power. They often get the family leftovers—already-used clothes, toys, and baby equipment—as well as the leftovers of parents' time, focus, and energy.

Youngest children are more likely to have been surprise pregnancies, and are often raised largely by their older siblings, since their parents may already be exhausted and used up with the needs of the older children. Or, on the other hand, they can be the most spoiled and least micro-managed of the children, as parents

232

seek to have a close and positive relationship with this last-chance child, before their parenting days are fully over.

Youngest children often survive by becoming the cutest, most entertaining, and personable of the children in a family. They find identity and importance in their family by making others laugh and smile. They are often bossed around by older family members, and will either comply with this pressure, becoming chronic people-pleasers, or they might resist this pressure, becoming chronic rebels and troublemakers. They are used to having other people take care of them, and may be less naturally responsible than their older siblings. So in peer relationships, they are often naturally engaging and popular, entertaining and cheerful. But they may have a harder time feeling taken seriously by the rest of the world, due to their chronic "baby" status.

Middle children have neither the natural dominance of firstborns, nor the natural "cuteness" of lastborns. So they have to carve out a unique identity for themselves, somewhere in the middle. They don't have the firstborns' need to be in charge, or the lastborn's tendency to be taken care of. Middle children may have to work extra hard to find a defined place in the family—a unique identity for themselves in the social system.

As a result, middle children may have the most social insecurities, lacking a clear sense of identity. On the other hand, middle kids are generally the best social "mixers," and do well forming and maintaining relationships with the broadest variety of people— because they've been doing it for a lifetime.

Only children are by definition the oldest child, the youngest child, and the middle child in a family—so they most often display a mix of all three sets of traits.

———

Your natural strengths, weaknesses, vulnerabilities, and preferences can be strongly influenced by all of these various factors—prior life experience, personality traits, attachment style, and birth order position. As a result, your manner of relating to others will be unique to you. Some things will be hard for you, others will come easy. Once you're aware of your natural tendencies, you can craft an individualized program for strengthening your social life that draws on your native strengths, and overcomes your natural weaknesses.

However, some principles and practices of relationship building seem to be virtually universal, and are useful to almost all people seeking to build stronger connections with others. Many of these core principles for social engagement can be found in books like Dale Carnegie's *How to Win Friends and Influence People.*

What follows are some of the best insights and ideas that over the years have proved to be most helpful for all kinds of individuals, of all ages, to strengthen their social connections. These strategies can help you emerge from the lonely "bubble" of social isolation, and enter a happier world of satisfying, meaningful relationships. *This is an important dimension of depression recovery and prevention*—and is also an essential ingredient for building a lifetime of joy, wellness, and resilience.

9–4   Six Strategies for Finding Your Tribe, and Building Your Social Network

1. **First, become the best version of you.** You will have the most to give to others socially if you are physically, mentally, emotionally, and spiritually well. Take good care of yourself, and be clear in identifying and consistently meeting your own personal needs. Ironically, one of the best things you can do for those around you is to become and remain well within yourself.

   Stephen R. Covey, in *The 7 Habits of Highly Effective People*, notes that before you can attain "public victory," you have to experience "private victory." Before you can positively impact other people or the world at large; before you can build a beautiful romance, marriage or family; before you can give yourself fully to any social relationship, you have to become available to *yourself*, in your finest form. Don't expect any outside relationship to "complete" you, or make you whole. You must become healthy and whole within yourself—*then* you will have that whole, healthy self available to relate with others.

2. **Find out what you love to do—and do it!** The most important and effective way to find other people who share your interests is—for *you* to discover your interests, and then be consistently, passionately engaged in carrying them out. You will be your best, most confident, most interesting self when you are doing what you love to do. Whether you're looking for a friend, a romantic partner, or a work associate, you will always find your best options

through doing what you love to do—and finding others who share that interest with you.

3. **Use social media—but don't overuse it.** Internet resources can be a significant tool to help you identify and strengthen your interests, and then find your "tribe" (others who share similar interests.) It has never been easier to find groups of people that share your passions than it is now, through search functions and other online tools. Use technology to find people who love to do what you love to do, and set up shared activities with them. But don't allow technology and media to dominate or control your life. Set limits on it. Use it as a *secondary* means of connection with those you care about or share interests with. Make sure you have plenty of face-to-face time with those individuals—don't just communicate with them electronically.

4. **Use books and other materials to find like-minded individuals.** Books, articles, music, paintings, movies, and other creative media store insights from creative minds in a form that allows these ideas to be accessed even centuries later. Some members of your "tribe" may be long dead, or live so far away that you will never be able to meet them face to face. But their ideas can enrich yours, their perspectives can speak to you from beyond the grave, or across the continents, in ways that can inspire and uplift you—wherever you are now.

Also, once you have discovered what authors, musicians, or artists you resonate with, you can often find other people, here and now, who share your interests. Though the original author or artist may be unavailable or even long dead, the fans or followers of that individual may be very much alive and accessible to you. Look for events and activities that can bring you together with people that enjoy the same things that you do, and actively participate. In so doing, you will be more likely to meet others that resonate with ideas important to you, which could be the beginning of a long, enriching social relationship.

5. **Invest in face-to-face continuing education.** Take classes, attend lectures, and sign up for workshops, seminars, and conferences that reflect your personal interests and skills. By doing so, you are more likely to meet others who share the same interests as you. This is a particularly valuable strategy if the learning experience is in a format that occurs more than once—for example, an eight-week course is better than a one-time two-hour lecture. You are more likely to form relationships with like-minded people when you're in a context that puts you in the same learning space more than once. Seek experiences that don't just expand your own knowledge and skill, but that can also foster relationships with others who share your interests.

6. **Be interested in others you meet, and show that interest in word and deed.** Be curious about what makes others tick, what interests them, and what they're good at. Ask them questions about themselves, and be sincerely interested in their responses. Be willing to learn from other people's strengths and interests. Look people in the eye when you talk to them with an open body posture (arms and legs uncrossed, breathing freely, leaning slightly

toward them.) Ask questions that help them talk more about what interests them. *If you struggle with shyness or self-consciousness, you will find that those challenges melt away when you focus on others, rather than wondering what others are thinking about you.*

Strengthening your **SOCIALITY** skills can bring great joy and satisfaction into your life. It can take courage and determination to get started, especially if you have experienced previous pain in peer relationships. But it pays tremendous dividends in helping you to leave depression behind, and build a life of joy and fulfillment.

9–5   The "4 Ts": Basic Elements of Relationship Building, Erosion, and Repair

How do relationships get built in the first place—whether in friendship, romance, marriage, family, work, or community? Once built, how do they erode? What tears a good relationship down, after it has already been established? Finally, if you are dealing with an eroding relationship (for example, a fading friendship, a struggling marriage, or a painful conflict with a cherished child), what can you do to strengthen and repair it?

Over the years, I have observed some simple relationship patterns that can help answer these questions, and promote more effective relationship development and maintenance over time. I call these patterns *"The 4 Ts,"* as they can all be described in these four short words: **1–Time, 2–Talk, 3–Trust, 4–Touch.**

This model has proven to be a tremendously useful resource to build and strengthen all kinds of relationships, including friendships, parent-child connections, romantic attachments, family ties, and professional relationships with coworkers, customers, and clients. It is also helpful for repairing marriages, as it was developed originally to help couples find their way through some particularly rough patches.

We will use these "4 Ts" to explore three basic stages of relationship development: **1) Relationship Building, 2) Relationship Erosion, and 3) Relationship Repair.**

Relationship Building—Four Phases:

Phase 1—*Time*: Relationships are built first through a *substantial investment of focused time*. The friends sharing common interests; the couple falling in love; the mother bonding with her baby; the fellow soldiers dodging danger together on the battlefield; the professional team sharing ideas in regular meetings—these are just a few examples of relationships getting built through spending meaningful time together.

This is most evident in romantic attachments, where couples often feel so consumed by each other that they spend every possible minute together—and feel pained and deprived by even a few minutes apart. In all relationships, *time* is the first crucial, irreplaceable element, building a sense of meaningful connection and shared experience.

Phase 2—*Talk:* As people spend *time* together, it is only natural that they also *talk* to each other. This deepens a sense of connection and mutual understanding. Couples falling in love often say that they can "talk to each other about anything," which is a major source of their mutual attraction. Friends, colleagues, and family members likewise deepen their connection through using *talk* to share their ideas and feelings—opening their hearts to each other and sharing their unique perspectives and insights to enrich each other's lives.

Phase 3—*Trust:* As people spend *time* together, and become acquainted with each other through *talk*, over time, a growing sense of *trust* results—a feeling of safety and comfort in each other's presence: "I know that you'll be there for me, and that I can safely share my inner self with you." This creates a sense of deep confidence and bonding in the relationship.

Phase 4—*Touch:* As *time, talk,* and *trust* unfold in the relationship, *touch* often becomes a means of expressing that sense of connection, warmth, and safety. Again, this is most true in couple relationships—but also has relevance in other relationships (except, perhaps, in professional relationships, where touch is mostly out of bounds.) *Touch* is often a gauge reflecting the level of emotional connection in a relationship.

Now, let's use the **"4 T's"** to explore what happens when a relationship becomes strained or distant.

Relationship Erosion—Four Phases:

Phase 1—*Time Erosion:* Relationships begin to fray when less *time* is devoted to them. This may occur because of conflicting demands from work, children, church, community service, or other worthy priorities. Often, it is results from too much time spent on electronic entertainment, or other less meaningful pursuits. The less time people spend together, the less experience they will share, and the less connection they will feel. *Time erosion* is often the beginning of the end of what was once a good marriage, a close friendship, or a satisfying parent-child relationship. Both *"quantity time"* and *"quality time"* are important, to develop and preserve the strength of meaningful connection in a relationship. When these begin to erode, the relationship tends to erode as well.

Phase 2—*Talk Erosion:* As people spend less *time* together, they inevitably *talk* less with each other. The less *quantity* of *talk* they engage in, the more the *quality* of that *talk* will suffer. *Talk* may then turn to criticism, blame, sarcasm, or other negative expressions that generate disconnection, not connection; pain, not warmth; misunderstanding, not understanding. This can very quickly strain or even destroy a relationship.

Phase 3—*Trust Erosion:* As *time* and *talk* become less abundant and less satisfying, inevitably *trust* becomes a casualty in the relationship. No longer do people feel safe and warm in each other's presence. Instead, suspicion, anger, or even fear enters the relationship. Defensiveness is a common reaction. The relationship stops feeling like a safe harbor—and begins to feel more like a threatening battleground.

Phase 4—*Touch Erosion*: As *trust* erodes, caring *touch* becomes next to impossible. *Touch* can feel scary, deceptive, or inauthentic when people feel unsafe or emotionally disconnected. The avoidance of *touch* can be a serious warning sign in a relationship that was once close and caring. It is often at this point that people seek help through relationship counseling. But by the time erosion has gone this far, it can be very difficult (though not impossible) to repair the damage and restore connection.

Finally, using the "4 Ts," let's discuss building blocks for repairing a relationship that has become damaged:

Relationship Repair—Four Phases:

Phase 1—*Time Repair*: A relationship that has become distant or strained will have to be rebuilt from its very foundations. This starts, as it did in the beginning, with the intentional investment of focused *time*. Setting aside time is harder after a relationship has been damaged. Life is more complex, feelings are more brittle, and people are more cautious after having been previously hurt or disappointed. But with the regular conscientious investment of focused *time*, significant relationship repair can begin to occur.

Phase 2—*Talk Repair*: As people intentionally begin spending more *time* together, there is greater opportunity to *talk* to each other. It is important at this stage to not just increase the *quantity* of talk, but also to improve its *quality*. (Techniques for this will be provided more thoroughly with Tool #15.) As people develop the skills to really *talk* to each other—including about difficult topics—with mutual respect and openness, Relationship Repair proceeds powerfully forward, rebuilding connections, and deepening trust.

Phase 3—*Trust Repair*: Shared *time* and positive *talk* lay the necessary foundation for the repair of that tender, fragile dimension of a relationship known as *trust*. Not just the simple assurance of not being lied to or betrayed in the relationship—but, far beyond that—the confidence that your feelings are important to the other person; that on a deep level, your needs and opinions truly *matter*.

Phase 4—*Touch Repair*: This is typically the final phase of relationship repair, as it builds on the other dimensions of *time, talk,* and *trust*. When these other elements are strong in a relationship, *touch* can be a crowning expression of that sense of connection. However, without these other elements, *touch* often becomes merely a painful and contentious battleground, disrupting these other dimensions of connection. So, *it is important to proceed in the sequence outlined here, in order to produce full relationship repair.*

I've found over the years that when people use **"The 4 Ts"** to assess the status of their relationship, and then follow the sequence of "relationship repair" to strengthen their connection, they can often rescue and revitalize even a badly threatened relationship, restoring it back to its full health and vitality.

Let's now summarize **"The 4 Ts"** in a simple table form for ease of reference and review:

THE 4 Ts:

1—RELATIONSHIP BUILDING:	2—RELATIONSHIP EROSION:	3—RELATIONSHIP REPAIR:
T-ime	T-ime Erosion	T-ime Repair *(Quantity and Quality)*
T-alk	T-alk Erosion	T-alk Repair *(Quantity and Quality)*
T-rust	T-rust Erosion	T-rust Repair
T-ouch	T-ouch Erosion	T-ouch Repair

Reviewing this table, it is easy to see why excessive media can disrupt the building or maintenance of positive relationships. Connection with another human being takes ongoing work. It requires significant amounts of focused *time*. It requires face-to-face, heart-to-heart *talk* (not just the voiceless exchange of tiny printed words on a small screen.) It requires the development of mutual *trust*—including, the trust that you'll really be there for that other person, and that they'll really be there for you. It often requires meaningful, palpable *touch*. **Excessive media drains away the time and focus required for all four of these important dimensions.**

A lack of social connection can greatly increase vulnerability to depression, anxiety, addiction, and other emotional challenges. So learning to build and maintain effective relationships is one of the most demanding but important skills you can develop, to prevent or heal depression, and to form the basis of a happy, fulfilling life. Whether you're seeking to build new relationships in the first place, or are striving to strengthen or repair existing relationships, these tools can assist you, in that important healing process.

Now—let's move on to the last of our Level 2 Tools— **SERVICE**—a tool that gathers all the previous tools together in purposeful and productive action—simultaneously bringing joy to you, and to others.

TOOL TEN

———

SERVICE:

*Joyfully Share What You Have
and Are with Others*

➤ **10–1** Giving Back—The Most
Joyful Expression of Ourselves

➤ **10–2** How Service Expands Our
Happiness, Over Our Lifetime

➤ **10–3** What Happens When
Service Becomes a Lost Art?

➤ **10–4** Finding Service Opportunities,
Balanced with Self-Care

➤ **10–5** Pulling Together All
You've Learned So Far

INBORN TRAITS

1. Action
2. Feeling
3. Positivity

4. Learning
5. Creativity

LEARNED SKILLS

6. Identity
7. Recording

8. Seeking
9. Sociality
10. Service

ADVANCED

11. Health
12. Activity
13. Order

14. Thinking
15. Connection
16. Healing

10–1   Giving Back—The Most Joyful Expression of Ourselves

Tool #10 in *YOUR* Happiness Toolkit is—the SERVICE tool. Together with Tools #8 and #9, SEEKING and SOCIALITY, this tool contributes to a balanced set of strategies for building positive connections with other people—a crucial ingredient for a happy and fulfilling life.

The SERVICE Tool completes this 3-part relationship-building system, like the third leg of a 3-legged stool. All 3 parts are useful and important; all 3 are necessary for living a joyful and productive life; all 3 balance and support each other. SEEKING and SOCIALITY help fill our emotional bucket, and SERVICE allows us to generously pour that bucket out to enrich others' lives—adding zest, richness, and meaning to our own lives.

When we serve others, we express the deepest and healthiest parts of ourselves. We learn more fully who we are, what we're capable of, and what legacy we can leave behind, when our time in this world is past. We find the best that we have to offer, and we offer it, extending it outward to benefit others—particularly those less fortunate or less experienced than ourselves.

SERVICE is the pinnacle of all we've discussed so far. All of our *Inborn Traits* (Level 1) and our *Learned Skills* (Level 2) feed into this tenth tool. SERVICE puts the spring in our step, and adds focus and purpose to our lives, at every point in the life cycle. It isn't always easy, and it isn't always fun. But SERVICE, in any of its many forms, opens the door to the best that we can be, and the finest that life can offer.

10–2   How Service Expands Our Happiness, Over Our Lifetime

Like the other four tools in Level 2, the SERVICE tool is one we generally get introduced to early in life. From the time we can stand on our own two little legs, we can engage in service to others. In our **preschool** years, that might be putting our own toys away, doing simple chores around the house, or putting loving arms around a family member or friend who's going through a hard time. As our capacities expand during our **school-age** years, we might provide assistence to a friend struggling with a homework assignment that came easily to us. Or, we might collect cans of food for our school's service project for the homeless; or invite the new kid in school to sit with us at lunch, and to play with our friend group during recess.

248

Children can be taught even at an early age to provide service—and they are happier and more productive in doing so than simply by sitting around, being passively taken care of or entertained all day. *Even at an early age, bringing happiness to others also brings us joy.* Tuning in compassionately to help meet others' needs is a skill that can be taught and cultivated. In proper sequence—first children need to receive appropriate care and nurturance for themselves; then they can be taught to reach out, in kindness, generosity, and service.

As we become **teenagers,** our service opportunities expand yet again. We are now bigger, stronger, smarter, and more self-aware. We have a broader range of emotions available to us—and from these, we can feel greatly expanded compassion for others. *Teens are happiest when they can contribute to their world in positive ways.* They can do more demanding chores at home, use their talents to cheer others' lives, help brainstorm and solve family challenges, gain employment and cheerfully serve customers at their workplace, or extend compassionate understanding and kindness to troubled friends and family members.

Our service opportunities extend still further when we become **adults.** Education opens the door to expanded capabilities for service in the workplace. Dating, marriage, homemaking, and parenthood all present opportunities to serve others daily—cooking, cleaning, grocery shopping, doing laundry, reading stories, wiping away tears, driving children to their important events, and so on. Opportunities may also arise for increased sharing of our talents through service in our church or community; or even for public service in the broad political arena.

It is in adulthood, with this vast range of service opportunities and expectations, that we are most vulnerable to overtaxing ourselves, and getting burned out. If we are not careful, we can fall into a pattern of obsessive codependence—caring excessively for other people's perceived needs, while neglecting our own. *It is crucial, particularly during these busy and demanding years, that we take time for self-care,* to replenish ourselves in the midst of all these various service demands that may be constantly tugging at us.

Finally, **retirement and aging** provide a new set of service challenges and opportunities. As children become grown and leave the nest; as formal service opportunities in the workplace end with retirement; as aging and health issues set in, leaving us less active than we once were—it can become more difficult to find meaningful service opportunities. We may grieve the loss of association and sense of purpose we had while raising our children, or while working full-time every day.

But retirement can be a rich time of new discovery and exploration, as we find new people to love and serve, new ways to use our talents and rich life experience. Life is more relaxed in these latter decades, without the constant press of demands that we may have experienced in earlier phases of adulthood. If we are wise, we will use these latter years in positive, productive ways to benefit the lives of others and to reach out publicly and privately in ways we may not have had the time or energy to do in our younger, busier days. The happiest retired people are those who remain tuned to others' needs, and keep finding meaningful ways to contribute.

10–3 What Happens When Service Becomes a Lost Art?

Unfortunately, we now seem to be living in a time when service to others has become a lower priority for many people than personal enjoyment, buying and consuming products, and constant media entertainment. Profit and financial growth have become the core guiding values for many businesses, rather than a mission to help others through their products and services. Hands-on customer service at the grocery store, at the gas station (once known as a "service" station), at the bank, or even on the phone helpline have largely become artifacts of the past, as machines and voice recorders have replaced caring human interaction, and automated functionality has replaced human connection in many (if not most) modern businesses.

At every stage of modern life, from childhood to old age, service opportunities are now largely eclipsed by ever-present entertainment options. We may not even *see* people that need our help, because our eyes and attention are already fixed on some screen or electronic device. Toddlers, children, teens, adults, and retirees alike can become seduced by the siren call of self-fulfillment, consumerism, and constant media distraction.

Of all the modern lifestyle patterns driving the recent increase in depression and even suicidality, this may be one of the most widespread and profound. *When service becomes a lost art, joy becomes a lost opportunity.* When pointless distraction fills our days and nights, life can quickly feel meaningless, purposeless, and devoid of real satisfaction.

Likewise, when we separate ourselves from each other to focus on our own entertainment, purchases, or self-fulfillment, the cost is often isolation and depressing loneliness—even if we're spending our time in so-called "social" media. Ultimately, that isolation and loneliness can become destructive—and at times, even potentially life-threatening. The more engaged we are listening to our own playlists through our own headphones, the less engaged we are with the actual human relationships that surround us. Correspondingly, the less joy and meaning we find in our daily lives, as we fall into these increasingly common lifestyle patterns.

Or, at times, we may feel forced to do our household chores, go to a joyless workplace to collect a needed paycheck to fund future purchases, or provide essential physical care to children or others who annoy us with their cries if they don't get what they need. In such instances, serviceable action might be carried out with resentment rather than joy. So it delivers less benefit to those we feel forced to "serve," and certainly brings less joy to us than loving service we extend willingly from the heart.

Rate your current pattern on the scale below:

LIST 1—*Patterns Feeding:*	LIST 2—*Patterns Feeding:*
Depression, Disease, Deterioration, and Disability	Happiness, Wellness, Resilience, and Productivity
10. ISOLATION: Stay Focused on Yourself (or, Serve Resentfully)	**10. SERVICE:** Joyfully Share What You Have and Are with Others

-3	-2	-1	0	1	2	3
Strong	Moderate	Mild	Neutral	Mild	Moderate	Strong

Fortunately, any time we choose, we can decide to refocus our lives on service and positive connection, rather than on self-absorption, distraction, or consumption. Though the world may continue to hurtle towards heartless machine-generated functionality, we can choose to keep our hearts open, keep our eyes open, and keep our schedules open to the compassionate and intentional exercise of heartfelt service to others.

10–4 Finding Service Opportunities, Balanced with Self-Care

How do we engage in a lifestyle of service and connection? Here's some ideas to help start the process:

1. *Where* **we can serve**

   The best place to get started with service is—right where you are! Service doesn't require an expensive passport to some distant village in the developing world. If you have the eyes to see, there are people to serve right in your own *home*, in your own *workplace*, in your own *school*, *church*, or *neighborhood*.

2. *Who* we can serve

Start with the people closest to you, especially family members, coworkers, friends, and neighbors. Then, expand your reach. You can serve both publicly and privately—serving the one, *and* the many. Anonymous service can bring you great joy, customizing your service to the needs of individuals (such as snow-blowing a neighbor's sidewalk, or leaving a treat on the doorstep for a friend). Public service allows you to impact many people at once—both those you know, and those you don't know. *You can serve people both far and near. But start with those near and dear.* They should always remain the most central focus of your service.

3. *When* we can serve

Look for opportunities *throughout each day* to serve, even in small ways, such as a smile, a small kindness to a family member, or an encouraging word to a struggling friend. *In every season of your life,* from childhood to old age, you can find meaningful ways to serve, bringing joy to yourself and others. Don't limit your service to big days, such as feeding the homeless on Thanksgiving or Christmas. Help is needed all *throughout the year.*

4. *How* we can serve

Service can be carried out in all four areas of life—mentally, physically, spiritually, and socially. The Wellness Grid introduced in Section I can help you structure and plan your service in a balanced way. For example:

MENTAL	PHYSICAL
Volunteer at your child's school	Rake an elderly neighbor's leaves
Share your musical talents at a rest home	Cook a nice dinner for your family
Teach a class or start an instructional blog	Help your brother's family move

SPIRITUAL	SOCIAL
Pray for someone who's struggling	Call a friend who looked lonely at church
Accept an assignment at your church	Visit someone who is sick or home-bound
Share an inspiring quote on Facebook	Serve on a public board or committee

Your service can extend from your particular talents and interests, so it is customized to you as you share the things you can uniquely share. If you struggle with a disability, don't focus on what you *can't* do—focus on what you *can* do, finding ways to serve that draw on your remaining abilities. Remember to serve with a positive and happy heart. This will extend the most benefit both to you *and* to those you serve.

If you find yourself feeling resentful in your service, stop and refocus on *who and why* you're serving. It might feel hard at first, sacrificing time away from personal interests to serve. But doing so can greatly enrich your life.

Some people, of course, have the opposite struggle. Their lives are *so* consumed in service, in taking care of other people, that they forget their own needs, and their own personal identity. These individuals have so many service obligations that they may be running day and night to meet a vast array of needs—yet they feel constantly depleted and discouraged, feeling they can never measure up to all that's required of them.

Often, these highly serviceable individuals are those who describe themselves as "people-pleasers"—and it can be very upsetting to them if they have to disappoint anyone. The irony, of course, is that disappointing *someone* is virtually inevitable in this physical world, where we can only be in one place at one time, and where there is a practical limit to how many hours a day we can feasibly serve.

If, for example, we choose to spend an hour visiting a sick neighbor, by definition that hour ends up costing us time away from our children, husband, friends, civic duties, house cleaning, church service, or the thousands of other good things we could otherwise be filling that hour with. So almost inevitably, as we engage in one act of service in one context, we eliminate the possibility of service in all the other contexts, to all the other people, during that same period of time. Hence, the old adage is true: **"You can please some of the people some of the time, but you can't please all of the people all of the time."**

The example of Mother Teresa may be useful to give perspective. As she began her vast service to thousands of the poorest of the poor, she was asked, "How do you think you're going to fix everything when there are so many who struggle?" She wisely responded, "*God doesn't expect me to fix everything. He just expects me to do what I can.*" And so it is with each of us. We are each just expected to do what we can—making sure we take the necessary time to keep ourselves well, happy, and strong, so that we can continue to serve.

Doing what we can, but not more than we can; keeping a manageable balance between service and self-care—these things are essential for effective, sustainable SERVICE over time. Balancing these elements with SEEKING and SOCIALITY helps create healthy relationships that contribute greatly to our overall well-being.

10–5 Pulling Together All You've Learned So Far

Congratulations! You have now completed Section III of this book, becoming acquainted with the next five tools in *Your* Happiness Toolkit. These are your Level 2 Learned Skills—gained initially at a young age, as a natural part of growing up; and then becoming further strengthened over time, infused with ever-increasing power, as part of your program to overcome depression, and build a joyful, fulfilling life.

As a review, these five new tools are:

Tool 6—IDENTITY:
Know and Value Your Unique Traits and Gifts

Tool 7—RECORDING:
Write and Preserve Your Life Experience

Tool 8—SEEKING:
Reach Out for Guidance, Support, and Insight

Tool 9—SOCIALITY:
Engage in Meaningful Social Connections

Tool 10—SERVICE:
Joyfully Share What You Have and Are with Others

Together with the **Transformational Tools** introduced in Section I, and the **Inborn Traits** introduced in Section II, these new **Level 2 Tools** can help you daily craft a positive lifestyle that promotes emotional recovery and enduring wellness.

Now, before introducing the **Advanced Level 3 Tools** in the following section, here is a worksheet to help summarize all you've learned so far:

THE LEVEL 1–2 TOOLS, AND THE 5 TRANSFORMATIONAL TOOLS:

LEVEL 1 TOOLS (INBORN TRAITS):	
Tool 1—ACTION:	Do what you love—and do what loves you back!
Tool 2—FEELING:	Feel and Express Your Actual Feelings
Tool 3—POSITIVITY:	Notice and Enjoy the Good Things
Tool 4—LEARNING:	Develop New Abilities and Skills
Tool 5—CREATIVITY:	Focus on Creating Rather Than Consuming

LEVEL 2 TOOLS (LEARNED SKILLS):	
Tool 6—IDENTITY:	Know and Value Your Unique Traits and Gifts!
Tool 7—RECORDING:	Write and Preserve Your Life Experience
Tool 8—SEEKING:	Reach Out for Guidance, Support, and Insight
Tool 9—SOCIALITY:	Engage in Meaningful Social Connections
Tool 10—SERVICE:	Joyfully Share What You Have and Are with Others

You can now mobilize all ten of these tools in *Your Happiness Toolkit*, to help fill in and activate the five change strategies introduced in Section I:

5 TRANSFORMATIONAL TOOLS:

1. WELLNESS GRID	Physical, Mental, Spiritual, Emotional
2. UP-OR-DOWN SPIRAL	Upward Direction or Downward Direction?
3. DIAMOND	Triggers, Thoughts, Behaviors, Spirituality, Relationships
4. MORE-OR-LESS GRID	"I Need More . . . / I Need Less . . ." in the Four Areas
5. *YOUR* HAPPINESS TOOLKIT	16 Strategies, Levels 1–3

	What Do I Need MORE of?	*What Do I Need LESS of?*
PHYSICALLY:		
MENTALLY:		
SPIRITUALLY:		
EMOTIONALLY:		

YOUR HAPPINESS TOOLKIT, LEVEL 3

Advanced Strategies

INBORN TRAITS

1. Action
2. Feeling
3. Positivity

4. Learning
5. Creativity

LEARNED SKILLS

6. Identity
7. Recording

8. Seeking
9. Sociality
10. Service

ADVANCED

11. Health
12. Activity
13. Order

14. Thinking
15. Connection
16. Healing

The six tools introduced in this section are very different than the previous ten. They are significantly more complex, requiring more specific training, and containing a wider variety of applications and component parts. They could be likened, in a physical toolbox, to a complex drill bit set, or a power saw with multiple settings.

You would be well advised *not* to start off with these tools—but rather to build first on the foundation of the Quick Start Strategies, and the ten tools already introduced in Sections I and II. Once these are in place, then the six tools described here can bring expanded power and capacity into your daily life.

These are literally the "power tools" in *Your* Happiness Toolkit. They can increase your effectiveness, productivity, and confidence vastly beyond what is possible without them. However, they can be demanding to learn, and require significantly more effort, energy, and willpower than the previous tools. So again, I advise you to start with the earlier sections, and work up to this one, so that the energy and vitality provided by the simpler tools can prepare you for the demands of these particularly powerful, life-changing strategies.

———

HEALTH:

Care Wisely for Your Body—And Your Brain

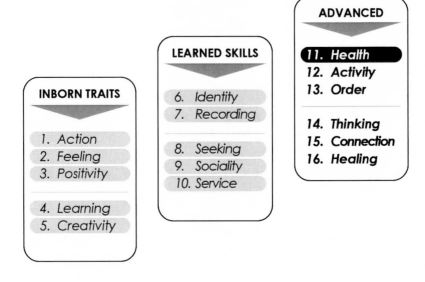

11–1 Healthy Body, Healthy Brain— The Foundation of Wellness

Tool #11 in *YOUR* Happiness Toolkit is—the HEALTH tool. It is no secret that our emotional health and happiness are largely impacted by our physical health. It is difficult, if not impossible, to feel sustained joy and well-being if we are feeling physically ill, fatigued, or depleted.

It is also no secret that *depression—at least in part—is physical.* Many of its hallmark symptoms include physical difficulties— including sleep problems, loss of appetite, reduced or eliminated sex drive, digestive difficulties, significant weight loss or gain, or a deep heaviness and crushing fatigue that makes everything feel hard. Indeed, it is because depression feels so physical that many people under its influence seek a doctor's intervention. Sometimes people don't even recognize that what they are struggling with is depression—they just want help with the exhaustion, difficulty sleeping, etc.

It is important to address these physical symptoms *early* in depression treatment—otherwise, the chronic exhaustion and resulting loss of motivation can make it almost impossible for people to engage effectively in any of the many healing actions that can contribute to depression relief.

In contrast—when people are physically healthy and vibrant, alert and energetic, pain-free and engaged in positive activity, the resulting sense of well-being is a natural antidepressant—a solid foundation for action that promotes both physical *and* emotional wellness throughout life.

11–2   Three Health-Killers in the Modern World, and How to Reverse Them

Over recent decades, depression has often been described in the media as a *"brain disease"* that supposedly resulted from a lack of serotonin in the brain. Antidepressants have been touted as the magic-bullet "answer" to this supposed deficiency—like insulin is needed by the diabetic to balance blood sugars. On the surface, this theory sounds plausible and scientific, and has been believed by millions of people all over the world.

But scientific research has never exposed *any* solid evidence supporting this widespread theory. In reality, it is impossible to measure serotonin levels in a living brain. Also, serotonin and other neuro-transmitters affecting mood and energy exist not only in the brain, but also in the gut and throughout the whole body. Their presence and action is affected by a wide range of highly adaptable lifestyle factors—not just by "bad luck" producing "random disease." **No depression was ever *caused* by a lack of antidepressant medication.**

Likewise, depression has often been blamed on faulty genetics—largely because it is so often observed in multi-generational families. However, genetic structure is only *one* of the factors handed down in families. Attitudes, lifestyle habits, diet, activity levels, social engagement patterns, and other day-to-day factors impacting depression also tend to be passed from generation to generation, exerting powerful influence.

Happily, these factors are significantly more changeable than genes themselves. And the emerging science of *epigenetics* is revealing that even if a particular gene *does* exist in an individual, it will only be "turned on" if the conditions exist that are required to activate it. Like the switchboard controlling electrical circuits in your home—these genetic "switches" can be "turned on" by certain conditions, and "turned off" by other conditions, including personal lifestyle choices. So even if depression has run in your family for generations, you can learn to "turn off" the genetic or lifestyle switches that might otherwise activate it in your own life.

Also, consider this—Depression in recent years has been emerging at an unprecedented, epidemic rate, including in those that carry *no* family history of it. It is extending through a broader and broader range of people of various ages, socio-economic statuses, genders, life histories, races, and nationalities. So this massive spread of depression cannot be accounted for simply by genetics—because *genetics themselves simply have not changed that much over recent decades.*

But a *lot* of other things *have* changed over the last few decades. These other changes have been identified as powerful factors in the spread of not just depression, but also of *heart disease, cancer, diabetes, autoimmune disorders, chronic pain, autism, Alzheimer's, infertility, eating disorders, sexual dysfunctions, obesity, anxiety,* and many other conditions that have become far more common throughout the world over the past thirty to fifty years—including in the very young. In fact, over recent years, each successive generation has become, by and large, more vulnerable to these troubling conditions than the previous one—developing these diseases earlier in life, and at a more severe and debilitating level.

These other physical conditions often intersect with depression. People with depression are more likely to suffer with one or more of these other diseases; and people with these diseases are more likely to struggle with depression. They complicate each other, feed off of each other, and make the cumulative impact more serious and disruptive of life and happiness for the individual, family, and society involved.

Remarkably, all of these diseases are spreading throughout the world, according to an absolutely consistent pattern. The more primitive a civilization is, the more resistant they are to these debilitating conditions. In fact, in those societies, these illnesses are largely non-existent. But *the more "civilized" a nation becomes, the more vulnerable they become to the spread of all of these illnesses, including depression.*

This unsettling pattern began to be observed first in the early twentieth century, when there were still sizeable pockets of "uncivilized" societies scattered throughout the world. For example, in 1939, Dr. Weston Price, a dentist, published his influential book *Nutrition and Physical Degeneration.* Concerned by increasing rates of tooth decay among his American patients, Dr. Price set out on a worldwide exploration to discover whether or not this pattern was universal.

Over and over, in society after society, on continent after continent, Dr. Price found the same repetitive pattern. The more primitive the society, the better their teeth, general bone structure, and overall health and mood. Though the aborigines, native Eskimos, primitive Pacific Islanders and others he studied had never owned a toothbrush, their teeth were white, shining, straight, and strong, without any of the deformities or decay he so often observed in his dental practice in the United States.

Dr. Price witnessed the same pattern in area after area that he studied. Where civilization had begun to arrive—for example, in coastal towns participating directly in free trade with more developed nations—tooth decay and deformity, as well as other *"diseases of civilization"* had begun to settle in. Meanwhile, in neighboring villages farther away from the trade route, people of the same race, even of the same family descent, showed a vastly different pattern. Their teeth were strong, their bodies were well-formed, their moods were upbeat.

In the 1930s, this research on lifestyle differences focused mostly on nutrition. It revealed that the more "civilized" people were consuming more processed or manufactured foods—canned and packaged goods, pasteurized milk, white bread, and highly sweetened foods and treats. Meanwhile, their "primitive" neighbors were still doing what had sustained prior generations for centuries—eating fresh, locally grown fruits, vegetables, grains, seeds, and nuts, in season along with fresh, locally cultivated animal foods.

Their particular diets varied by geographic area. Primitive cultures in South America lived on corn, beans, and a wide range of local fruits and vegetables. Pacific Islanders ate tropical fruits, tubers, and fresh fish. Asian cultures ate rice, land and sea vegetables, and freshly caught seafood. Native Eskimos ate less plant food, and more animal fat, including in the form of whale blubber. Primitives in Northern Europe raised cattle and included lots of fresh, non-pasteurized milk and cheese in their diets. Despite the vast difference in these traditional diets, what they all had in common was—a reliance on *fresh, locally grown, natural foods*, in season, recently drawn from the earth—*not* from a factory.

Later health professionals observed similar phenomena and came to similar conclusions. John McDougall, Joel Fuhrman, Neal Barnard, Dean Ornish, T. Colin Campbell, Caldwell Esselstyn, Mark Hyman, and Henry S. Lodge are among the many twentieth-century medical pioneers who have observed, researched, and documented the profound health differences between people who eat whole, natural food, versus those who eat processed, manufactured food. Different researchers focus on different conditions—some on diabetes, some on cancer, some on heart disease, some on Alzheimer's, some on aging, etc. But the preponderance of research contributes to one overwhelmingly consistent conclusion: *The way we are typically eating in the civilized world is literally making us sick—and ultimately, is killing us.*

The *standard American diet (SAD)* being literally exported all over the world is spreading these patterns of disease from country to country, and from civilization to civilization. Depression is only one of the myriad of debilitating conditions that is literally being *fed*, day by day, by denatured, manufactured, fake food.

What is good for the body is good for the brain—for it is an essential part of the body. What heals the heart, what reverses diabetes, what strengthens the immune system, what slows aging, what promotes healthy weight control, what builds actual overall wellness, from the inside out, is likewise protective against the debilitating *physical* aspects of depression.

These doctors who study these other illnesses often mention the relief of depression as an unintended but happy side benefit of overall health improvement. Individual professionals may be focusing on reversing obesity, heart disease, diabetes, Alzheimer's, or some other degenerative condition. But frequently they mention the *emotional benefit* that positive health modification brings to patient after patient. Dr. Mark Hyman, in fact, calls himself "the accidental psychiatrist" because so many of his patients have reported emotional recovery, including the lifting of depression, in response to his physical healing regimen. He is not the only "accidental psychiatrist." Anyone who learns and practices the principles of positive health enhancement will likewise experience the happy side benefit of emotional improvement.

As stated before, depression is partly physical, and is often experienced in a highly physical way. So it is sometimes assumed, "Because it's physical, it requires a medication." What these and many other professionals (including myself) have experienced in administering treatment is—chemical symptom management is a poor substitute for actual health-producing, health-maintaining behaviors that generate wellness and vitality throughout the entire physical system, from the inside out. There are simply better answers that work—more comprehensively, and far more safely than chemical intervention.

This is exhilarating and liberating news, once you grasp it. Because *the same strategies that fight physical degeneration also combat the physical elements of depression—and vice versa.* Strong teeth and bones, clean hearts and livers, healthy digestive and immune systems, pain-free bones and joints, *and* thriving, balanced, resilient brains are all composed of the same processes and materials. And they can all be compromised by the same processes and materials. Once you learn the difference between what *heals* you and what *endangers* you, daily you can make powerful educated decisions to guide yourself and your loved ones into a happier, healthier condition, for years and decades to come.

So—what are the three fundamental health-killers in the modern world and what can *you* do to reverse them?

In summary, they are as follows:

1. **Food**—a lack of needed nutrients from natural food, and an excess of processed, manufactured substances.

2. **Movement**—a lack of exercise and whole-body movement, and an excess of low-activity, sedentary time.

3. **Light and Sleep**—a lack of sunlight by day and sleep by night, and an excess of artificial light and screen time.

Rate your current pattern on the scale below:

LIST 1—Patterns Feeding: Depression, Disease, Deterioration, and Disability	LIST 2—Patterns Feeding: Happiness, Wellness, Resilience, and Productivity
11. ILLNESS: Eat Junk; Get Little Sleep, Exercise, and Sunlight	**11. HEALTH:** Care Wisely For Your Body—And Your Brain

-3	-2	-1	0	1	2	3
Strong	Moderate	Mild	Neutral	Mild	Moderate	Strong

It may at times seem like the whole world is going in the direction of processed, fake "food"; inactive, sedentary lifestyles; and constant, ever-present artificial light, often flickering at us day and night from electronic screens. From super-sized IMAX screens in public theatres, to oversized TV screens in our family rooms,

274

to the tiny, ever-present phone screens we each carry with us everywhere in our purses and pockets—we are inundated with cultural messages and norms that, if followed, will continue to lead us, as individuals, families, and nations, to the ever-expanding tragedies of destroyed physical and emotional health. *But it need not be so.* We can choose a happier, healthier course for ourselves and for our loved ones—starting *today.*

11–3   Food Is Fuel: Choosing a Wellness-Promoting Nutrition Program

For a moment, imagine your dream car. Envision its sleek, attractive shape; its perfect color, personalized to your exact preference; the hum of its powerful engine. Imagine sliding into the driver's seat of that dream car, turning on the speakers to hear your favorite tunes, and turning the key to rev up that powerful engine.

Imagine speeding along in that well-crafted machine, down streets and highways to some of your very favorite fantasy destinations. Maybe you drive to a pristine ocean beach, for an active day of fun in the sun. Maybe you navigate, with powerful four-wheel drive, up steep, snowy mountains to enjoy a weekend of skiing. Maybe you visit historical sites that interest you, national parks filled with wondrous vistas, or crowded shopping areas full of quaint little boutiques and restaurants. Wherever you drive, the power and instrumentality of your vehicle carries you comfortably and speedily to wherever you want to go, to do whatever you want to do.

Now—imagine that after several days of driving, your fuel gauge starts to indicate that you're about to run out of gas. But, let's say that you choose to ignore the gauge. and just keep on driving. After all, you reason, you're the owner of a perfectly engineered, top-quality dream machine that exists only to do your bidding.

If you continue on such a course, then no matter how powerful the engine, how dynamic the paint color, or how cool the gadgets and features of that vehicle might be—before long, *it will simply run out of fuel, and then will entirely cease to function.* Despite all of that carefully crafted circuitry, and those well-designed components, the unfueled vehicle becomes merely a very heavy and expensive chunk of metal on the road.

Worse yet, imagine that as you realize that fuel is running low, you stop at a local market, and pick up some fluid to fill up the tank. Maybe you choose Diet Coke, root beer, vodka, or even fresh-squeezed orange juice. You fill the fuel tank with this substance, get back in the car, and turn the key, expecting it to rev into motion, as it was designed to do. What happens? Answer—*nothing.* Or actually—*worse* than nothing. You've just done significant additional harm to the inner workings of that well-crafted machine. The longer that inappropriate "fuel" stays in the tank, the more lasting and harmful the damage will be.

In real life, of course, none of us would ever be foolish enough to let an expensive dream car run out of gas; and we would never even think of filling its tank with an inappropriate substitute for fuel, knowing how badly such an action could damage the structure and function of our prized vehicle.

But while we are generally smart enough to provide basic fuel and care to our motor vehicles, we are *not* always so smart about the way we care for our bodies. These priceless, personal vehicles—these intricate organic machines we live inside of—are more complex than any Maserati, more miraculous and intricately designed than any NASA rocket ship. Our amazing human bodies carry us from place to place, and from activity to activity. *But they can only continue to do this if we treat them properly.* If we neglect to fuel our bodies, we will inevitably run out of energy, stamina, and eventually the capacity to even move. Likewise, if we fuel our bodies with junk, with inappropriate fuel they were never designed for, comprehensive physical harm will be the result.

Fortunately, **our bodies are far better than human-built machines, because they have the capacity to regenerate and heal themselves,** if proper supplies are provided. Our bodies innately know how to build healthy new cellular structures—in our blood supply, in our muscles, in our teeth and bones, and, yes, even in the complex circuitry of the brain. But in order to do that, we need to provide proper fuel, and we need to stop dumping in improper substances.

11–4   Identifying and Correcting a Depressed Eating Pattern

It has been my experience, both personally and professionally, that when we are depressed, we will either:

1. **stop eating altogether,** or

2. **only eat what's most easy, tasty, or entertaining** (consuming mostly sugary, fatty junk food, fast food, or convenience food.)

But food avoidance *and* improper food consumption will both significantly impede depression recovery, and increase the overall harm to the system. Not eating at all is like not fueling the car at all, guaranteeing inaction. Eating junk is like filling the car's gas tank with Dr. Pepper. It corrodes, impedes function, and does additional damage—*besides* not providing needed fuel in the first place. In my experience, these two destructive conditions must be corrected early in the treatment process, if depression recovery is to occur.

It has also been my experience that rarely if ever do medical professionals even *ask* depressed patients about their nutritional habits—what they are eating or drinking, how often, or what time of day they are eating—if they are eating at all. Even patients receiving heavy-duty medications, or complex "drug cocktails" producing significant side effects, often tell me their medical providers never asked about their diets.

What kind of auto mechanic would dive into replacing the transmission on a vehicle without at least checking the fuel gauge first? In the mechanics industry, such a practice would be seen as misguided, incompetent, or even downright shady. But in medical practice, it has virtually become standard procedure for practitioners to pull out the prescription pad, to offer chemical symptom management, without checking first on the basic health and nutrition practices of the patient sitting right in front of them.

If a patient is not eating regularly, is not drinking pure water consistently, or is only consuming "junk" foods and beverages high in sugars, unhealthy fats, excessive salt, artificial flavors and colors, preservatives, and a range of other unnatural chemicals, there is simply no way for that individual to enjoy long-term good health. The negative impact of such "food" will show up differently in different individuals. In some it may present as diabetes, cancer, or heart disease. Others may suffer with chronic pain, obesity, or sexual dysfunction. In still others, it presents as anxiety, ADHD, or depression. Or, there may be a mix of these and other ailments.

But across the board, what researcher after researcher has found is—good physical and mental health absolutely require an abundance of good healthy food. **In a very literal sense, *you are what you eat.*** Your physical cells are literally composed of the materials you have provided them through your mouth, year after year, multiple times per day. Over time, those physical cells either get stronger, healthier, and increasingly resilient to illness and infection—or they get weaker, sicker, and more vulnerable to a variety of illnesses and ailments, both physical and emotional.

Food is certainly not the only factor in producing health or illness—but it is a massively influential one, determining much of your physical and emotional condition over time—whether positive or negative. We will discuss some of the other major health factors (movement, light, and sleep) in the next chapter. For now, however, we will focus on this foundational factor of health-promoting nutrition.

So, here are some practical suggestions, seen over and over throughout the scientific literature, that can help you, multiple times each day, to make wise food choices that can help promote wellness, rather than illness.

11–5 Fifteen Nutritional Tips to Help Overcome Depression and Disease

1. **Eat plenty of whole, natural, nutrient-rich, living food.** This is the *first* priority, to provide plenty of needed, appropriate "fuel" to the living cells of your body and brain. Even if you're currently eating lots of junk food, like chips, cookies, and junk beverages like soda pop, supplement those substances with pure, natural salads, fresh-made juices and smoothies, whole fruits and vegetables, and raw nuts and seeds.

2. **Drink lots of pure filtered water.** Your brain, like your heart, is composed of seventy-three percent water. For these organs and others to be fully functional, you need a fresh abundant supply of water daily, to cleanse out impurities, and to replenish needed fluid. Think about it—would you shower the exterior of your body in Diet Coke? Of course not! That would be ridiculous, because it would leave a sticky, corrosive, chemical residue on your skin. Likewise, successful *internal* cleansing requires actual *water*, not some manufactured, chemically produced, highly sweetened, unnatural substitute. Herbal tea or adding to water a few flavored stevia drops, ice, or a squeeze of fresh lime or lemon offers alternative ways to consume water, adding a little variety in taste or temperature. But the crucial thing is—in whatever form, drink plenty of water *daily*, throughout the day, morning to evening.

3. **Eat lots of high-water natural foods.** High-water natural foods include fruits, vegetables, and other products that naturally contain a lot of water. Watermelon, celery, citrus fruits, fresh vegetable juice, smoothies, and whole-food soups deliver added hydration, together with lots of vitamins and nutrients. Nutrient-rich water goes directly through your bloodstream to the cells and organs of your body, bringing life-giving resources that can go to work right away to cleanse, repair, and nourish your body, inside and out.

4. **Consume natural foods in a variety of colors.** Fruits and vegetables naturally come in many different colors—each color indicating the presence of different nutrients. The deep yellows and oranges of squashes, carrots, and yams; the vibrant greens of spinach, romaine lettuce, and broccoli; the tranquil whites and browns of mushrooms, raw nuts, and whole grains; the dark purples or deep reds of grapes, blackberries, blueberries, tomatoes, and purple cabbage—each color indicates a different mix of nutrients and health benefits. To get a more balanced combination of nutrients, as well as a more attractive presentation on your plate, include a variety of natural foods at every meal, in a variety of colors and textures.

5. **Eat locally grown, organic produce, as much as possible.** For maximum nutritional benefit and freshness, support local farmer's markets and organic food producers. You may spend a little more in the short term, but will reap expanded health benefits that accumulate more and more over time.

6. **Avoid sugar and caffeine like the plague.** These substances in particular supercharge anxiety, depression, and other mood disorders. If your goal is recovery and wellness, you want to stay away from these destructive substances—as well as from alcohol, drugs, tobacco, and other addictive products.

7. **Build in food variety, through a variety of national cuisines.** As mentioned earlier, many traditional cuisines are built upon simple but health-promoting foods. Expand your repertoire of food tastes and experiences to include more of these traditional cuisines—Italian, Greek, Indian, South American, Asian, etc.

8. **Make it easy.** Find healthy things you can do consistently. For example, get a filtered water pitcher, and make it a point to fill it and drink the contents several times daily. Keep a large cup or bottle of water with you at all times when you're out and about, and drink from it throughout the day. Buy bags of bite-sized vegetables, such as baby carrots or miniature sweet peppers, that you can easily "grab and go" for a quick healthy meal. Keep raw nuts and dried fruit in your purse, car, or office for a nutritious snack when needed, to avoid turning to more processed snacks later in the day, when hunger strikes.

9. **When grocery shopping, shop only in the fresh-food aisles.** This will save you significant time, money, temptation, and stress. Spend most of your time in the produce aisle, selecting a wide variety of fresh fruits and vegetables. Spend some time in the bulk-foods section,

gathering dry beans, lentils, seeds, dried fruits, whole grains, and raw nuts. If you choose to include dairy or meat products, choose the leanest, cleanest, most natural selections you can find. Avoid time in the aisles selling cookies, chips, canned foods, soda pop, alcohol, and other processed junk foods. They will not nourish you—they will just impede your recovery.

10. **Find a few reliable and guides and mentors.** It can be a little challenging at first, figuring out what to do with simple foods you may not be used to. You'll probably need a few good cookbooks, websites, or video collections to give you some tips to get started and to keep going. Look for mentors who specialize in improving physical health and wellness through nutrition. Some of my personal favorites that I recommend to my clients are *FoodMatters.com* and *Eat to Live* by Dr. Joel Fuhrman.

11. **Find and post some short quotes that inspire and motivate you.** Some of my personal favorites are:

    "If man made it, I don't eat it."—*Jack LaLanne*

    "If it didn't grow out of the ground, or it didn't have a mother, don't eat it."—*Jillian Michaels*

    "Eat food that can remember where it came from."—from *What to Eat When You're Expecting*

    "The more you eat green, the more you get lean."—*Dr. Joel Fuhrman*

    "Let thy food by thy medicine, and thy medicine be thy food."—*Hippocrates*

12. **Explore the emotional reasons for unhealthy eating.**
Get to the bottom of these, and find ways to resolve them.
Some of these reasons may include—eating for comfort,
for distraction, for protection, for socialization, or simply
out of habit or family tradition. My favorite resources
on this topic include *Love Hunger: Recovery from Food
Addiction* by Frank Minirth and Paul Meier, and *The
Gabriel Method* by John Gabriel.

13. **Remember—it's not just *what* you eat, but *when* you eat
it.** Our bodies, like the bodies of many plants and animals,
are designed to take in nutrients most effectively during
the day, when the sun is high in the sky. Try to eat your
meals beginning a little after sunrise, and ending before
sundown. This will help not only your mood and energy,
but also your sleep, so your body can spend its nighttime
hours resting and refueling, rather than depleting energy
digesting more food late at night. Also, to avoid mood-
disrupting blood sugar crashes, eat small portions at
regular intervals throughout the day, rather than just one
big meal all at once.

14. **When eating out, make the best possible choices.**
Modern life often keeps us out of the kitchen, and
needing to obtain food elsewhere. When eating out,
apply the principles on this list to make the best possible
choices, as you decide on eating locations and menu
options.

15. **If you don't "feel like eating"—do it anyway.** Remember—depression tends to make you want to do more of what feeds it, and less of what fights against it. If you struggle with depression, you probably won't *feel* like eating healthy—or even feel like eating *anything*. But remember your "dream car." Unless you fuel it, it simply cannot take you where you need to go. Eating when you don't "feel" like it can actually be really effective—because then your logical mind can be in charge of what goes into your mouth, rather than your emotions or impulses. Over time, healthful eating will become its own reward, giving you increased stamina, a more stable mood, and greater energy to apply to *all* the things you hope to do in life.

Providing consistent, health-promoting nourishment to your body and brain is one of the most important, but often neglected, aspects of depression recovery. It is literally the fuel for *everything* else you need to do to help yourself heal. Enjoy the adventure of learning to eat in a way that helps balance your brain chemistry, even out your mood swings, and provide the consistent energy resource needed for a joyful, fulfilling life.

ACTIVITY:

Enjoy Daily Health-Promoting Movement

➤ **12–1** Movement and Activity: Building Positive Energy and Vitality

➤ **12–2** How Inactivity Contributes to Depression and Illness

➤ **12–3** The Transformative Power of Physical Exercise

➤ **12–4** Non-Exercise Activity: A Powerful New Wellness Tool

➤ **12–5** Sleep and Sunlight: Balancing Natural Cycles, for Daily Renewal

12–1   Movement and Activity: Building Positive Energy and Vitality

Tool #12 in *Your* Happiness Toolkit is—the ACTIVITY tool. Along with positive nutrition, this tool promotes depression recovery and prevention on a *physical* level, and is a significant contributor not only to basic wellness and joy, but even to exhilaration, peak experience, and cheerful zest in life.

Movement is a quality naturally seen in young children and in primitive cultures, but it is frequently discouraged or even crushed by "civilization," which tends to be more sedentary. Where movement is lacking, its absence is one of the core factors in all of the "diseases of civilization" mentioned in the previous chapter—contributing not only to depression, but also to heart disease, diabetes, cancer, chronic pain, dementia, autoimmune disorders, etc. In contrast, **where movement is abundant, it contributes to both physical and mental health,** in proportion to the quantity and quality of its presence in a person's individual life.

Whereas nutrition, in the Health chapter, was likened to the engine of a dream car, fueled through the gas tank, movement is literally the "wheels" of recovery and lifetime wellness. Without an engine, the vehicle cannot even start up. Without wheels, the car might start, but it won't *go* anywhere. Without wheels *or* an engine, even the most finely crafted Porsche or Maserati would be nothing but a motionless pile of tin—unable to move, go anywhere, or provide any positive use. In contrast, with a functioning engine and wheels, that same vehicle can provide vivid, breathtaking, exhilarating experiences. *So it is with your body!*

12–2   How Inactivity Contributes to Depression and Illness

The first law of physics states, "A body in motion tends to stay in motion. A body at rest tends to stay at rest." The physical dimension of human life works the same way—and has a direct impact on emotional well-being. If an individual is moving, active, vibrant, *in motion*—they tend to stay in motion, day after day— experiencing, contributing, accomplishing, relating, learning. However, if someone is chronically "at rest"—essentially, without wheels, just *sitting* day after day, like a lifeless collection of steel and plastic parts—then each day their body becomes more and more accustomed to inactivity—and each day, it becomes harder to change that debilitating and progressive pattern.

Over time, *without meaningful movement, experience, and contribution—life may begin to feel meaningless, purposeless, or even worthless.* An immobile individual may begin to feel like a burden to those around them. This adds immeasurably to their depressed mood, and can launch a powerful downward spiral. The longer they "just sit there," the more useless they feel. The more useless they feel, the longer they sit there, ruminating about their supposed "worthlessness." This deeply painful state has a tendency to grow into more severe and disabling forms of depression—and sometimes, even of suicidality.

Fortunately, this is an *entirely* reversible pattern. The sooner it is reversed, the sooner this principle can work in a positive way, rather than in a negative way. For while an unmoving body tends to stay unmoving—so, according to the law, a body in motion tends to remain in motion. Once someone *gets* moving, it's far easier to *keep* moving.

It can be difficult to begin such a process. But even if movement just begins slowly, in small, short doses—once the wheels are back on the Maserati, so to speak—even if movement is only occurring at five miles an hour, that's far more productive than just sitting there. And once movement is occurring at five miles an hour—it's not hard to slowly increase speed from five miles an hour, to ten, to twenty, to fifty, to ninety, or more. As movement increases, so does life energy, improving overall mood—because low life energy contributes to depression, while high life energy contributes to radiant wellness and enduring joy.

Depression will always fight against good intentions. It will make you *want* to just sit there and do nothing. It will make you *not* want to get up and do anything—particularly anything active or physically demanding. Remember—it is the known tendency of depression to make you *want* to do things that feed it, and to *not* want to do things that can fight it.

But you do not have to obey the dictates of your depression. You can *decide* to build a life that works better for you. Making yourself move—getting yourself in motion—is one of the most important, powerful things you can do to overcome depression, and build a joyful, fulfilling, even exhilarating life.

Rate your current pattern on the scale below:

LIST 1—*Patterns Feeding:* Depression, Disease, Deterioration, and Disability	LIST 2—*Patterns Feeding:* Happiness, Wellness, Resilience, and Productivity
12. INACTIVITY: Spend Hours Sitting and Remaining Sedentary	**12. ACTIVITY:** Engage in Consistent, Health-Promoting Movement

-3	-2	-1	0	1	2	3
Strong	Moderate	Mild	Neutral	Mild	Moderate	Strong

There are various forms of movement that are useful for fighting depression, and building positive life energy. Let's explore several of these in turn:

12–3 The Transformative Power of Physical Exercise

It has long been recognized that physical exercise has powerful transformative effects *physically*—helping people lose weight, build muscle, increase energy, manage stress, prevent disease, and improve heart health. It has often been observed that if all the health benefits of exercise could be captured and packaged in a pill bottle, it would quickly become the best-selling drug in history. Physical exercise transforms bodies, helping them become leaner, more muscular, and more stress-resistant and resilient. Physical exercise slows and reverses aging, increases confidence, improves sleep, and strengthens overall immunity and well-being.

In addition, over the past several decades, the **depression-fighting power of physical exercise** has become increasingly recognized. Around the year 2000, researchers at Duke University discovered that moderate physical exercise was as effective as antidepressant medication for short-term depression relief. Beyond that, exercise was shown to be *more* successful than medication in preventing depression relapse in the long term.

Duke University researchers located 156 older patients diagnosed with major depression, and divided them into three groups. One group was given a standard dose of the antidepressant Zoloft. A second group was given a regimen of brisk but moderate aerobic exercise, for thirty minutes, three times a week. A third group received both the Zoloft *and* the exercise regimen.

After sixteen weeks, all three groups experienced relief from depression, at approximately the same level. This surprised the researchers, who had assumed that the combination group would show a significantly greater improvement, since they were receiving two treatments, rather than just one. They were surprised that the Zoloft seemed to contribute *no* additional benefit, beyond the exercise alone.

As Duke researchers continued to study these same participants for another six months, they were surprised again as they observed a significant difference in relapse rates between the three groups. Only **8%** of patients in the exercise group experienced the return of their depression. In contrast, relapse occurred in **38%** of the drug-only group. But what really stunned the researchers was— in the combination group that received both exercise and Zoloft, relapse occurred in **31%** of patients—almost as much as in the Zoloft-only group.

James Blumenthal, the lead researcher in the study, noted, **"We had assumed that exercise and medication together would have had an additive effect, but this turned out not to be the case."** Instead, they found that the combination was not nearly as effective as exercise alone. Indeed, the medication seemed to *reduce* the positive effects of the exercise—rather than strengthen it. This shocked researchers, who had begun the research assuming that the combination group would show the most benefit, both short-term and long-term.

In seeking to understand this, Blumenthal observed, *"Simply taking a pill is very passive. Patients who exercised may have felt a greater sense of mastery over their condition and gained a greater sense of accomplishment. They may have felt more self-confident and competent because they were able to do it themselves, and attributed their improvement to their ability to exercise."*

In other words, it appeared that the lower relapse rates among those who "only" exercised was due to the personal sense of victory and accomplishment of having overcome the depression themselves—and having the confidence of knowing how to maintain their own well-being, through action they were able to continue independently. Blumenthal also noted:

> *"We found that there was an inverse relationship between exercise and the risk of relapsing—the more one exercised, the less likely one would see their depressive symptoms return.* **For each 50 minute increment of exercise, there was an accompanying 50 percent reduction in relapse risk.** *Findings from these studies indicate that a modest exercise program is an effective and robust treatment for patients with major depression. And if these motivated patients continue with their exercise, they have a much better chance of not seeing their depression return."*

Physical exercise can do far more than simply improve general physical health. It can also improve brain health—fighting depression, and helping to prevent depression relapse. Active people often affirm that when they are active, their mood is more positive, and their energy is more abundant. So it makes sense to include physical exercise, in a program designed to strengthen both physical and emotional wellness.

There are three general categories of physical exercise, each delivering unique benefits:

1. **Cardio Exercise**—Large-muscle exercise that strengthens the heart, builds endurance, and improves heart health. Varieties of cardio exercise include running, jogging, walking, jumping, biking, dancing, and swimming.

2. **Strength Training**—Also known as resistance training, this kind of exercise uses free weights, machine weights, or your own body weight to provide resistance—building muscle by lifting extra weight. Different strength exercises strengthen different muscles, reducing overall strain on bones and joints in the process.

3. **Flexibility**—This kind of exercise tends to be slower, with more flowing motions designed to stretch out the muscles and joints—for example, through yoga, general stretching, or Tai Chi. Flexibility work is more gentle than the other two types of exercise, and can be an excellent way to start an exercise program. Cardio and strength training should also include flexibility training, to protect joints and build balanced fitness.

Some exercise programs include elements from all three of these categories of exercise. These include Pilates, kickboxing, and many forms of dance, sports, or skiing.

So there are many ways to exercise, with varying levels of demand, intensity, and proficiency. *Find some type of exercise you can enjoy, and do it regularly—ideally, every day, for at least a few minutes.*

Depression recovery is benefitted by all three types of exercise, but seems to respond most effectively to cardio training, particularly high intensity interval training (HIIT). *Generally, the more intense the exercise, the more the benefit*—and the greater the mood lift and exhilaration resulting from the movement. However, it is always wise to **start slowly right where you are—then move up gradually, rather than jumping ahead too quickly.**

Make sure you don't exert yourself too much too soon. You don't want to wear yourself out, or get too sore on day one—and then be too tired or sore to exercise the rest of the week. *Pace yourself wisely.*

Be honest about where you are currently with your fitness level, and then be a little more active today than you were yesterday. If your energy is low, start with some mild flexibility exercises, yoga, Tai Chi, or gentle walking. If your energy is high, maybe you'll want to go on a run, attend a kickboxing class, do an hour of Zumba, or take the steepest slope on a downhill ski run.

Energy levels will change from day to day. So start where you are, and gradually become more and more active. Your brain, as well as your body, will thank you!

12–4 Non-Exercise Activity: A Powerful New Wellness Tool

For some people struggling with severe depression, physical challenges, or time limitations, the mere thought of exercise may feel overwhelming—or even impossible. Such individuals may need to build their strength first through improved nutrition or rest, before engaging in demanding physical exercise.

But also, recent scientific discoveries have revealed new insights about the benefits of less intense but regular physical activity, carried out calmly within the normal routine of daily life. Indeed, over the span of human history, most people have remained physically fit not through weight-lifting at the gym or doing a structured aerobics class—but rather, by simply *remaining on their feet, being physically active throughout the day.*

In most areas of the world, throughout most of the millennia in which human life has existed, **high-level physical activity was built into the structure of daily life.** Hunter-gatherer cultures throughout time and all over the world by definition had to physically move throughout the day, if they wanted to sustain life. Daily they wandered over miles, seeking and gathering berries, fruits, nuts, roots, and other edible substances. And in order to obtain meat, they literally had to run for it—following and chasing quick-footed live animals.

They didn't do these things because they wanted to "exercise." They did these things because they wanted to stay alive! And that very movement, over miles of terrain, seeking out daily nourishment, helped keep their bodies, muscles, joints, bones, and teeth strong and well-formed.

These are among the same cultures that Dr. Weston Price studied in the early twentieth century. Besides their natural whole-food diet, these primitive cultures maintained their health through their natural whole-body movement. Besides the white, straight, perfect teeth and bones of these people, Dr. Price noted their overall health, immunity, leanness, and muscular definition. These people had never seen a treadmill or done a single crunch or bicep curl; yet they were lean and muscular. Depression was unheard of; cancer, heart disease, diabetes, obesity, and other "diseases of civilization" were non-existent in these people.

Similarly, early agricultural cultures were based on hours per day of natural, whole-body movement. From sunup to sundown, men in these cultures worked for hours caring for their fields, crops, and herds. Other tasks included clearing ground, chopping wood, and chasing away predators or invaders—all highly physical tasks. Meanwhile, their women were also on their feet throughout the day with their necessary, life-sustaining chores—scrubbing clothes and hanging them to dry; sweeping floors, grinding grain, kneading and baking bread, gathering wood and lugging it to the fire, bearing, training, and running after their numerous children.

People in these traditional cultures likewise never took a Zumba class, ran a marathon, or did a single bench-press. But the highly physical requirements of their daily lives kept them active and on their feet, throughout most hours of most of their days—and, as a result, kept them in stellar physical condition.

Vast cultural change began less than two hundred years ago when industrialization set in. For the first time in human history, massive numbers of people began to *sit* immobile for hours at a time each day, rather than stand and move. Their daily work began to occur mostly indoors, rather than outdoors, and under electric light, rather than in sunlight. Likewise, children became almost universally required to sit for long hours every day in school settings.

Most recently, technological advances have resulted in both adults and children sitting immobile for hours a day, indoors, under electrical light, their eyes fixed on electronic screens, eating mostly manufactured edible products, rather than whole, natural food— and often consuming chemical medications, trying to minimize the inevitable aches, pains, and illnesses resulting from this inactivity, lack of sunlight, and artificial nourishment.

In recent years, a number of authors have begun to reveal the devastating effects of this highly sedentary lifestyle. Consider some of the titles of these books:

- *Sitting Kills, Moving Heals* and *Designed to Move* by Joan Vernikos

- *Get Up! Why Your Chair Is Killing You and What You Can Do About It* by James Levine

- *Is Your Chair Killing You?* by Kent Burden

These and other authors reveal that sitting for hours at a time is even more deadly a behavior than smoking cigarettes. Our bodies were simply *not* designed to sit. They were designed to stand and move constantly over the hours of each day. *The further we get away from the natural requirements of our bodies, the more our bodies break down and become sick.* Consider these statistics, gathered from the authors cited above:

- Eleven or more hours a day of sitting results in 40% or higher risk of dying in the next three years than people who sit four hours or less.

- People who sit all day are 54% more likely to die of a heart attack.

- People who sit a lot have two to three times the rate of heart disease, diabetes, and obesity.

- Exercise, even for an hour a day, isn't enough to offset the effects of prolonged sitting.

- At least 34 modern diseases, including depression, are associated with excess sitting.

These authors likewise note that our modern lives and environments have become almost constant invitations to sit for prolonged periods. After waking in the morning, we sit to eat breakfast, then sit to drive to our workplace or school, and then sit for hours at work or school (often staring for hours into a small screen). At the end of the workday, we sit to drive home again, to eat again, and then we sit for hours of "relaxation and entertainment"—usually staring at yet another screen displaying video games, movies, TV, or social media.

Public places are now places for large numbers of people to sit for long periods of time. Schools, workplaces, restaurants, bars, movie theatres, stadiums, concert halls, and lecture halls are all designed for extended sitting. *Sitting for prolonged periods has become a virtually universal feature of modern life.*

But this increasingly common lifestyle pattern is literally destroying our bodies and our brains. It weakens our muscles, strains our spines, breaks down our joints, compromises our eyesight, and, yes—makes us vulnerable to depression, anxiety, and other emotional and mental illnesses.

It has become literally counter-cultural to move throughout the day, as we were designed to do. Just as it has become counter-cultural to eat whole, natural food, as we were designed to do. But these widespread cultural patterns are literally the physical engine driving disease into ever-expanding, worldwide epidemics.

However—*once we recognize these destructive patterns in our own lives, we can immediately begin to replace them.* We can intentionally build more movement and activity into the structure of each day. Here are six general suggestions to get you started:

1. **Make it a point to get up on your feet at least once every thirty minutes.** This will result in 32 times a day that you engage the large muscles in your back, glutes, and legs. Best is if you can walk, run, jump, or otherwise move around during this time. But even if you just stand and stretch, that can be helpful.

2. **Intentionally choose more activity whenever you have the option.** Park your car farther away from your destination, to build in a longer walk there and back. Take the stairs, not the elevator. Get out of your chair to change the channel, rather than reaching for the remote. Walk or bike to work, rather than drive. Use a standing desk at work or school. Exercise while you watch TV or videos

in the evening. *Look for every opportunity you can to build more physical activity into your day.*

3. **Limit media time as much as possible.** Staring into a screen for hours at a time, in a stationary position, isn't good for your eyes, body, or brain. So minimize that time. Find ways to fill your free time that *don't* involve an electronic screen. When you must use a screen for work or school, shift your physical position as much as possible. Focus on the human beings around you. Be outside as much as you can, drawing in healing sunlight and fresh air. Don't let media devices be the center of your life. Such a course is bad for your body, brain, and mood. Fill your life with *life*, not just screen images.

4. **Think strong, even with ordinary behaviors.** Use more muscles than you have to, to get more exercise and stretching benefit out of your normal routine. When you crouch to pick something up, crouch deeper. When you extend your arms to make your bed, extend them longer, enjoying the stretch. When you walk somewhere, walk faster. When going up steps, skip every other step. Think of normal movement as exercise, and use as many muscles as you can to carry it out, as often as possible. In this way, you can turn your normal life into a constant opportunity for healing movement— whether or not you get to the gym that day.

5. **Seek out NEAT opportunities, each hour of each day.** NEAT is an acronym used by the authors cited above. It stands for *"Non-Exercise Activity Thermogenesis."* Researchers found that non-exercise activity, performed

throughout the day, burned more calories and produced more physical and psychological benefits than an hour of focused exercise, and is crucial for human health.

6. **Walk as much as you can, in as many different ways as you can.** Being on our feet walking is what our human bodies were mostly designed to do. It distinguishes us from all other species of living things. Walking engages our largest muscles, connects us with gravity, and increases our balance.

Walking is one of the easiest but most important things you can do, to become more consistently active throughout each day. But it can feel a little boring, unless you build some variety into it. Here are eighteen different ways of walking that you can begin incorporating into your daily life, starting today:

NORMAL WALKS:	
The Functional Walk:	walk to work, get mail, shop, walk to your parked car, etc.
The Working Walk:	housework, gardening, childcare, etc. (This used to be built into everyday life.)
The Listening Walk:	walk while listening to an audiobook or music. Don't overuse this one.
The Thinking Walk:	go on a long stroll to gather ideas or brainstorm solutions to a current problem.

The Talking Walk:	walk with a friend or loved one, or have a phone conversation while walking.
The Nature Walk:	feast your eyes and ears on a mountain hike or beach, park or scenic byway stroll.
The Dog Walk:	walk your dog at least once daily. You both will be happier and healthier for it!
The Elevation Walk:	mountain hike, stairs, stadium seating, stepper machine, or treadmill.
The Emotional Cool-Down Walk:	let yourself cry, think, cool down after an argument, etc.

SPECIALTY WALKS:	
The Reading Walk:	read, review, or study a book while walking.
The Working-Mind Walk:	jot down ideas, review study notes, memorize lines, etc.
The Royal Walk:	walk with a book on your head, to improve grace and posture.
The Power Walk:	swing or punch your arms, breathing deeply to get more cardio benefit.

The Breathing-and-Stretching Walk:	breathe deeply, and do long stretches to work out tension.
The Barefoot Walk:	to experience total mindful contact with your physical environment.
The Run-Walk:	alternate walking and running outside, or even in circles around a small room.
The Dance-Walk:	turn on music and groove as you walk, do housework, childcare, etc.
The Crazy-Weather Walk:	walk in rain or snow—amazingly invigorating! Warm clothes help.

Walking and other NEAT activities performed throughout the day can play an essential role in improving your health, lifting your mood, and greatly contributing to your wellness and joy, throughout your lifetime.

12–5   Sleep and Sunlight: Balancing Natural Cycles for Daily Renewal

The last element for naturally healing the physical side of depression is—*engaging in adequate sleep, rest, and sunlight, in adequate amounts, at the right times to fit your built-in biology.* This is another element that was virtually guaranteed for earlier human civilizations, but that can be more problematic in our modern society.

In primitive cultures, when the sun came up, the workday began; and when the sun went down, the workday ended, because of inadequate light. Sleep came easily, after a long physically-demanding day of sustained movement and activity. Sleep began shortly after sundown, and ended around the time the sun came up.

These natural rhythms are built into the very cells and structures of our bodies. The more closely we adhere to these rhythms, the healthier we remain. The further away we stray from these rhythms, the sicker and more exhausted we become—emotionally as well as physically.

These natural rhythms reflect our *circadian rhythms*—the way our bodies relate to the daily movement of the sun across the sky. All organisms have circadian rhythms—even simple plants. If you have a dog, you might have noticed that he naturally puts himself to bed when the sun goes down, and wakes when the sun comes up—even if electric lights are on in the house all night. You would be wise to follow his example.

Night-time sleeping is literally the biologically designated time for the body to clean house and repair itself—building new cells, removing impurities, and refreshing the whole system. You would never think of facing a new day without having plugged in your phone or computer to recharge overnight. But many of us daily drag ourselves to work or school, without having gotten the recharge we needed, through deep, adequate sleep.

The optimal repair and cleansing times for our bodies are between 11 pm and 1 am. If we miss that window by staying up later, we miss our optimal recharge opportunity for the whole twenty-four-hour period—leaving us feeling groggy, irritable, exhausted, and depressed. Even if we sleep twelve hours at a later time, it doesn't have the same reparative impact as sleeping deeply at night, after a day full of activity and wholesome nutrition.

So, here's some suggestions to put this final element to work in your life:

1. **Try to be in bed falling asleep by at least 10:30 pm each night.** The more of that 11 pm to 1 am time you can spend being deeply asleep, the more refreshed you will feel when you awake.

2. **Wake up around sunrise each morning.** You will find that early morning hours can be the most refreshing, important hours of your day—*if* you get adequate sleep at night.

3. **Remove and turn off all media devices at least an hour before bedtime.** Otherwise, the blue light from your media screens can interfere with your body's natural signals to enter the sleep cycle.

4. **Charge your phone and other media devices far from your sleeping area.** This removes media temptations overnight that might otherwise interfere with sleep, and also removes light pollution that can come from your media devices. Use a cheap alarm clock if you need help waking at a certain time.

5. **Keep a notebook, pen, and small lamp by your bed.** This way, if you are awakened during the night by disturbing thoughts or dreams, you can quickly jot them down, get them out of your system, and then return to sleep. Deal with these issues by daylight—not at night, when you're tired and vulnerable.

6. **Find a way to take in sunlight during the day.** During winter months, this may include getting an artificial lamp that replicates sunlight, and basking in its glow first thing in the morning.

7. **Don't eat or drink later than around 7 pm.** Otherwise, your body will be busy digesting food overnight, rather than entering the needed rest and repair cycle.

8. **Live in harmony with your body's natural rhythms—** and enjoy the many brain and body benefits!

By providing the simple ingredients and processes your body was designed to function on, you can repair and strengthen your physical system far more powerfully than you ever thought possible. Mental acuity, physical energy, stable elevated mood, and resistance to physical and mental illness are just a few of the many benefits you will find, as you learn to consistently provide what your brain and body need, for optimal wellness.

TOOL THIRTEEN

ORDER:

Organize Your Time, Resources, and Living Space

➤ **13–1** Bringing Order to Your Life, Increasing Positive Control

➤ **13–2** How Disorder Interferes with Emotional Wellness

➤ **13–3** Time Management—Balancing Your Most Valuable Resource

➤ **13–4** Resource Management—Managing Your Finances and Belongings

➤ **13–5** Home Management—How to Dejunk and Organize Your Home

INBORN TRAITS

1. Action
2. Feeling
3. Positivity

4. Learning
5. Creativity

LEARNED SKILLS

6. Identity
7. Recording

8. Seeking
9. Sociality
10. Service

ADVANCED

11. Health
12. Activity
13. Order

14. Thinking
15. Connection
16. Healing

13–1 Bringing Order to Your Life, Increasing Positive Control

Tool #13 in *Your* Happiness Toolkit is—the ORDER tool. As human beings, we all long for a sense of control. Control helps us feel powerful and worthwhile. Some things in life we truly cannot control, like past trauma, or other people's decisions. Some things we can *entirely* control, like what we eat and how often we exercise.

Controlling what we can control, and learning to let go of what we cannot control, is a crucial skill for our mental and emotional well-being. One of the things we *can* control is—the use of our time and resources. Managing these things wisely can contribute greatly to our overall happiness and productivity.

Bringing order to our lives requires that we identify what we truly value, and then make choices—sometimes hard choices—about what to include, and what not to include in our lives. The very act of choosing one thing involves *not* choosing other things. There is simply not enough room in our time, our living spaces, or our budgets to accommodate *all* possible options. Order means choosing which options to hold on to, and which to let go of; what to give priority to, and what to assign lesser priority to—or to eliminate altogether.

The crucial thing, for health and happiness, is that we order our lives, our time, and our resources in ways that reflect our deepest priorities and values—rather than let outside forces "choose" these things for us.

13–2   How Disorder Interferes with Emotional Wellness

A disordered life is a life out of control—a life bounced around by a swirling variety of outside forces. Disorder rarely reflects our deepest values. It increases our stress, sucks up our energy, and sometimes even causes us embarrassment or shame. In the process, it can intensify depression, anxiety, and low self-esteem.

Disorder leaves us at the mercy of what life throws at us, or what other people decide for us. It leaves us in reactive mode, rather than in powerfully proactive mode. It leaves us feeling overwhelmed and inadequate. When we do not set our lives in order, outside forces will rush in to fill the void for us.

Rate your current pattern on the scale below:

LIST 1—Patterns Feeding: Depression, Disease, Deterioration, and Disability	LIST 2—Patterns Feeding: Happiness, Wellness, Resilience, and Productivity
13. DISORDER: Live in Chaos, Clutter, and Disorganization	**13. ORDER:** Organize Your Time, Resources, and Living Space

-3	-2	-1	0	1	2	3
Strong	*Moderate*	*Mild*	*Neutral*	*Mild*	*Moderate*	*Strong*

13–3   Time Management—Balancing Your Most Valuable Resource

Benjamin Franklin wisely observed, *"Dost thou love life? Then do not squander time, for that is the stuff life is made of."* Truly, our lives are composed of the minutes, hours, days, years, and decades we spend in this world. Of all our resources, *time* is the most important for us to order wisely and well.

Having the freedom to decide how to spend our time is a relatively new problem for humanity. During most of the world's history, nearly all available hours were spent simply doing what was necessary to sustain life—hunting and preparing food, warding off predators, etc. However, in our time, modern conveniences have given us expanded freedom and opportunity to choose from many different options in how we spend our **time.** We can "squander time," as Franklin warned against—wasting our newfound freedom on endless entertainment and pointless pastimes. We can be the slaves of time, punching a clock to spend our time and energy meeting other people's expectations. Or, we can use this modern gift of time intentionally, in fulfilling and productive ways, bringing our personal dreams, goals, and values joyfully to life.

Stephen R. Covey's classic book *The 7 Habits of Highly Effective People* encourages readers to think carefully about the use of time in their lives. To become "highly effective," Covey suggests that readers *"Begin with the End in Mind"* (Habit 2); *"Put First Things First"* (Habit 3); and *"Sharpen the Saw"* (Habit 7).

- **"Begin with the End in Mind"**—Covey notes that in order to fulfill your most important objectives, you have to first know what they are. *What are your personal dreams and priorities? What is on your "bucket list"*—the list of things you want to experience and accomplish by the time you finish your time here on earth? What is your guiding life mission? What things are the most important to you? Knowing these things about yourself is a crucial ingredient for effective time management. If you don't determine and make plans for what is important to you, your time and energy are likely to get used instead in the service of someone else's goals—or simply sucked up in mindless entertainment. So *start by clearly identifying what is important to you personally.*

- **"Put First Things First"**—Once you know what your personal priorities are, you can *make space for those things on your personal schedule.* Maybe there are relationships you want to preserve and strengthen, that you need to allocate specific time for. Maybe there are talents you want to develop or things you want to learn, that will only be yours if you set aside the time for needed development. Maybe exercise, spirituality, preparing healthy meals, or community service is important to you. These values will likewise require the specific allocation of time, if they are to be fulfilled in your life. Your schedule will be different than anyone else's, because your personal mix of priorities and preferences is different than anyone else's. Be sure to create intentional time for those things that are most important to you. *"Don't let the things that matter most be at the mercy of the things that matter least."* Put first things first.

- **"Sharpen the Saw"**—An effective life does not consist of 24–7 work and productivity. As a car requires regular fueling and tune-ups to remain serviceable, so we require regular replenishment and renewal, in all of the four basic areas of life: *mental, physical, spiritual, and social.* We need to schedule in regular time for such renewal—otherwise, the noisier demands of life could crowd it out, depleting our energy, exhausting our joy, and distracting us from our deepest priorities and truest enjoyments.

Another book containing useful insights about values-drive time management is *Lifebalance* by Linda and Richard Eyre. These busy parents of nine children share principles and strategies they found useful to balance the competing demands of work life and managing their large family. Key insights from their book include:

- **Three Balance Points: Work, Family, Self**—The Eyres recommend building a happy balanced life by setting goals on each of these areas of focus—including daily "balance points," identifying the top priority in each of these areas each day, and making sure those top priorities get done. So even if *everything* on your schedule doesn't get done, at least the most important things are done, balancing the needs of these three important areas of life. For example—**Work** goals could include: writing an important paper for your job; completing a needed repair or cleaning task in your house; or finishing a crucial homework assignment for school. **Family** goals could include—helping your child finish their science fair project; going on a date with your spouse; or calling your aging mother to chat. **Self** goals could include— getting that haircut you've needed; working out at the gym; or taking a long personal walk to develop some needed plans about your future. Retaining a daily balance between these three areas of life enriches each area, and creates a more solid and sustainable base for a balanced life.

- **Relationship Bands**—The Eyres likewise recommend that specific periods of time get allocated each day to maintain and strengthen important relationships. On a paper planner, this regular time could be indicated by a yellow band, marked with a yellow highlighter. On an electronic calendar, this time could be given an identifiable color on your regular schedule. For example—you may want to allocate fifteen minutes first thing in the morning to check in, cuddle, and review daily plans with your spouse. You might want to plan time after school or work, to give some focused attention to your kids. You might want to allocate fifteen minutes before bed for prayer, inspirational reading, or other activities to strengthen your spiritual connection. *Relationship bands are visual reminders of the people that are the most important to you— so you can make sure they get top priority in your plans for each day.*

- **Serendipity Line**—The Eyres note that frequently life doesn't go according to plan, especially when you're dealing with many people's conflicting needs—for example, in a big family or a large business. To absorb impact from unexpected changes to your schedule, they recommend that you draw a vertical line down the middle of your day planner page. List planned activities on the left of the line. On the right of the line, record unplanned "serendipity" events—things that come up unexpectedly that prevent the completion of your planned activity. Documenting these unplanned events helps you take joy in these unexpected but often enriching life experiences—rather than just be frustrated when your original plan has to be adjusted to accommodate these unplanned experiences.

In addition to these six suggestions, here are three additional insights to help you plan and balance your time:

- **Don't Be Afraid to Set Goals**—Some people are reluctant to set any goals, fearing that they will disappoint themselves or others if those goals are not met as planned. Set "best-guess" goals as a general road map for action—daily, weekly, monthly, yearly, and long-term. Certainly, you will need to make some adjustments along the way. But if you start with a general plan, you at least know where you're headed, and can get back on course more easily—or adjust course, if needed, as life unfolds.

- **Beware of Chronic "People-Pleasing"**—While it is important to be sensitive to others' needs, it is simply true that "You can please some of the people some of the time, but you can't please all the people all of the time." Kind-hearted people who seek to please everyone else often end up making more promises than they can ever keep, and find themselves overly fatigued and depleted, ultimately unable to serve anyone. *Decide who your priority people are, and focus on meeting their needs first.*

- **Balance Your "Me-O-Meter"**—Some people entirely forget their own needs, and consume themselves in the service of others, sometimes to the point of exhaustion. (This is a frequent pattern with depression, particularly with *"depletion depression."*) In contrast, some people focus so much on themselves that the needs of others get entirely forgotten—which breaks down those relationships, thus *also* feeding depression. To maintain a healthier, more sustainable balance, imagine a gauge with your own needs on one side, and the needs of others on the other side. You'll want to maintain balance between those two sets of needs, rather than let either side entirely outweigh the other.

13–4 Resource Management—Managing Your Finances and Belongings

In an age of abundance and prosperity, it can be tempting to buy more than we need, keep more than we can use, and go into debt to support a lifestyle that we can't maintain effectively over time. In contrast, over most of human history, people lived in small, simple dwelling places; ate simple, inexpensive, but nourishing food; acquired only what was truly needed; and kept only what remained actually useful to them over time.

A common factor feeding depression and anxiety in our time is financial stress. This often results from over-extending our purchasing power, often through the overuse of credit cards and loans. The resulting debt and financial commitments can hang over our heads day and night—interrupting sleep, adding stress, negatively impacting health, and creating conflict and strain in our close relationships.

A happier course is to order our finances according to these basic principles:

- **Live within Your Means.** Don't buy what you can't afford. Don't spend more than you make. Don't make expensive purchases now, hoping someday your income will expand to accommodate those inflated purchases. Be frugal, buying only what you truly need, as economically as you can.

- **Budget Your Expenses.** Keep track of your expenses, including: 1) *fixed-payment bills*; 2) *variable-payment bills*; 3) *regular expenses*, such as groceries or music lessons; 4) *discretionary expenses*; and 5) *savings and retirement*. Then use these records to plan a manageable budget for future expenses.

- **Purchase Mindfully.** When you decide to buy something, don't do it reactively. For example, don't go to the grocery store while you're hungry, as you're likely to toss into your cart a number of things you don't really need, and that aren't in your best interest. Be mindful in your purchases. Consider the pros and cons of each purchase, and whether or not you really need or will use the item you're considering.

- **Communicate, Cooperate, and Coordinate.** If you share finances with someone else, particularly a spouse or other family members, communicate openly and regularly about finances. Learn early what financial needs are coming up for everyone involved, so you can anticipate those upcoming expenses when you're deciding whether or not to buy something you want. Cooperate and coordinate regularly with those you share the budget with, to make decisions together about important purchases.

13–5 Home Organization—How to Dejunk and Organize Your Home

Few experiences in life are more depressing than walking into your living space, and finding it so crammed and cluttered with things you don't need that you can't find or get to things that you actually *do* need. There are those, for example, who are unable to eat a meal in their own kitchen, because the table and counter are piled so high with clutter that there is literally not enough space to lay out a meal. There are those who are embarrassed to let anyone into their living room for a brief visit, because the chairs, sofas, and coffee tables are so full of extra items that there is nowhere for the intended guest to even sit down. There are those whose closets and drawers are so full of old clothing that hasn't been worn in years that it's nearly impossible for them to find a clean, suitable outfit to wear today.

Strange but true—*clutter, disorder, and depression often go together.* The condition often develops into a negative, self-perpetuating cycle. As clutter accumulates, the person feels increasingly overwhelmed and depressed. The more depressed they feel, the more unable they become to get rid of the clutter—so it grows even more, leading to even more depression, and so on. This cycle also can strain family relationships, as conflicts erupt over whose job it is to remove clutter, and to restore order and tranquility to the living space.

In contrast—when life sometimes feels overwhelming and out of control, it can be incredibly comforting to come home to a neat and orderly environment, where there is a place for everything, and everything is in its place. Order soothes the soul, even in frightening or disruptive times. *Building a place of order and peace can be a strangely powerful antidote to emotional distress.* Here are some ideas to help you do that:

- **Feng Shui:** This ancient Chinese philosophy teaches that you should only keep that which is useful or beautiful to you currently—otherwise, energy will be drained from you by items that no longer serve you. A particularly helpful guide for removing non-essential, energy-depleting items is *The Life-Changing Magic of Tidying Up* by Marie Kondo. She suggests first selecting those items that give you consistent joy and positive use—and then eliminating the others. Creating open space in your daily living environment is amazingly effective for promoting inner relaxation and tranquility.

- **Three-Box Dejunking:** Another useful method for removing clutter and restoring order is as follows: Find three large boxes. Label these 1) *The Keeper Box*—these are items that are still useful or beautiful to you, that you still want to keep in your home. 2) *The Giveaway Box*—these are items that are still useful, but not to you personally— clothes you no longer wear, toys your kids no longer play with, cooking items you no longer use, etc. These items can be given to those in need, sold at a garage sale or secondhand store, or donated to charity. 3) *The Throwaway Box*—these are items that are in such poor condition that even the poor wouldn't want them! Toss these useless items right into the trash. This includes old papers, magazines, broken or ripped items, outdated products, etc.

- Choose an area of your living space to focus on first, and put each item from that area into one of the three boxes. Some items, of course, are too large to actually fit in the boxes, but still fit these three basic categories. *Large items that you don't need to keep, that take up a lot of space, should be the first to go, whether to "give away" or to "throw away."* It is truly amazing how much emotional relief can come from removal of unnecessary items, especially those large ones. People often comment that as the extra items are removed, a great boost of energy quickly follows.

"Keeper" items should be assigned a clear and consistent place in your home, so they can be found and used easily, with a minimum of effort. It is truly amazing how emotionally rejuvenating it can be to remove what is no longer useful or needed, and keep only what you currently use and enjoy.

"Giveaway" items are those you remove from your home, and pass on to someone else (whether through donation or sale). These bring benefit to both you and to the new owner. You benefit by having the item gone, leaving more needed space in your home. The new owner benefits by having an item they can now put to use to serve their current needs. Truly, *"One man's junk is another man's treasure."* What was "junk" to you—no longer usable by you, that had just been in your way—now can become someone else's "treasure."

"Throwaway" items might include old papers or items with sentimental value, but with no remaining practical

value to you or to anyone else. If so, take pictures of these items, so you retain the memory associated with them. But then, throw the actual items away, out of your current living space.

- **Form follows function.** As you identify the "keeper" items throughout your home, organize them by function. Enjoy doing crafts? Gather all your craft supplies in a single craft room, rather than scattered throughout your home. Have a lot of exercise equipment? Pull it together into an exercise area. Love to read? Gather your books and bookshelves into a clear library area, with comfortable seating and good light. Your home will become more expressive of your needs and personality, as you identify the "functions" served in your home, and then create "forms" or spaces to serve these specific functions.

- **Engage also in "emotional dejunking."** As you choose to let go of old physical things you no longer need, allow the experience to help also cleanse your heart, mind, and memory. Let things go emotionally, as you let the physical relics of old experience go. For example, emotional grief work can be greatly facilitated by removing and passing on the personal belongings of a departed loved one.

- **Enlist help if needed.** If you get stuck while organizing and dejunking, don't be afraid to ask for (or even hire) competent help. Letting go of old physical items can be a strangely emotional process—letting go of relics from past seasons of your life, or past reminders of someone who used to be in your life, but is no longer present due to death, divorce, miscarriage, or other challenging circumstances. You may need the objectivity and emotional support of someone else, to help you dejunk and reorder your home. Someone without emotional attachment to your old belongings can help you be much more objective about which items you should keep, and which should be removed or replaced.

- **Share the burden of care.** If you live with others, develop an equitable plan for keeping your living space clean, tidy, and uncluttered. Distribute tasks and chores among *all* members of your household.

Creating and maintaining ORDER in your schedule, your finances, and your living space can bring a new sense of control and well-being into your life. Use this tool daily to help lift your mood, improve your energy level, reduce your stress, and invite tranquility and joy into your everyday life.

———

THINKING:

Direct Your Thoughts in Positive, Productive Ways

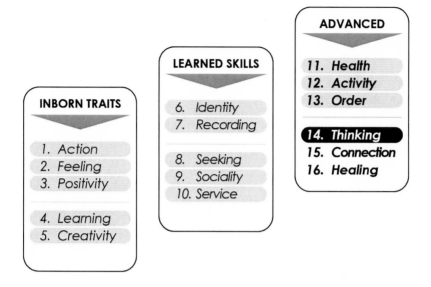

14-1 Thoughts, Beliefs, and Moods— How They Affect Each Other

T
ool #14 in *Your* Happiness Toolkit is—the THINKING tool. The previous three chapters have provided information on ways to improve your *external* environment, using Tools #11, #12, and #13—HEALTH, ACTIVITY, and ORDER. It is now time to dive *inward*, using this THINKING tool to start transforming your *inner* environment—the unseen but very real world of your personal thoughts and feelings.

In a remarkably direct way, your private thoughts and beliefs impact your feelings and moods. This can happen in an instant, turning what might have been a perfectly satisfying day into what suddenly feels like a devastating catastrophe. If you struggle at times with sudden mood swings like that—before you assume purely random biological causes and reach for a pill bottle—first, examine the pattern of your thoughts. *You may be pleasantly surprised to discover that your moods are far more manageable than you thought,* once you become more aware of the specific factors driving those moods from moment to moment.

Or, you may have struggled for years with a consistently dark and discouraging mood that feels like a heavy, ever-present storm cloud above your head, that's been there for as long as you can remember. You may have assumed that these persistently negative feelings result from a flawed personality; from a bad childhood; from a traumatic experience in your past; or even from bad DNA passed down through your family genetics. These seemingly hopeless explanations feed the cloud of despair, and may feel unchangeable and permanent. But as you will soon learn, even those long-term dark moods can dissipate—*if* you learn to use the right tools.

14–2   The A-B-C Response Pattern— Putting *You* in the Driver's Seat

We often assume that our emotions are the direct result of our surrounding circumstances, or of other people's behavior toward us—and early models of psychology reflected that belief. In the late nineteenth century, Sigmund Freud's *psychoanalytic approach* built on the theory that the troubled feelings and behavior of his patients resulted from negative experiences in their early childhood. Then, in the early twentieth century, the *stimulus-response models* of behaviorism dominated psychology. Behaviorism basically theorizes: *This* happened to you; therefore, you feel and do *that*. Behavioral scientists studied the stimulus-response pattern of animals, including dogs and lab rats, and then applied their findings to human psychology.

These early theories are often described as **A-B** models. **A** occurs; therefore, **B** results. Stimulus and response. Action and reaction. Cause and effect. Trigger and impact.

There is certainly some truth in the ideas taught in these early psychological models. There is no question that our early experiences *do* tend to affect our later responses; or that our emotions *can* be influenced by surrounding circumstances, or by other people's decisions or behaviors toward us. These cause-and-effect reactions are, in fact, our *default* response—our natural, instinctual reaction to external "trigger" events.

But such reactive patterns leave us fully at the mercy of outside influences. Our daily moods and well-being, according to these models, are controlled by external circumstances and require, for our well-being, that everyone treat us in kindly ways. But *these are conditions over which we personally have no direct control*. We can't control what others do or think; nor can we control everything that happens around us. As a result, the reactive feelings and behaviors that arise instinctually within us also feel uncontrollable, in an **A-B** pattern.

Later theories of psychology, developed in the later twentieth century, included a third vitally important and empowering element. Rather than just simple **A-B** models, these later approaches expanded to **A-B-C** models, in which "**A**" is the "*activating event*," "**C**" is the "*consequence*" (expressed in behavior and feeling); and "**B**" is "*belief*"—that uniquely human ability to form a chosen attitude about an external event. In other words, *our beliefs are powerful filters between our circumstances and our reactions.* What we believe about our circumstances affects our feelings and behavior far more than just the circumstance itself. As Epictetus, the ancient Greek philosopher, wrote: *"Men are disturbed not by things, but by the view they take of them."*

An **A-B-C** model can be a powerful instrument for maintaining emotional wellness. Because while we cannot control everything that happens to us, or the automatic emergence of our own feelings—in contrast, we *can* learn to powerfully direct our own filtering internal beliefs. We can learn to harness the power of our own thinking and attitudes about our circumstances in ways that can help us, rather than hurt us. We can learn to move beyond the natural default of being simply "triggered" when challenging events occur.

Rate your current pattern on the scale below:

LIST 1—Patterns Feeding:	LIST 2—Patterns Feeding:
Depression, Disease, Deterioration, and Disability	Happiness, Wellness, Resilience, and Productivity
14. TRIGGERING: Believe Negative Thoughts, Get "Triggered"	**14. THINKING:** Direct Your Thoughts in Positive, Productive Ways

-3	-2	-1	0	1	2	3
Strong	*Moderate*	*Mild*	*Neutral*	*Mild*	*Moderate*	*Strong*

14–3 Your Interpretive Style—How and Why to Choose an Optimistic Mindset

A fine example of an **A-B-C** model is the work of psychologist Martin Seligman. In his masterful book *Learned Optimism: How to Change Your Mind and Your Life*, Dr. Seligman observed that habitual emotions result from patterned thoughts that he called our "*interpretive style.*" In other words, again, we are affected not so much by what *happens* to us, as by how we *interpret* what happens to us. Our "interpretive style" tends to naturally be either more **optimistic** (seeing the positive side of things) or more **pessimistic** (seeing the negative side of things.) In general, he observed, optimistic people tend to be more happy, healthy, and influential with those around them than pessimists are.

Seligman observed that the "interpretive style" associated with pessimism could be described as *"The 3 Ps."* When challenging or difficult events occur, a **pessimist** tends to view these situations as:

1. **Permanent** (*"It's not just now—it's **forever**."*)

2. **Pervasive** (*"It's not just this—it's **everything**."*), and

3. **Personal** (*"It's about **me**—it's because of me."*)

These pessimistic thought patterns expand the impact of the original trigger situation, making it feel more catastrophic, or perhaps even hopeless. In contrast, an **optimist** in the same situation would see it as:

1. **Temporary** (*"It's hard now, but it will pass."*)

2. **Specific** (*"It's just this one thing, right now."*)

3. **From Multiple Causes** (*"A lot of different things brought this on."*)

Seligman's research revealed that individuals—even children—can be taught to consciously recognize a pessimistic thought (characterized by the 3 Ps) and intentionally replace it with an optimistic interpretation, which brightens their mood, and leaves them feeling more hopeful. His research found that when these simple strategies were taught to elementary school children, these children proved, over time, to be significantly more resilient against depression and emotional distress than their untrained peers. These findings are reported in Dr. Seligman's book, *The Optimistic Child: A Proven Program to Safeguard Children from Depression and Build Lifelong Resilience.*

For clear contrast, let's view these interpretive styles in table format:

PESSIMISM *("The 3 P's")*	OPTIMISM
1. **Permanent** *("It's not just now—it's **forever**.")*	1. **Temporary** *("It's hard now, but it will pass.")*
2. **Pervasive** *("It's not just this—it's **everything**.")*	2. **Specific** *("It's just this one thing, right now.")*
3. **Personal** *("It's about **me**—it's because of me.")*	3. **Multiple Causes** *("A lot of different things brought this on.")*

Consider, for example, the situation of a young woman who met an attractive young man one day during lunchtime in their university cafeteria. As they prepare to return to their various classes, he concludes their brief conversation by asking for her phone number, and telling her, *"I'll call you tonight!"* She provides the number—and then spends that entire evening, hour after hour, sitting expectantly by the phone, waiting for his promised call—which never comes.

If she has a **pessimistic mindset,** then with each hour that goes by, she will feel more and more despondent over these circumstances. Her pessimistic interpretation of this event will reflect the 3 Ps as follows:

1. **Permanent** *("He probably won't **ever** call. I'll never see or talk to him again.")*

2. **Pervasive** *("Probably **no** guys will ever call me. I probably won't ever date or marry **anyone.**")*

3. **Personal** *("I guess I'm just not very attractive. Guys just don't like me. I'm a guy repellant.")*

These negative thoughts, spinning hour after hour, may intensify over time, in even more generalized, destructive forms. After waiting the entire evening without a call, she might, for example, end up thinking:

1. **Permanent** *("My entire life is going to be lonely, meaningless, and miserable. Why stick around?")*

2. **Pervasive** *("I fail at everything. Nothing ever works out for me. Why am I even going to school?")*

3. **Personal** *("I am an unattractive, unwanted, worthless failure. I'll never amount to anything.")*

These thoughts will leave her feeling miserable, worthless, and without hope for the future. If unchecked, they can launch her into a serious state of depression, even suicidality. But—that is *not* an inevitable reaction.

In contrast, if she chooses an **optimistic mindset** in responding to this event, she might still feel disappointed that things didn't turn out as she hoped. But, her disappointment will be mitigated by thoughts such as:

1. **Temporary** (*"He must have had something come up tonight. Maybe he'll call me another day."*)

2. **Specific** (*"This just one guy, out of thousands at this school. Others may be more reliable."*)

3. **Multiple Causes** (*"He might have gotten sick, or found out about a pop quiz he needed to study for. Or, he may have lost my number; or he might just be scared of dating. It's his loss."*)

In this way, she moves beyond simply being "triggered" by this disappointing event. She intentionally takes control of her reaction, and deactivates the potential trigger. She retains emotional control, rather than relinquishing it to forces outside of herself. She responds to the "micro-aggression" of this non-ideal event by talking herself through it, and then moving herself optimistically onward—rather than getting stuck in it.

Remarkably, Seligman's research revealed that when *positive* events occur, the whole pattern is reversed. Optimistic people interpret positive events as Permanent, Pervasive, and Personal, while pessimistic people see those positive events as Temporary, Specific, and With Multiple Causes.

For example, when given a raise at work, the optimistic person might think, *"Wow, I'm moving forward now! All my professional goals are coming to pass. I'm finding success and will continue to climb the ladder, just as I always dreamed. This is the direct result of all my hard work and dedication!"* But the pessimistic person might think, *"I'll probably be fired within two months, when they find out how useless I am. This just another rug waiting to be pulled out from under me. They only chose me because they were desperate. I'll just disappoint them soon enough, like I always disappoint everybody. I'm guaranteed to fail at this, like everything else I do!"*

Seligman found in his research that some people are naturally more optimistic, naturally choosing positive interpretations in the face of adversity. Many people, however, are naturally more pessimistic. Those with a pessimistic mindset are far more vulnerable to the development of depression throughout their lives.

But even the most naturally pessimistic person, old or young, can learn to trade in "The 3 Ps" for a more optimistic interpretation of events—which can lift their spirits, improve their outlook, and empower them to move productively forward in their lives.

"Learned optimism" is a simple, easy-to-learn **A-B-C** model that can help you more effectively weather adversity, and increase your general resilience. Let's now explore a more complete and comprehensive A-B-C strategy for the identification and replacement of negative thoughts.

14–4 Cognitive Therapy—Identifying Thought Patterns That Feed Depression

Cognitive therapy was developed in the mid-twentieth century originally as a strategy to help heal depression, particularly in treatment-resistant patients for whom psychoanalysis, medication, or other existing therapy methods had been unsuccessful. Over time, cognitive therapy has proved to be one of the most powerful and successful treatment protocols available—not only for depression, but also for anxiety, OCD, anger, relationship problems, low self-esteem, and other challenges. *It is a well-respected, research-supported approach that deserves an honored place as one of the key "power tools" in* Your *Happiness Toolkit.*

Its one downside is that it has a fairly steep learning curve—which is why it appears later in this book. Hopefully by now, you have already applied some of the simpler strategies discussed in the earlier chapters, to help lift your mood and relieve your stress. If so, you are now ready to take on the challenge of learning to use this extraordinary "power tool" known as *cognitive therapy.*

This method began with psychiatrist Dr. Aaron T. Beck, who observed that traditional methods such as psychoanalysis were not providing satisfactory relief to his more depressed patients. In fact, in many cases, he found that psychoanalysis made these distressed individuals feel even worse, as it broadened their awareness of their current misery, and intensified their focus on past disappointments and deprivations.

Determined to help, Dr. Beck listened carefully to these deeply depressed patients and, over time, observed a consistent pattern among them. This he termed the "cognitive triad"—a trio of negative thought patterns that he found almost universally among his depressed patients.

This "cognitive triad" consisted of a pattern of negative thoughts about:

1. **Self**
2. **The World,** or People in the World
3. **The Future**

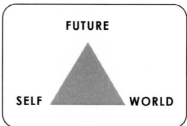

Almost universally, Dr. Beck observed that his depressed patients thought negatively about them**selves**, with thoughts such as: *"I'm worthless. I'm stupid. I'm ugly. I can't do anything right."* Negative thoughts about the **world** included phrases such as: *"The world is a dark and threatening place. There's no happiness or safety for me here. All that happens to me in this world is that I get hurt and rejected. People hate me. People hurt me. People are trying to make me miserable."* About the **future**, his depressed patients would think things such as: *"Things will never get better. I'll be depressed forever. Bad things will always happen to me. I'll always be just as miserable as I am today—so why try? Why stick around in a world that will always make me miserable?"*

Under the influence of these persistently negative thought patterns, Dr. Beck's patients struggled with serious depression, and sometimes even suicidality. Over time, he began to wonder if these negative thought patterns, rather than just being *symptoms* of a depressive disorder, might also be some of the *causes* and maintaining factors in the depression itself.

He turned to his colleagues at the University of Massachusetts to help explore, research, and test this hypothesis further. Over time, they developed together the "the new mood therapy" known as *cognitive therapy*—in other words, **changing negative feelings, through changing negative thoughts and beliefs.**

One of Beck's colleagues, Dr. David D. Burns, popularized this new treatment method in a series of reader-friendly books, including *Feeling Good: The New Mood Therapy* and *The Feeling Good Handbook.*

Significantly, it was found in research that whether people used these books as part of a treatment process guided by a professional therapist, or whether they simply engaged in independent *bibliotherapy,* reading and applying the books on their own, they experienced remarkable recovery from their depression and other emotional challenges. Furthermore, research revealed that cognitive therapy was at *least* as effective as medication in the short term, and far more effective in the long term, without any negative side effects.

Cognitive therapy is grounded in the idea that there are certain patterns of thought that are guaranteed to create and escalate emotional misery. In his books, Dr. Burns documented these identified patterns, calling them the *"Ten Forms of Twisted Thinking."* Cognitive therapy seeks to first *identify* these negative patterns, and then *replace* them with more positive thoughts, bringing profound emotional relief in the process. These

Ten Forms of Twisted Thinking that feed depression and other emotional challenges are the following:

1. **All-Or-Nothing Thinking**

   Also known as "black-or-white thinking," this pattern works like a light switch. Things are either good or bad, perfect or worthless, acceptable or unacceptable—with no gradations in between. So, if you or someone else displays *any* imperfections, however small, it is unacceptable and catastrophic, according to this distortion.

2. **Overgeneralization**

   This pattern takes specific unfortunate events, and expands them into broad and devastating patterns, by applying such words as "always" or "never" to describe the situation.

3. **Mental Filter**

   This pattern influences people to focus only on the negative aspects of an experience, and in the process, to remain unaware of the positive aspects—making the whole situation feel dark and disappointing.

4. **Discounting the Positive**

   This pattern diminishes or explains away the positive aspects of an experience, finding reasons to assume that they're not real or lasting, and that the negative aspects are what truly matter.

5. **Jumping to Conclusions**
   This pattern has two varieties: 1) **Mindreading**—
   assuming that others are responding to you negatively; or
   2) **Fortune-Telling**—anticipating future disasters (also
   known as *"what-if" thinking*). This pattern, in both of its
   varieties, is the major springboard for anxiety, as well as a
   known contributor to depression, and also to anger.

6. **Magnification**
   Comparing someone else's strongest qualities against your
   weakest ones (also known as *"the binocular trick"*).

7. **Emotional Reasoning**
   Assuming that how you feel is evidence that something is
   real, without actual evidence to support that belief.

8. **Should Statements**
   Believing that something "should" be different than it
   is. Directed against oneself, these thoughts foster guilt,
   depression, and low self-esteem; directed against others,
   they trigger anger and frustration.

9. **Labeling**
   Attaching broad negative labels to yourself or others
   (stupid, worthless, lazy, fat, hopeless, etc.)

10. **Personalization and Blame**
    Assuming that a negative situation is "all" your fault, or is
    "all" someone else's fault.

The first task with cognitive therapy is to *identify* these thought distortions as they occur, so they can be rooted out and replaced with more positive thoughts. These thoughts emerge in one of two ways:

1. **Automatic Thoughts**—These seem to bubble up unexpectedly on the brink of consciousness, often in response to current events. These negative thoughts tend to set off negative feelings and behaviors, often out of proportion with the seriousness of the original event.

2. **Schemas**—These are belief systems that may have been in place for years, or even across generations. They are often unconscious—but can be significantly powerful in generating deep emotions and repeated behaviors that persist over time.

Cognitive therapy generally focuses first on automatic thoughts, which bubble up regularly in response to each day's unique events and challenges. The *Daily Mood Log* introduced earlier in this book is a cognitive therapy exercise, used to gather awareness of factors associated with troubled emotions on a day-to-day basis. The early version of this exercise contained three steps. Now that you have been introduced to The Ten Forms of Twisted Thinking, you are ready to progress to the more complete Five-Step Daily Mood Log, as follows:

FIVE-STEP DAILY MOOD LOG EXERCISE:

When you feel upset, write down:

1. **The Situation** (*day, date, time, location, and trigger event/s, if applicable*)

2. **Your Feelings** (*name them, and rate their intensity level, on a scale from 1 to 10*)

3. **Your Thoughts** (*ask yourself, "What's my head saying to me right now?" and write it down verbatim*)

4. **Identify Distortions** in these thoughts (*referencing the Ten Forms of Twisted Thinking*)

5. **Replace Distortions** with more positive ways of thinking (*to help ease troubled emotions*)

Over time, as you record these various events in your Daily Mood Log, notice any repeated patterns that begin to emerge. For example: *what day of the week, time of day, locations, people, or circumstances tend to be present when you struggle the most emotionally?* Once you know what these repeated patterns are, then you can start targeting and replacing them—first, the day-to-day *automatic thoughts*; then the underlying, repetitive *schemas* that often lie at the ground-level foundation of these negative thought patterns.

When you are first starting, you won't have many replacement strategies available to plug into step 5. That's fine. Just recognizing that a type of thought is "on the list" of distortions is often very helpful, in and of itself, because you know you don't have to *trust* thoughts that are "on the list." You can start experimenting, asking yourself, *"How could I think about this situation in way that **doesn't** involve that distortion?"* In this way, you can begin talking *back* to your negative thoughts, rather than just accepting and believing them at face value.

Likewise, as you start identifying negative thought distortions, you can quietly recognize those patterns not just within yourself, but also within others. Recognizing someone *else's* distortion, especially if it is launched forcefully against you, can help insulate you against the harmful impact of that person's negative point of view. It puts things in perspective, and essentially becomes personalized, protective, internal armor for you—protecting you from the impact of your own negative thoughts, and also from the negative views of others.

The faster you can identify a distortion in yourself or others, the faster you can interrupt its negative force in your own mind and heart. In fact, the negative feelings arising from negative thoughts can, in essence, become an *early-warning system* for you—an emotional "lightning rod" of sorts. If you *feel discouraged* and blue, you may be doing *any* of the Ten Forms of Twisted Thinking, all of which feed depression. If you feel *anxious*, you're probably doing #5—Jumping to Conclusions (either Mindreading, Fortune Telling, or both.) If you feel *frustrated or angry*, you're most likely doing #8, #9, #10, or some combination thereof (Shoulds, Labeling, or Blame.) As soon as you know what you're dealing with, then you can go to work to replace it.

14–5   Positive Self Talk—Techniques to Silence the Negative Chatterbox Within

There are many methods you can use to replace negative thinking, once you identify it. All of these constitute what has been called *"Positive Self-Talk"*—changing the way you communicate with yourself on the inside.

We all naturally tend to have a *"Negative Chatterbox Within"*—a negative internal voice that speaks to us in disparaging, discouraging terms. If we listen to this voice, it will bring us down, leaving us depressed, anxious, or angry. Silencing this voice, and replacing it with positive helpful thoughts, is the core purpose of cognitive therapy, and has proven helpful in reversing and preventing depression and other emotional challenges.

Some thought-replacement strategies you will discover for yourself, with some personal experimentation, as you apply the Five-Step Daily Mood Log. Some you can learn from books by Dr. Burns and other cognitive therapy experts. And some time-tested replacement strategies will be summarized here in this section:

TIME-TESTED ANTIDOTES

for Each of the Ten Forms of Twisted Thinking

1. **The Dial** (*Antidote for* **All-or-Nothing Thinking**)

   Trade in the "light switch" of black-and-white thinking for continuum thinking. Imagine moving from a light switch, with simple on and off positions, to a dimmer switch with a variety of settings—all the way from complete darkness to full radiant light. Or, imagine a dial, with numbers all the way from −10 on the left side, to +10 on the right side, with 0 in the middle. Rather than judging yourself or others based on the "light switch" (on or off; good or bad; perfect or worthless, etc.), assess current behavior "on the dial." Perfect, flawless performance will be a +10 (those are very far and few between.) Terrible, destructive behavior is a −10 (again, significantly rare.) Behavior that is neither positive nor negative is a 0. Placed "on the dial," most behavior falls somewhere between −7 and +7. Progress can, thereby, be incremental, with one small improvement at a time increasing the score, over the process of time. *Note: This is a powerful antidote to destructive perfectionism, where anything lower than a 10 is regarded to be a "failure."*

2. **Stay Specific** (*Antidote for* **Overgeneralization**)

   Rather than describe situations as "always" or "never" in their scope, limit yourself to thinking about and resolving the specific situation at hand. This keeps the problem solvable and manageable.

3. **Positive Focus** (*Antidote for* **Mental Filter**)

   Rather than focusing only on the negative, intentionally expand your vision to include the positives. Keep a gratitude journal, express appreciation to others, and consciously look for good things to enjoy each day.

4. **Full Appreciation** (*Antidote for* **Discounting the Positive**)

   Find reasons to fully enjoy and appreciate success, accomplishment, and positive behavior, in yourself or in others. Graciously accept compliments, and give positive feedback to others without "*Yes, but . . .*" limitations.

5. **Decatastrophizing** (*Antidote for* **Jumping to Conclusions**)

   Rather than envisioning only the worst-case scenario as you imagine a future event, intentionally focus on the best-case scenario and the most-likely scenarios that could unfold from current circumstances.

6. **Cherish Diversity** (*Antidote for* **Magnification**)

   Rather than comparing yourself negatively against others, enjoy and appreciate your own strengths, while at the same time enjoying and appreciating the strengths of others. Appreciate the powerful synergy created by combining the different gifts and perspectives of different individuals.

7. **Examine the Evidence** (*Antidote for* **Emotional Reasoning**)

   Rather than just assume that your feelings reflect reality, use your head as well as your heart. Look at the actual evidence in a given situation, before drawing conclusions based only on your untested feelings.

8. **Three-Part Replacement** (*Antidote for* **Should Statements**)

Rather than thinking *"So and so"* should do *"such and such,"* use this three-part formula:

1. ***"It would be nice if . . ."*** (*"So and so" would do "such and such."*)

2. ***"But the reality is . . ."*** (*Fill in with as many relevant facts as possible.*)

3. ***"Therefore, given these realities, my best course of action in this situation could be . . ."***

(*Fill in with as many positive action plans as possible, to meet the needs of the situation.*)

What makes this strategy powerful is that it stops the ineffective rumination about what "should" happen—and nudges you instead toward positive practical action that you can begin to launch today.

9. **Behavioral Description** (*Antidote for* **Labeling**)

Rather than using broad negative labels against yourself or others (resulting in character assassination, and a sense of hopelessness)—instead, describe the specific behaviors observed in the situation at hand. For example, rather than labeling yourself an "idiot," think, *"In the future, I would be wise to study longer than I did, before taking such a challenging test."* Rather than labeling a classmate a "jerk," think, *"He seemed to be highly stressed when he gave me that feedback yesterday."* Behavioral description allows you to discuss problems without generalizing them, so they remain specific, manageable, and solvable.

10. **Personalization and Blame** (*Antidote for* **Blame Pie**)

Any problem involving two or more people has at least two active contributors. Rather than assume that the difficulty is *"all"* your fault, or *"all"* someone else's fault, identify *all* the various pieces of the "Blame Pie"—all of the diverse factors contributing to the problem. Then, take responsible action to correct *your* piece of the "pie"—but leave it to others to correct their "pieces."

For ease of reference, here is a short table summarizing the "negative thought patterns" and "antidotes" discussed in this section:

NEGATIVE PATTERNS 1–5	ANTIDOTES 1–5
All-Or-Nothing Thinking	*The Dial*
Overgeneralization	*Stay Specific*
Mental Filter	*Positive Focus*
Discounting the Positive	*Full Appreciation*
Jumping to Conclusions	*Decatastrophizing*

NEGATIVE PATTERNS 6–10	ANTIDOTES 6–10
Magnification	*Cherish Diversity*
Emotional Reasoning	*Examine the Evidence*
Should Statements	*Three-Part Replacement*
Labeling	*Behavioral Description*
Personalization & Blame	*Blame Pie*

Identifying and replacing negative thought patterns, whether short-term "automatic thoughts" or longer-term "schemas," is a powerful tool in overcoming depression and other emotional challenges. It takes some work and effort early on to learn these change strategies. But the benefits over time are life-changing and enduring.

Even more powerful than cognitive therapy alone is the treatment strategy known as **CBT,** which is short for **"cognitive-behavioral therapy."** CBT consists of thought-replacement strategies, such as those discussed in this chapter, together with behavior change strategies, including those we've discussed in prior chapters. *This powerful combination produces benefits far greater than either strategy can produce alone.*

Now, let's proceed to the next of the "power tools" you can add to *Your* **Happiness Toolkit.**

TOOL FIFTEEN

CONNECTION:

Communicate and Relate Well with Others

➤ **15–1** Relationship Building—An
Important But Demanding Venture

➤ **15–2** Turn Toward Others, Not
Against or Away from Them

➤ **15–3** Know and Respect Others' Needs
and Perspectives, As Well As Your Own

➤ **15–4** Building Effective Communication,
to Foster Mutual Understanding

➤ **15–5** Patterns of Connection or
Disconnection: A Review and Summary

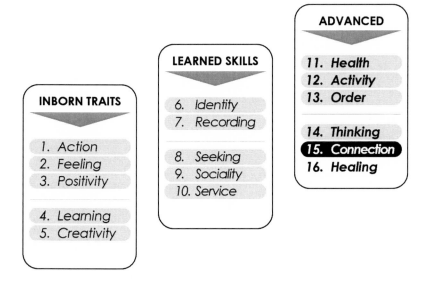

15–1 Relationship Building—An Important But Demanding Venture

Tool #15 in *Your* Happiness Toolkit is—the CONNECTION tool. The ability to communicate and relate well with others is perhaps one of the most important, complex, and demanding of all the tools you can possess. Many hundreds of books have been written on this topic, and many more will surely yet be written. The basic question is— are the habits, thoughts, and behaviors you are currently engaged in *strengthening* positive connections in your life? Or, are they *weakening* or preventing positive relationships with others?

While this chapter cannot within itself provide a comprehensive guide to relationship building, it can provide some helpful guidelines, and summaries of various approaches that have proven to be useful in this area.

It is human nature to long for meaningful human connection—to dream of the perfect fulfilling relationship. But dreams and realities can be two very different things. *A good, solid relationship cannot simply be "found." Instead, to be effective, it must be conscientiously and intentionally **built**, over the process of time.*

What are the most important building blocks of a happy, successful, lasting relationship? What are some of the dangers and pitfalls to watch out for? How can depression disrupt effective relationships? And what can be done to repair a relationship that has already become strained or troubled? These are some of the questions we will seek to address, as information is presented throughout this chapter.

15–2   Turn Toward Others, Not Against or Away from Them

John Gottman is one of the most prolific and influential of researchers in the area of human relationships. For decades, he has led the field in the scientific study of marriage and other important connections. He shared some of his most important findings in his book *The Relationship Cure.* Here, Gottman gathered insights from his many years as a marriage researcher, and applied his findings to *all* kinds of relationships. He reported that out of all he has learned over the years about effective and ineffective relationships, ultimately it all seemed to boil down to two simple principles:

1. **Bidding:** People in *effective* relationships frequently "bid for connection" with one another—intentionally initiating mutual contact and interaction. In contrast, people in *ineffective* relationships (or without significant

relationships) tend *not* to bid for connection very frequently, if at all.

2. **Reponses to Bidding:** In *effective* relationships, bidding for connection is responded to with a ***"turn toward"*** response that is pleasant, friendly, and accepting—completing the connection that began with the initial "bid." Gottman noted that this "bid and response" cycle that he observed in effective relationships could be likened to watching a pair of master tennis players—who, after the initial ball is served, both connect with that same ball over and over, back and forth across the net, with mutual skill and cooperation.

In contrast, in *ineffective* relationships, those infrequent bids are responded to by one of two patterns. The responder might ***"turn against"*** the bidder, in a hostile, critical, or attacking way, which greatly discourages any further attempts at connection. Or, the responder might simply ***"turn away"*** from the bidder, in silence, avoiding any connection at all. Remarkably, Gottman found that these "turn away" responses (often motivated by a kindly-intended desire to avoid conflict) destroyed relationships even faster and more deeply than the more volatile "turn against" response pattern.

This finding is highly significant in a discussion of depression recovery—because very frequently, under the influence of depression, people are more likely to *"turn against"* or *"turn away"* from others, and to not initiate relationship *"bidding."* These common depressive behaviors can directly damage or prevent relationships—and can, thereby, lead to even more loss and conflict for depression sufferers. This can result in yet another downward spiral in the depressive pattern.

Building positive relationships, therefore, requires "bidding" for connection, and "turning toward" others when they seek connection with us. Any effective relationship requires these two core elements— whether in a marriage, dating, friendship, family, workplace, or community context. In his book, Gottman powerfully challenges readers to carefully consider the day-by-day, moment-by-moment nature of their interactions. He affirms that *each day contains precious opportunities to either connect—or disconnect—with others.*

Gottman is not the only researcher who has identified these kinds of comparative dynamics in relationships. In their book *Fighting for Your Marriage,* researchers Howard Markman, Scott Stanley, and Susan Blumberg report that relationship trouble begins when differences of opinion are responded to by four destructive communication patterns. They found that these patterns constitute **"danger signs"** for relationships:

1. **Escalation**—*small issues intensifying into bigger and bigger conflicts*

2. **Invalidation**—*putting down the other person's point of view*

3. **Mind-Reading**—*thinking you know what the other person is thinking*

4. **Avoidance and Withdrawal**—*refusing to engage with the other person*

These patterns are often initiated when people believe that they are "right," and feel that it's their duty to prove the other person "wrong." The fight over "who's right" is the most common factor generating conflict in relationships—regardless of the topic being discussed. The problem with fighting over "who's right" is that it belittles the point of view of the other person—invalidating their perspective and needs. This is directly in conflict with the elements required to build a fulfilling, safe, caring, trusting, happy, enduring relationship.

Not all communication is positive. Some kinds of communication, in fact, can do significant and lasting harm—to individuals, and to relationships. Positive communication helps people understand each other's different perspectives and experiences. Negative communication disrupts connection, destroys trust, and cuts off understanding between people. Battling for the dominance of your own way, while seeking to break down the opinions of the other side, leads to escalated conflict, not connection; to greater despair and loneliness, not satisfaction and joy.

Rate your current pattern on the scale below:

LIST 1—Patterns Feeding:	LIST 2—Patterns Feeding:
Depression, Disease, Deterioration, and Disability	Happiness, Wellness, Resilience, and Productivity
15. CONFLICT: Attack or Invalidate Others, in Word and Action	**15. CONNECTION:** Communicate and Relate Well with Others

-3	-2	-1	0	1	2	3
Strong	Moderate	Mild	Neutral	Mild	Moderate	Strong

15–3   Know and Respect Others' Needs and Perspectives, As Well As Your Own

To truly connect with someone else does not mean to transform them into an identical clone of yourself, or to persuade them to give up their own perspectives and needs, in order to serve yours. To really connect with someone, you have to know and value them as they are—recognizing that what they see, need, feel, and experience is just as real and important as what you see, need, feel, and experience.

The personality test described in the IDENTITY chapter can be a great asset in helping you to see into the heart of a person who's different from you—to glimpse a point of view that you do not necessarily share. *A happy, successful connected relationship is the result of two different people coming together to enrich each other's lives, and to expand each other's life experience*—whether they are naturally very similar to each other, profoundly different, or somewhere in between.

Harmony, by definition, is a musical term describing the rich interplay of distinct musical elements. In music, some notes may be high, and some notes are low. Some are short, and some are long. They resonate at different frequencies, producing different pitches. But the harmonic interplay between these distinct musical elements creates a richness that would never result from just repeating one single note over and over again.

Similarly, a symphony orchestra is composed of many different instruments, each playing different notes and producing different qualities of sound. The violin section, high and sweet, sounds very different from the bold trumpet, the mighty timpani, the cheerful flute, or the delicate harp.

But these very different instruments can come together to produce a symphonic masterpiece—rich with variety, balance, and interest that a solo instrument, in and of itself, could never even begin to replicate.

Similarly, as human beings, we see, feel, and experience different things. We make different contributions, and offer different views and perspectives. Like the symphony orchestra, we are more full and complete when we allow each other the freedom to be who we really are, and to offer what we uniquely have to offer.

The second half of Stephen R. Covey's *The 7 Habits of Highly Effective People* focuses on building harmonious relationships between people with different characteristics. These powerful insights can be summarized as follows:

- **Habit 4—"Think Win-Win"**

  Building and maintaining effective connections requires that when we encounter conflicts or problems, we learn how to resolve them with "win-win" solutions. These are solutions that are satisfying to everyone involved in a situation. These "win-win" solutions contrast with "win-lose" solutions (*"I get what I want, and you don't"*); "lose-win" solutions (*"I give up what I want, so you can get what you want"*); or "lose-lose" solutions (*"I'm not going to win, but I'll make sure you don't either."*) Of the four types of solutions, win-win solutions are the only ones that are sustainable in long-term relationships.

- **Habit 5—"Seek First to Understand, Then to Be Understood"**

Being understood is something we all naturally desire and seek for in our relationships. We often regard effective communication as an interaction in which we share our view, others "listen" to us, they are convinced by our perspective, and they fall in line with our desires—which, of course, we regard as "the right way." If this does not occur, we tend to feel that communication is unsuccessful.

Habit 5 teaches a different and more effective form of communication, in which we first engage in respectful, empathic listening, to make sure we hear the perspective of others involved in the situation, and that they hear us. Then, when all sides are heard and understood, we have the ingredients necessary to craft a win-win solution that effectively addresses *all* of those conflicting needs, and balances those different perspectives.

- **Habit 6—"Synergy"**

A truly effective solution, like a truly effective relationship, is more than the sum of its parts. So in a synergistic equation, 1+1 doesn't equal 2; but rather, it equals 3 or more. Because, besides the unique elements that each individual person brings to the table, the interaction and balance occurring *between* people creates new, additional benefits. Each person enriches the other's capacity and understanding; each unique insight adds valuable dimension to the eventual solution. Like a symphony orchestra, the various parts are balanced, and no one part is allowed to dominate or silence the others.

These "habits of highly effective people" are *not* natural to us, as are the tools in Levels 1 or 2. Indeed, they go fully against the natural grain. They require work, patience, humility, and sacrifice. *They are new habits that we have to learn, cultivate, and practice, over time, in order to experience the benefits.*

What *does* come naturally to all of us, as we have already discussed, is what every infant is born with—an awareness of our own desires and the capacity to request—or demand—what we want. Newborns do this from the day they enter the world. They scream, cry, and insist that their needs be met—even if the person they are crying to is already exhausted, frustrated, frazzled, or overwhelmed. Infants have not yet developed the capacity to care for others, or to experience empathy for others' needs. Nor have they developed impulse control, or the capacity to wait their turn. They are built for instant gratification—wanting what they want, the way they want it, *now*. They are egocentric little creatures who are aware only of their own individual needs, impulses, and desires. This is the age-appropriate condition for a cute little newborn. It is not so attractive in a more mature individual.

As we grow up, moving beyond infancy, it is vitally important that we learn to see more than we alone see; to recognize that other people are just as real and valuable as we are; and that their needs are just as important as ours. To build healthy, mature, sustainable relationships, we need to develop compassion, respect, and empathy for others.

Likewise, however, as we grow to maturity, it is important that we not lose sight of our own needs, desires, and perspectives.

Constantly seeking to "please" others by giving up what is important to us is not healthy, sustainable maturity—it is, in fact, *codependence.* To build healthy, mature, sustainable relationships also requires that we retain (or develop) self-respect, self-awareness, and the courage to clearly speak up.

David D. Burns, in the latter half of his *Feeling Good Handbook*, provides valuable guidance on building effective relationships and mature, balanced communication. As he insightfully observed:

> **Good communication has two properties:**
>
> 1. *You express your feelings openly and directly.*
>
> 2. **And,** *you encourage the other person to express his or her feelings.*
>
> *You say how you are thinking and feeling, and you try to listen and understand what the other person is thinking and feeling.*
>
> *According to this definition, the ideas and feelings of* **both** *people are important.*

How, then, do we engage in communication that creates this kind of mutual respect, balance, and synergy? The next section gives some suggestions.

15–4   Building Effective Communication, to Foster Mutual Understanding

1—Improve the Communication between Your Own Two Ears

As discussed in the previous chapter, our thoughts and interpretations of events directly impact our feelings, far more than the original event itself. If our internal self-talk is inundated with negative distortions, then inevitably our communication with others will reflect that negativity—driving others away, and making effective interpersonal communication next to impossible.

So, particularly when you are feeling depressed, anxious, or angry, it is important that you first deal responsibly with your *own* negative thoughts, so that these do not interfere with your interpersonal communication. One way of doing this is to write your thoughts and feelings on paper, so you can see them objectively, and work through them as much as you can by yourself, before sharing your concerns with others.

Communication is *always* a description of reality *as we each see it*. So communication will be more effective if "how we see it" is already cleansed of negativity that otherwise can lead to defensiveness and conflict.

2—Avoid Bad Communication (Communication That Makes Things Worse)

There are certain styles of communication that will inevitably worsen a challenging relationship situation. David D. Burns has identified many "bad" communication styles, which include:

1. **"Truth"**—fighting about who's right or wrong, seeking to "win" over the other.

2. **Blame**—arguing about whose "fault" something is and denying any personal responsibility.

3. **Put-Down**—saying mean or belittling things about one another.

4. **Demandingness**—insisting on your own way without regard for the other person's needs.

5. **Defensiveness and Counter-Attack**—which always makes a bad situation worse.

Likewise, John Gottman identified four negative communication patterns that he found to be so toxic that they consistently predicted the strong likelihood of divorce. He called these the *"Four Horsemen of the Apocalypse,"* since they are so powerfully destructive. **These four negative patterns to avoid at all costs are:**

1. **Criticism**—finding fault with the other person, describing complaints in broad, defaming terms that attack the other person's basic character and integrity (*character assassination*)

2. **Contempt**—verbally and nonverbally expressing scorn for the other person, their needs, and their point of view. This directly obstructs communication and mutual understanding

3. **Defensiveness**—responding to criticism and contempt by defending yourself, meeting accusation with accusation, and hurtful comment with hurtful comment

4. **Stonewalling**—becoming silent, unresponsive, and inaccessible—often in response to criticism, contempt, and defensiveness; also known as the *"silent treatment"*

Where these negative communication patterns occur, relationships are guaranteed to struggle. It is important to recognize and extinguish these destructive patterns, along with the 4 "danger signs" mentioned previously:

1. **Escalation**—small issues intensifying into bigger and bigger conflicts

2. **Invalidation**—putting down the other person's point of view

3. **Mindreading**—thinking you know what the other person is thinking

4. **Avoidance and Withdrawal**—refusing to engage with the other person

These negative patterns are literally the "weeds" that can destroy the "garden" of your relationship. Catch them early, call them by their names, root them out, and replace them with better techniques. *Stop engaging in communication styles known to divide and destroy.* Instead, learn and engage in communication styles designed to build trust, safety, connection, mutual respect, and understanding.

3—Express Yourself Clearly Using "I Messages" Rather Than "You Messages"

Your opinions and experiences are valuable elements of your relationship, and need to be expressed. But *how* you express those perspectives can greatly impact the success (or failure) of your attempt to communicate.

Using accusatory language is virtually guaranteed to result in defensiveness and resistance from the other person. Because when people feel attacked, they will be more likely to defend themselves and counter-attack. This is most often the cause of what is frequently reported in therapy: *"I was just telling him how I felt. But then, he turned the whole thing around and blamed it all on me!"* Or *"I was just making some suggestions on how she could improve things. But then she yelled at me, calling me a controlling jerk, stormed out of the room, locked the door, and wouldn't talk to me for hours!"*

Sensitive information is best shared as an **"I Message,"** sharing information about how *you* feel, and why.

As previously mentioned, a helpful formula for an "I Message" might be:

I FEEL:	
ABOUT:	
BECAUSE:	

For example, *"I'm feeling concerned about all the expenses that have shown up on our credit card the last few weeks, because our taxes will be coming due next month, and I'm getting worried that we won't have enough money left to pay them."* This shares the concern in a clear and specific way. But it has a very different impact than a **"You Message"** version would be, such as: *"I'm so sick and tired of you frittering away every available dollar in our account. You're always so irresponsible and selfish! You only think about you, ALL the time!"*

Let's explore another example. Imagine that a man gets home from work late one evening, exhausted after a long and demanding workday. His wife meets him at the door with a scowl, saying:

> *Why in the world are you home so late? Don't you remember that Sally's dance concert starts at 7:30 sharp? And here we are, as usual, with me doing EVERYTHING to get dinner on the table, and everything prepared for a nice evening— because YOU can't ever stand up to that stupid boss of yours, and tear yourself away for once at a decent hour! I'm so sick of you always putting your job first, and not caring one bit about your family!*

That kind of accusatory, character-assassinating, overgeneralized "You Message" cannot help but complicate the existing problem, and make an already tense evening even more tense. Imagine how different the impact would be with a short but clear "I Message," such as:

> *Hi honey. I'm glad you're home safe. I'm feeling a little worried, though, because we need to be at Sally's dance concert in forty minutes, and there's still a lot to pull together before then.*

This "I Message" version stays specific, clearly expressing the need at hand, and inviting cooperation to solve a specific but manageable problem. "I Messages" provide a safe, effective, respectful way to share your concerns and feelings, without putting the other person on the defensive.

4—Listen with Empathy and Understanding, Using Reflective Listening

This fourth technique is one of the most difficult, though simple, tools in your toolbox. It's not at all difficult to understand—but it can be challenging to carry out, especially when things feel heated, and *most* especially if you're feeling unfairly attacked or blamed. It is in those situations, however, that this tool is most needed, and most effective to create and maintain a sense of connection—even in the midst of conflict or stress.

The basic technique for using **Reflective Listening** (otherwise known as "empathic listening") is to hear the other person without interrupting—listening to them carefully enough that you can calmly repeat back to them the basic message they just shared with you. Let's revisit the earlier example, to observe the difference between a Reflective Listening response, and a Defensive Counter-Attack response.

> *Speaker (**using an "I Message"**): I'm feeling concerned about all the expenses that have shown up on our credit card the last few weeks, because our taxes will be coming due next month, and I'm getting worried that we won't have enough money left to pay them.*

> *Listener (using Reflective Listening): So, you're getting worried that we won't have enough to pay our taxes, because of the recent expenses you're seeing on our credit card?*

Simple enough, right? But now, let's replay that same scenario, observing the difference when the response is a Defensive Counter-Attack:

> *Speaker (using an "I Message"): I'm feeling concerned about all the expenses that have shown up on our credit card the last few weeks, because our taxes will be coming due next month, and I'm getting worried that we won't have enough money left to pay them.*

> *Listener (using Defensive Counter-Attack): Oh, so now you're blaming ME for all those charges, huh? Who brings the money in around here, while you sit around watching TV all day? If you're so worried about money, then why don't you stop wasting money every single month, going to that fancy salon to get your hair cut!*

The **Reflective Listening** response keeps things calm, so the original question can be discussed, and the actual issue resolved. In contrast, the **Defensive Counter-Attack** response escalates the situation, and fails to resolve the original identified problem.

In that first example, the speaker expressed their concern calmly as an "I Message," rather than a "You Message." Now, let's look at the how the two response patterns operate in the more challenging environment of a conversation that begins with an accusatory "You Message":

Speaker (using a "You Message"): I'm so sick and tired of you frittering away every available dollar in our account. You're always so irresponsible and selfish! You only think about yourself, ALL the time!

Listener (using Defensive Counter-Attack): Well, I'm even more sick of you complaining constantly, when I'm the only one bringing in money in the first place! You call ME selfish? REALLY?? When I go to work for HOURS every single day to support this family, while you sit here at home doing absolutely NOTHING?

That conversation, brimming with mutual accusation, can spin quickly out a control. It can easily escalate into an all-out fight that can last for hours (or days), as each person tries to justify their own position, and get the other person to "admit" that they are "wrong."

Now, consider how a Reflective Listening response pattern can help to de-escalate this situation—even if it started with an accusatory "You Message":

Speaker (using a "You Message"): I'm so sick and tired of you frittering away every available dollar in our account. You're always so irresponsible and selfish! You only think about yourself, ALL the time!

Listener (using Reflective Listening): Sounds like you're pretty worried about money. You're angry with me over these various expenses you're seeing on our charge account.

That calmer response won't instantly solve the problem—but at least it doesn't add additional venom to it, like the Defensive Counter-Attack did. A consistent Reflective Listening response, used over time, tends to de-escalate conflict, and promote an environment where problems can be discussed, understood from both sides, and then resolved.

Moreover, *a Reflective Listening response provides you a protective shield*, so you don't get sucked into the negative mindset of an overwhelmed speaker. Used correctly, Reflective Listening is like a glass shield that allows you to see and respond compassionately to the person in front of you, even in the face of conflict.

Though simple in concept, Reflective Listening can be challenging, and requires lots of practice to master. Stephen R. Covey has observed that most often in conversation, we tend to *"listen to respond,"* rather than *"listen to understand."* We listen to the other person long enough to develop our clever "come-back" or self-defense—but not long enough to really understand and feel the *other* person's concern. Reflective Listening doesn't require that we agree with the other person's perspective. But it does require that we be willing to hear them out, and recognize that their feelings are real to them, though we may see the situation differently.

The best communication, of course, occurs when *both* people use "I Messages" consistently to express their views, and Reflective Listening consistently to respond to each other's observations. But, we are all human. We have our good days, and our bad days. You will never have full control of how others communicate with you. But over time, you can learn to consistently be a positive force in your conversations—de-escalating conflict through Reflective Listening; and sharing your own views respectfully through using I Messages.

In the heat of battle, in the face of conflict, in the sting of accusation, it can be very difficult to feel a sense of positive connection with another person. *Learning to effectively manage interpersonal conflict is one of the most challenging but important life skills any of us can obtain.* It requires self-awareness, maturity, patience, and courage. It doesn't come naturally to any of us. But with persistence, determination, and practice, it is a skill we can develop over time, to strengthen, preserve, and protect our most cherished relationships.

5—Give Others the Benefit of the Doubt

In our relationships, conflicts often emerge because of differing expectations or worldviews. In the face of resulting conflicts, people will sometimes assume, *"You're just TRYING to hurt me!"* or *"You're always pushing my buttons!"* This accusatory view tends to escalate any problem we may be facing. But the truth is—almost always, people are doing the best they know how, within their own frame of reference. Giving others the benefit of the doubt, especially when conflicts arise, is always more productive than assuming negative intent.

6—Trade in Unrealistic Expectations for Realistic Expectations

It has been observed: *"The level of misery in any situation is equivalent to the distance between expectations and reality."* Most of us begin our relationships with unrealistic expectations—that our needs will always be met, that we'll always want the same things, that our relationships will always make us happy. The truth is: relationships require hard work, self-sacrifice, and lots of patience. But they can also bring us profound personal growth, meaning, and joy, if we are willing to truly understand and connect with others.

15–5 Patterns of Connection or Disconnection: A Review and Summary

In concluding this chapter, let's compare and contrast patterns that contribute to connection, versus those that feed disconnection:

DISCONNECTION PATTERNS:	CONNECTION PATTERNS:
Expecting to **"find"** the perfect relationship	Working to **build** a strong relationship
Initiating **few or no "bids"** for connection	Initiating **frequent "bids"** for connection
Turning **against or away** from others	Turning **toward** others
Seeking to be **"right"** and proving others "wrong"	Validating and understanding **both sides**
Building w**in-lose, lose-win,** or **lose-lose** solutions	Developing **win-win** solutions
Conflict Response: **Escalation, Invalidation, Mind-Reading, Avoidance, and Withdrawal**	Conflict Response: Think **Win-Win**; Seek to **Understand**, Then to Be Understood; **Synergy**
Expecting **instant gratification** of our desires	Exercising **patience** and **compassion** for others

Egocentricism—focusing only on our own needs	**Empathy** and **respect** for others' needs
Spewing unfiltered negativity	**Improving positive self-talk** before speaking
Codependence and people-pleasing	**Self-respect, self-awareness, boundaries, self-care**
Bad Communication: "Truth," Blame, Put-Down, Demandingness, and Defensive Counter-Attack	**Good Communication**— mutually respectful sharing of *both* people's thoughts and feelings
Four Horsemen of the Apocalypse: Criticism, Contempt, Defensiveness, Stonewalling	**Appreciating differences,** learning from each other, expanding each other's perspective
Expressing Yourself in **"You Messages"**	Expressing Yourself in **"I Messages"**
Responding through **Defensive Counter-Attack**	Responding through **Reflective Listening**
Accusing others; assuming negative intent	Giving others the **benefit of the doubt**
Maintaining **unrealistic expectations**	Developing **realistic expectations**

Tool #15—CONNECTION is one of the most demanding but significant of the "power tools" we can learn, over time, to add to our Happiness Toolkit. Now, let's proceed with the last of our 16 Tools.

HEALING:

Repair Old Wounds and Move On with Joy!

- ➤ **16–1** How Old Wounds Get in the Way, and Impede Current Happiness

- ➤ **16–2** Original Pain—Finding the Courage to Finally Face and Overcome It

- ➤ **16–3** Grief, Loss, and Transition—Finding New Meaning to Help You Through

- ➤ **16–4** Why All of This Matters—Balancing and Unifying the Tri-Partite Brain

- ➤ **16–5** Abuse, Trauma, and Addiction— Breaking Old Chains, and Moving On

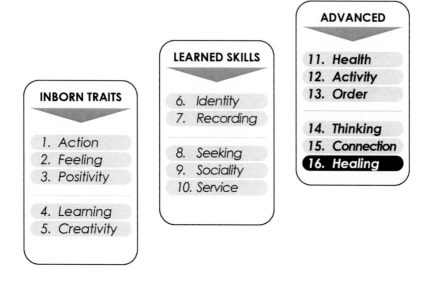

16–1 How Old Wounds Get in the Way, and Impede Current Happiness

Tool #16 in *Your* Happiness Toolkit is—the HEALING tool. This is the last of the 16 Tools, saved for this final chapter because it is the most complex and demanding "power tool" in your Toolkit. It is a resource to help overcome those most tender, painful trigger experiences that live at the core of our beings. *After using Tools #1 to #15 to create safety in the present, this tool exists to help you heal old pain from the past.*

It is human nature that when something significantly hurtful happens to us, we try to set it aside at a safe emotional distance— and just try to forget it, and move on. Particularly when we are young, dependent, and vulnerable, this almost universal strategy of just "bucking up" and trying to "forget about it" (whatever "it" is) helps to keep us from being entirely overwhelmed by the problem, so we can continue to try to face the normal challenges of growing up and finding our way through this challenging world.

However, old pain that is just "forgotten," set aside, and not dealt with doesn't *really* go away. It just goes deep inside, quietly continuing to impact us from the sidelines of our consciousness. It can bring up fears and insecurities, based on past experience, that aren't really relevant to our current circumstances. It can contribute to hair-trigger anger; to unexplained physical aches and pains; to seemingly unshakable addictive patterns; and to relationship problems that can arise from these various struggles. More than anything else, these old unresolved pains can eat away continuously at our sense of self-worth and our basic ability to feel happiness in our lives—even when, on the outside, things might seem to be going reasonably well for us.

Pain from the past gets in our way. It keeps us stuck. It sabotages good intentions. It disrupts positive relationships, and impedes personal joy. As Harvey Jackins insightfully observed: *"The person ... in the grip of an old distress says things that are not pertinent, does things that don't work, fails to cope with the situation, and endures terrible feelings that have nothing to do with the present."*

It has been said that therapy is like peeling an onion. The toughest, hardest layers are on the outside, acting as a protective shell, and can be difficult at first to penetrate or remove. The next layers are thick and strong, defending the soft inner core. Then each successive layer, going deeper and deeper, tends to be thinner and thinner, more and more tender and vulnerable. The innermost layers are the ones that make you cry. It is not wise—or even possible—to go immediately to that central core. You arrive there carefully, one layer at a time.

Likewise, it is generally not wise to deal much with this tool, until you are consistently and successfully using the others. You will need the strength of good health, a tranquil environment, a safe way to express your feelings, positive management of your thoughts, a solid support system, and other benefits derived from the previous tools, before you'll be able to work productively with this one.

Used too early, this tool can destabilize or overwhelm you. Diving into the past before feeling safe in the here and now can result in too much overall stress to handle effectively. *Make sure your life feels reasonably steady and manageable in the present, before you venture into resolving issues from the past.*

But, when you are ready for it, this HEALING Tool can help set at rest those old issues that may have weighed you down for decades, helping you remove significant obstacles to your mental health and happiness.

16–2   Original Pain—Finding the Courage to Finally Face and Overcome It

It can be challenging and scary to enter the realm of old pain. That original pain that sits at the sensitive core of our beings tends to be exquisitely tender and vulnerable. Most often, it remains hidden—even from ourselves. It frequently lies just outside the realm of conscious awareness. We have, after all, decided "not to think about it," to "just forget about it," and to "put it out of our minds." But that decision doesn't really remove the memory—or the emotional impact—of the original experience. It just shoves it out of consciousness, into the unseen, uncontrolled realms of the unconscious mind. There, it mostly just sleeps.

But it can be awakened instantly and forcefully in a moment of current stress. All the old alarms suddenly go off. All the old coping mechanisms spring back into action—even the ones that proved destructive in the past. Old habits and defense mechanisms re-emerge—unbidden, unwelcomed, and seemingly uncontrollable. This can be triggered by a conflict with our spouse; a moment of weakness with a temptation or addiction we thought we conquered long ago; or with any new trigger experience that might emerge in the present.

Rate your current pattern on the scale below:

LIST 1—Patterns Feeding:	LIST 2—Patterns Feeding:
Depression, Disease, Deterioration, and Disability	Happiness, Wellness, Resilience, and Productivity
16. DECAY: Emotionally Deteriorate; Get Stuck in Old Pain	**16. HEALING:** Repair Old Wounds, and Move On With Joy!

-3	-2	-1	0	1	2	3
Strong	Moderate	Mild	Neutral	Mild	Moderate	Strong

The first defense against these unbidden automatic reactions is to allow yourself to become consciously aware of what's behind them. We have to unmask the enemy, face the dragon, and enter the territory where old pain lives, in order to finally set it at rest.

Again, this should only be done when you feel strong enough and ready enough to directly face these hard things, in addition to whatever challenges you're managing in your current circumstances. If you currently feel overwhelmed and anxious about your everyday concerns, it may not be time yet for you to uncover and deal with these *old* issues in your life. Return to your attention to Tools #1 to #15, strengthen yourself here and now—and then, when you feel ready, return to this chapter.

But if you *do* feel ready to proceed in setting these old pains to rest, then what follows are some specific techniques you can use to begin the journey. *Take this process at a slow and manageable pace.* If you begin to feel overwhelmed, then stop for a while, and do something positive that helps re-anchor you in the present. Keep using Tools #1 to #15 consistently to keep yourself healthy, balanced, and grounded throughout the process. Then, choose the following strategy or strategies that seem most helpful for *you* now (these may vary over time).

Practical Techniques for Identifying and Resolving Old Pain

1. **Timeline:** This classic technique is a good starting point. The traditional method is to draw out a horizontal line; then indicate chronologically when various trigger events occurred throughout your life. For example:

Birth	Younger brother born	Parents' divorce	1st grade bullying	Best friend moved away
1985	**1988** (age 3)	**1990** (age 5)	**1991** (age 6)	**1995** (age 10)

And so on...

2. **Timeline with Positives:** Or, you can adjust your timeline, adding positive experiences above the line, and negative experiences below the line. This gives a more balanced and hopeful picture of your life:

Dad playing with me	Kind kindergarten teacher	Mom finding a better job	Finding out I'm good at math

Birth	Younger brother born	Parents' divorce	1st grade bullying	Best friend moved away
1985	**1988** (age 3)	**1990** (age 5)	**1991** (age 6)	**1995** (age 10)

3. **Life Review Grid:** As an alternative, rather than a timeline format, you may find it more helpful to do your life review in a grid format. This is easiest to do on a computer, creating columns and rows in a table. As you do this exercise, you'll generally find that *for every negative factor in your life, there's been a positive one* to help you through the struggle, as well as lessons and growth resulting from each experience— including the hard ones. Gathering those lessons can foster hope, giving a greater sense of meaning to your life.

Year/Age	Basic Condition	Negative event	Positive event	Lessons/ Growth
1985 / 0	Birth	Parents fighting	Bond with both parents	I am loved
1988 / 3	Brother born	Feeling forgotten	Becoming the big kid	Caring for others
1990 / 5	Kinder-garten	Parents' divorce	Kind kindergarten teacher	Making friends
1991 / 6	1st grade	1st grade bullying	Mom getting a better job	Things work out
1995 / 10	4th grade	Best friend moved	Find out I'm good at math	I can solve problems

4. **Mood Log Analysis:** Keep recording and reviewing your "mood logs," as taught earlier in the FEELING and THINKING chapters. As you notice the *situations, feelings,* and *thoughts* that are present when you are upset, begin looking for patterns: when it happens, where it happens, who you're with, and so on.

In particular, watch for events in which your negative feelings seem *out of proportion* with the event at hand. What was the "little thing" you were arguing about with your spouse that blew up into that huge fight? What was that tiny slight from a friend that left you feeling utterly devastated? What was the small provocation that occurred right before that disabling panic attack? These can point you to old issues still needing resolution.

Watch also for the times when *nothing* bad happened, yet your emotions became uncontrollably intense. Often, these episodes of "getting upset for no reason" include clues about leftover feelings from long-past events that were never fully healed, and may still need direct attention, in order to set them finally to rest.

5. **Personal History:** You may find it useful to write out a personal history of your life, or periods or elements of your life that have been especially troubling for you. For example, if you've been abused, you may need to write about what happened to you. If you struggle with an addiction, you may need to write about what was going on in your life when the addiction first began, and how it has progressed over time. If you recently lost someone you love, you may want to write about that person, and your experiences and memories with that individual. *Writing things out on paper tends to stop them from swirling around in your head,* keeping you awake night after night, and interrupting your focus and happiness day by day. Write your past story on paper; let the paper remember those hard things for you—and then, you go forward and live your actual life.

6. **Inner Child Work:** As you do your life review, you may find a number of negative experiences, including in childhood, that continue to interfere with happiness or productivity in your life today. If so, you may want to do some Inner Child Work, to help you process and resolve those difficult experiences. The full method for this process lies beyond the scope of this book; but these two excellent books can help guide you through it:

1. *Homecoming: Reclaiming and Championing Your Inner Child* by John Bradshaw

2. *Recovery of Your Inner Child: The Highly Acclaimed Method for Liberating Your Inner Self* by Lucia Capacchione

Bradshaw's book identifies the various developmental stages of life, and how you can get emotionally stuck at any of those stages. He observes that a wounded "Inner Child" can significantly "contaminate" your adult life, as the unmet needs of the "Child" crash unexpectedly into your current circumstances. Bradshaw wisely observes, ***"Of all of the people you will ever meet, you are the only one who will never leave you."*** If you can become a strong, solid, caring "Adult" in your own life, you build a solid emotional foundation that follows you wherever you go, making you less dependent on others. Bradshaw describes his book as "original pain work," as it first reveals and then heals old layers of pain, so these cease to be obstacles in your current life.

Capacchione's book uses an innovative method to reveal to you what is happening inside your deeper, more vulnerable "Inner Child" self. She uses a *two-handed writing method* throughout her book, that assigns your more dominant hand the role of the inner "Adult," and your non-dominant, less skilled hand the role of the more vulnerable "Inner Child." It is remarkable how this simple method can bring up powerful insights and feelings, so they can finally be resolved.

You will probably find, through these various techniques, that some of your old pain lives in the *recent past* (over the past few weeks and months); and some lies in the more *distant past*. You may have thought that these older experiences don't matter anymore, that they're just "ancient history." But stress tends to accumulate over time—any unresolved stress yesterday can be a springboard for escalated stress today.

So take whatever time you need to first identify and then resolve these hard experiences, so they don't continue to get in your way. Much of this healing work you might be able to do by yourself, using the techniques and books mentioned here. Some of it may require additional perspective and guidance from a competent therapist, life coach, or spiritual leader. Trusted friends and family members can provide crucial support along the way. Seeking spiritual guidance from a Higher Power is a life-transforming resource for many. However you go about *your* healing journey, you will find that your life today becomes more and more satisfying and tranquil, as you strip away your old baggage from the past.

16–3 Grief, Loss, and Transition—Finding New Meaning to Help You Through

Something you (and everyone else) are likely to face multiple times throughout life is—dealing with grief, loss, and transition. You may recall that these are three of the "depression triggers" mentioned early in this book. These three common but disruptive trigger experiences can be described as:

- **Grief:** losing someone important to you, through death, divorce, separation, romantic breakup, moving away, chronic illness, etc.

- **Loss:** losing other things that had been important to you such as: your health, your job, your faith, your figure, your reputation, an important opportunity, a cherished physical possession, etc.

- **Transition:** a major turning point in life that results in significant change. This can be grief or loss experiences, such as those mentioned above. Or, surprisingly, it can also be a happy, long-anticipated transition, such as a graduation, retirement, birth of a child, move to your dream home, growing into the "empty nest years" as your children leave home, or the final accomplishment of any cherished goal you've worked toward for a long time.

  Transition always involves loss—including loss of identity, loss of purpose, loss of familiarity, loss of structure, and loss of relationships associated with the experience you're now leaving. Often, we are blindsided by the emotional impact of "happy" transitions. Since we expected to be happier after going through the transition, we are often hit by surprise when the impact of the transition erupts.

If you are dealing with one or more of these common trigger experiences, here are some ideas that can help:

Practical Strategies for Moving Through Grief, Loss, or Transition

1. Recognize and Honor the Five Stages of Grief

This classic model first appeared in Dr. Elizabeth Kubler-Ross's book *On Death and Dying.* As a medical doctor working with terminally ill patients and their families, she often witnessed the emotional process people move through when facing grief. She described this process occurring in five stages:

1. DENIAL	feeling shock, numbness, disbelief: "This isn't real." "This can't be happening."
2. ANGER	projecting anger on everyone, including God: "It's not fair that this is happening!"
3. BARGAINING	pleading with God to take it away: "I'll do anything; please spare us this tragedy."
4. DEPRESSION	feeling empty, sad, hopeless: "There's nothing that can fix this."
5. ACCEPTANCE	accepting reality; finding a way to move on to a "new normal."

Different people experience grief differently. Some are more verbal, some are less verbal; some need more social connection, some need more alone time. Some people experience the five stages in the order presented here; others experience those stages in a different sequence, or cycle through the stages in various orders.

The ideal time to work through grief is immediately after the loss occurs. But that doesn't always happen. Sometimes life is just too busy, demanding, or even unsafe to work through it at the time. In those cases, *grief goes underground. But it doesn't go away.* Sooner or later, the difficult feelings associated with grief will need to be identified and worked through. However and whenever grief is experienced, it's important to recognize that the pain is valid, and requires resolution.

2. **The 4 Fs—A Path for Moving Productively Through Grief**

The five stages of grief mentioned above are mostly descriptive, drawn from medical observations of "what is normal" in people passing through grief. But often, just knowing that difficult feelings are normal doesn't really point the way *through* them.

In contrast, the **4 Fs** presented below can provide a clear, four-step path *through* a grief experience:

1—*Face* the reality of the loss and its consequences.
2—*Feel* your feelings—*ALL* of them.
3—*Free* yourself from thoughts and
feelings that make it worse.
4—*Find* yourself, others, and God more
deeply through the experience.

Facing the reality of a loss means—getting past denial, and recognizing that the loss is real and consequential. *You can't really recover from a situation that you don't recognize as real.* Facing the consequences of a loss means becoming consciously aware of all of the ways in which life is different because of the loss.

Feeling ALL of your feelings means—letting yourself experience the depth of pain, anger, fear, guilt, hope, love, faith, affection, appreciation, and all of the other emotions that may arise within you, in the face of grief. *You can't heal what you don't feel.* Emotions must be unfrozen and experienced, in order for you to heal.

Freeing yourself from thoughts and behaviors that make it worse means—identifying and removing patterns of thought and behavior that work *against* you, rather than *for* you, in the recovery process. *Examples include:* blaming yourself for the loss; believing that the loss means that everything in your life will turn out badly; isolating yourself from others; engaging in self-sabotage or self-injury; raging at other people; or turning to addictive substances or behaviors to numb pain. *Eliminate those patterns that hurt rather than help you.*

Finding yourself, others, and God more deeply through the experience means—the experience of grief can open up significant new reservoirs of personal growth, compassion, self-awareness, and faith. Getting through something so difficult can help you to become acquainted with deeper strengths inside yourself than you ever knew existed.

Passing through deep pain can bring you to a whole new level of understanding, empathy, and connection with others who have experienced similar pain. And learning to survive and transcend those hard things can foster spiritual perspective, resilience, and supercharged faith in God, as you learn for yourself that you are never truly alone—even on your most difficult and overwhelming days.

Moving productively through grief, loss, and transition can be a powerfully transformative experience. It is often on your very worst days that your very finest strengths become apparent—*if* you move courageously *through* your pain, rather than letting yourself be overcome by it.

3. Actively Engage in "Letting Go"

Emotional healing includes releasing whatever or whomever it is that you are grieving. This can be facilitated by finding a way to let go of something physical, providing a clear marking point for the emotional clearing.

Physical letting-go experiences could include: letting go of helium balloons and watching them fly away; throwing old leaves or flowers, one at a time, into a mountain stream; or physically dejunking items from your home, that represent whatever it is that you're letting go of. Physical letting go can also occur through intense physical exercise—running, high-energy dancing, punching a punching bag, playing basketball, etc.

4. **Recognize and Move Consciously Through the Three Stages of Transition**

Working through life's transitions, even the more benign ones like graduation, marriage, or retirement, can sometimes be challenging. William Bridges, in his book *Transitions: Making Sense of Life's Changes,* identified three stages of passing through a transition experience:

1—The "**Goodbye**" Stage

2—The "**Limbo**" Stage

3—The "**Hello**" Stage

In the "**Goodbye**" stage, we let go of the people, situations, and environment that were part of our prior life experience. This is usually the most painful of the three stages, because it involves elements of loss or grief—even if our current transition is a positive, desirable one.

As we move on to the "**Limbo**" stage of a transition, we no longer have our old situation available to us—but we have not yet arrived in creating our new situation. So we find ourselves uncomfortably "in limbo"—caught between the old life that we left behind, and the new life that is not yet fully developed.

As we continue into the "**Hello**" stage of a transition, we become acquainted with the people, circumstances, and opportunities that are part of our new life situation. This can be an exciting journey of discovery and personal growth, as we learn to stretch our wings in new ways, and slowly become familiar with the new context that will shape our lives and fill our time.

———

All four of these models and strategies—1) the **5 stages of grief;** 2) the **4 Fs;** 3) **letting-go exercises,** and 4) the **3 stages of transition**—can provide helpful perspective and guidance, as you work through grief, loss, or transition. By using these guidelines, you can turn tragedy into triumph, setting many of your old pains to rest, and moving forward into a new life of growth and happiness.

16–4   Why All of This Matters—Balancing and Unifying the Tri-Partite Brain

Why does writing or talking about old pain promote emotional healing? This is important to understand—especially when you're dealing with emotionally charged issues. You need a rationale, a *why* for all this hard, demanding work.

A little brain science can offer valuable perspective. Over recent decades, brain research has uncovered important explanations for the enduring impact of an unhealed past on present mood and experience. The human brain has at times been described as a *"tri-partite brain,"* because it consists of three basic parts:

1. **The Thinking Brain**—also known as the *cerebral cortex, conscious mind,* or *neo-mammalian brain.* The Thinking Brain is able to be conscious of itself. It can think, reason, analyze, strategize, order, and plan. It is like the screen on a computer: it only displays a tiny portion of what is contained in the entire machine—the portion specifically

chosen and called to appear on that visible screen. Once "on the screen," it then becomes possible to *decide intentionally* what to do with that information.

This part of the brain is called *"Neo-Mammalian"* because human beings developed last of all the organisms, and have the most complex structure—including this section of the brain, which *no* other organism possesses. Problems are understood, conceptualized, and solved in the Thinking Brain; and the Thinking Brain can clearly discern the difference between the past, present, and future. This is a *crucial* ability that is needed to heal past troubles. However, when we "choose not to think about" our challenges, we essentially push them out of that powerful Thinking Brain—and into the brain's murkier, less developed, more reactive areas.

2. **The Emotional Brain**—otherwise known as the *limbic system* or *mammalian brain*. This area of the brain stores *every* emotional and physical memory. It filters nothing, and stores everything. It is like a large sponge that sucks up and retains every experience and feeling. Unlike the Thinking Brain, it can't tell the difference between past, present, and future. So *feelings arising from the Emotional Brain can feel exquisitely raw and fresh—even if they are in response to experiences that originally occurred decades earlier.*

This section of the brain is remarkably similar to the brains of other warm-blooded mammals, such as dogs, cats, horses, wolves, and lions. This section of the brain is the seat of basic emotion (fear, pleasure, and anger) and of impulsive drives (hunger, sex, dominance, and care of offspring.) Mammals feel, bond, and react—but *cannot* think, plan, discern, or reason. Our Emotional Brains work in exactly the same way.

3. **The Survival Brain**—otherwise known as the *reptilian brain* or *brain stem*. This tiny portion of the brain, located at the base of the skull, is responsible for keeping the body alive, at a basic level. It keeps the heart beating, the breath going, the blood flowing. In the face of perceived danger, it instantaneously sends out "fight, flight, or freeze" messages throughout the body, through adrenaline and other stress hormones. Its basic job is to assure the organism's survival, no matter what. It is the *"law of the jungle"* part of the brain.

This part is called the *reptilian brain,* because it is similar in structure and function to the brains of reptiles—cold-blooded vertebrates, like snakes, lizards, turtles, and crocodiles. *These creatures focus exclusively on their own survival.* They do not form attachments to a pack, a mate, or a master. They do not feel on an emotional level. They live for this moment in time, and for no other. They live for themselves, and feel no attachment or loyalty to anyone or anything else—not even to their own offspring. They do not bond to protect or train their young, as mammals do. They live to live, and exist to exist—and that's about it. *Our Survival Brain becomes dominant when high-level stress makes thinking or even feeling seem too hard, and mere survival becomes the only remaining objective. But surely, this is not the most fulfilling way to live.*

Our tri-partite human brains contain all three of these elements. We are at our best when all three are functioning and working harmoniously together, resulting in a high quality of life. Our *Thinking Brains* can help us solve problems, establish order, and set goals. Our *Feeling Brains* can provide emotional richness, warmth, and attachment. Our *Survival Brains* alert us to danger, and preserve life even in the face of adversity.

However, under stress this naturally balanced system can be disrupted. When we "push something out of our minds" (out of our Thinking Brains), we lose the ability to problem-solve. The issue then goes into the Feeling Brain, which cannot make sense of it, put it in perspective, or resolve it. In the case of severe, life-threatening stress, such as war trauma or severe abuse, we can't afford even to *feel*, let alone to *think* clearly. So we go into exclusively Survival Brain mode. If that mode persists, our quality of life can become severely disrupted.

Restoring, repairing, and balancing these natural brain functions is not an easy or automatic process. It requires courage. It requires facing and resolving what we may have been hiding from for years. It requires hand-to-hand combat with the old dragons of memory and heightened feeling. It requires honesty and authenticity—with oneself, and with others. It requires hope to press forward, even when things get difficult. But activating the full powers of our tri-partite brain produces balance, healing, and growth.

This is certainly not something that can be found in any pill bottle. Building tranquil perspective, emotional strength, and problem resolution comes not from *numbing* our feelings about difficult situations, but from *facing* them—and then working courageously *through* them. This is done by: 1) bringing these situations to full consciousness, 2) feeling their impact appropriately, 3) coming to resolution about them, and then—4) joyfully moving *on*. Writing exercises, Inner Child Work, talk therapy, and open conversation are among the strategies that can be used to bring old sensitive issues into Thinking Brain awareness, so that they can finally be resolved, and personal peace can be restored.

16–5   Abuse, Trauma, and Addiction— Breaking Old Chains, and Moving On

Some of the most difficult circumstances requiring healing involve a history of abuse, trauma, or addiction. Not everyone deals with these specialized challenges—but here are some guidelines for those that do:

1. **Use Tools 1–15 to Strengthen and Ground Yourself in the Present**

    This must always be the first priority in dealing with difficult patterns and issues from the past. It has been said, *"The best revenge is a well-lived life."* In other words, don't let tragic experiences from your past keep you from engaging in positive patterns in the present. Use the previous fifteen tools, as well as the Quick Start Strategies in Section I, to guide you in building good health, positive thoughts, meaningful goals, healthy relationships, an orderly home, and so on. *You will be more effective in facing and resolving your past challenges, if you have a stable base of operations in the present to work from.*

2. Use Writing to Strengthen Your Thinking Brain

Writing things down on paper is a particularly powerful tool to assist the brain in this healing discrimination process. *Writing activates the Thinking Brain in a direct way, because you literally cannot form the symbols and words required for writing without the participation of the Thinking Brain.* So, if you find troubling memories or feelings swirling around endlessly in your head, use a pen and paper to capture them in written words. You will most often find that this simple action helps you feel more in control, and more at peace. You invite the Thinking Brain to help you discriminate between the past and the present; and so you are able to more effectively separate past feelings from current events, and move on to a happier future.

3. Apply the "Old Pain Resolution" Techniques Discussed Earlier in This Chapter

The timelines, writing assignments, and other strategies presented earlier are particularly important if you have experienced significant disruptions in your past, such as abuse or trauma. They are also crucial resources if you are dealing with an addiction, which usually develops as an attempt to deal with significant pain. *To truly overcome an addiction, you must face and work through the pain that motivated its development in the first place.* Seek professional support if you need it, as you use these techniques to identify past issues and patterns, and replace them with healthier ones. Remember to *pace yourself* through this past-resolution work. If you find that it becomes overwhelming, then take a break, and refocus on using Tools #1 to #15 to solidly re-ground yourself in the present, before proceeding further.

4. **Let Yourself Grieve, Drawing on Techniques Introduced in the Previous Section**

Grief is a powerful dimension of abuse recovery and trauma resolution. Depending on your particular situation, you may need to grieve a lost childhood; shattered innocence; lost opportunities; damaged relationships; disrupted ability to trust; loved ones who are no longer with you; or the life you might have lived, if your circumstances had been different. The grief-resolution strategies presented in the last section can be especially valuable to you, as you work to resolve the demands of your specialized challenges.

5. **Actively Engage in Discrimination Training**

If you have experienced abuse or trauma, those events are typically stored deep in your Feeling Brain. Remember—*that part of your brain is not capable of distinguishing between past, present, and future.* The reactive cry of the traumatized brain, when exposed to a trigger resembling the original traumatic event, is *"It's just the same! It's happening all over again!"* This can result in a reactivation of the raw feelings that belonged to the original event—even if that current event is significantly less toxic.

Trauma is stored in the brain at the age level the traumatized person was when the event originally occurred. So, for example, if an individual experienced abuse when they were five years old, any trigger event reactivating that trauma later in life will generate the feelings and reactions of that five-year-old child—not of the adult that person has chronologically grown into since the original trauma.

To correct this, you will need to actively and intentionally retrain those automatic responses. You do this by consciously engaging your Thinking Brain to clearly discern the difference between your current circumstance and the past traumatic one. Identify the *specific* elements of the original traumatic event, and then compare these elements with the *specific* elements of the recent event. Most commonly, you will find that only a small number of those elements match up, and that most of the elements in the later experience are substantially different and less toxic than the original experience.

6. **Set Time Boundaries on Your Healing Process**

As you engage in recovery work, make sure you don't let it consume your daily life. *Set boundaries on the time you invest in emotional healing.* A good practice is to set a regular time each day to engage in recovery work. During this time (fifteen to forty-five minutes a day), you can grieve, cry, write, talk, read, and otherwise engage fully in your recovery work. *Then when that time is up, you are done for that day.*

If other thoughts, memories, or feelings come up that day (or that night), jot them down quickly in a notebook as a personal reminder. Then resume dealing with those identified issues during your assigned "recovery time" the next day. When it's not "recovery time," engage fully in your current opportunities and responsibilities, in your present circumstances. Focus all those other hours of the day on your job, children, chores, friendships, health, sleep, and other elements of your present-day life. In this way, you will move steadily and consistently through your recovery work, without letting it consume the rest of your life.

7. **Learn to Forgive—For Your Own Sake**

When you have been deeply hurt by the actions of others, it is human nature to hold on to old resentments against those who hurt you. But doing so just keeps *you* trapped in the long-term consequences of their destructive actions. *Free yourself by letting go of bitterness—and choose to refocus your attention instead on your present circumstances and opportunities.*

8. **Engage in Spiritual Healing, by Turning to a Higher Power**

When you are dealing with overwhelming circumstances or feelings that seem beyond your capacity to bear, that can be a particularly important time to rely on a force stronger and smarter than yourself—for comfort, guidance, perspective, and strength. Turning to a Higher Power is a core principle of the *12 Steps,* a well-respected recovery program that has helped many addicts to escape the fierce and relentless grip of their hopelessly enslaving addictions. Likewise, whatever your challenges, turning to a Higher Power can help you to find your way out of the darkness of old pain, and into the light of a joyfully transformed life.

For some, turning to a Higher Power means turning directly to God through prayer, meditation, or personal worship. For others, it means getting out in nature—scaling a tall mountain, watching a sunrise in the early morning sky, or leaving soulful footprints on a peaceful ocean shore. Some may look to a support group, drawing on the power of mutual support for increased strength and insight. Others may find solace in inspirational music that soothes the soul, lifts the spirit, and expands needed hope and perspective.

In one form or another, *turning to a Higher Power moves you beyond the natural limits of what you are capable of,* in and of yourself. When you are feeling stuck, when you have exhausted your own abilities to change, when you have almost lost hope, when you feel determined to carve out a more productive life, but don't know where to start—those are some particularly important times to look above and beyond yourself.

Reach out to a force stronger and wiser than yourself to guide and support you, as you continue in your ongoing journey of discovery and healing. Over time, as you use these tools and techniques, you will find that even a once-shadowed life can become one of light and peace, as you move step by step into a better and happier future.

ADDITIONAL RESOURCES

For Further Understanding, Study, and Mastery

The resources in this section are optional, and are intended for those who wish to do the following:

1. **Understand** more deeply the problem of depression, its expansion in our modern world, and what can be done to stem the tide of its destructive reach in society.

2. **Study** the various tools introduced here, for purposes of professional research, or to build skill and understanding in sharing these tools with others.

3. **Gain mastery** of these skills for implementing them more effectively in your own life, or to more fully understand the wide applicability of these tools to help others.

The resources found in this section may be most useful for professionals or policy-makers. They may also be useful for general readers who, having finished this book, may be asking "What's next?" for their continued journey of healing, recovery, and positive growth over time.

YOU CAN OVERCOME DEPRESSION AND FIND JOY

Even in a Challenging World

- ➤ **Beyond** Symptom Management— Choosing a Path of Healing and Joy

- ➤ **"Under** Construction"—Growing Gradually, Over the Process of Time

- ➤ **Integrative** Wellness Training—Building a Balanced Wellness Program

- ➤ **Blending** the Wisdom of the Ages with Modern Tools and Resources

- ➤ **Powerful** Tips and References, for Your Continued Growth and Progress

Beyond Symptom Management—
Choosing a Path of Healing and Joy

ongratulations! You've now been introduced to all of the tools in *Your* Happiness Toolkit, and are equipped to start using these tools now and for years to come, in order to truly overcome depression, and build a life of lasting fulfillment and joy.

You have seen that these tools consist of much more than just simple symptom management, or passive healing in response to external treatment. Using these tools effectively requires knowledge, skill, and effort. This method consists of many things you can begin doing TODAY to start helping yourself and others.

"Under Construction"—Growing
Gradually, Over the Process of Time

As you consider the many new resources available to you, you might feel overwhelmed at times, wondering how you can apply so many techniques all at once. Remember—**this is a menu, not a prescription.** You can't (and shouldn't!) try to do everything all at once, any more than you should order everything on the menu at the same sitting.

"A little at a time, over the process of time" is the best way to incorporate the various elements of this program. Work on one area at a time, and then move on to the next area. Think of yourself as a living construction site. A building is not built in a day. The roof cannot be added on the same day the foundation is being dug;

nor can the electrical circuits be added before the supporting beams are in place. Most often, you'll want to apply strategies in the order they are presented in this book—first, the foundational Quick Start Strategies in Section I; next, reactivating the Inborn Skills in Section II; then, strengthening the Learned Skills in Section III; then finally, adding the Advanced Strategies in Section IV.

These ideas were gathered over 30 years' time, and have been developed by the contributing authors and theorists over decades, or even centuries. So you're not going to perfectly master them all at once. *You—and everyone you will ever meet—are "under construction"*—and gradual growth, over the process of time, is the goal you should shoot for, and the schedule you should apply, in implementing the material found here.

Integrative Wellness Training—Building a Balanced Wellness Program

The skills and techniques taught in this book are drawn from many different sources, and reflect different aspects of wellness—physical, mental, social, and spiritual. They have been introduced in these pages in a sequence that allows you to grow and heal in a balanced way, over the process of time.

You can think of this material as *"integrative wellness training"*—training that draws from and integrates ideas from many different disciplines, to help you develop emotional balance and resilience. Keep doing your Wellness Grid as you implement this material, and make sure that your healing process continues to address all four of these important areas—*physical, mental, social,* and *spiritual.*

Blending the Wisdom of the Ages with Modern Tools and Technologies

We live in a rich and astonishing time, with knowledge and opportunity literally at our fingertips. Draw on these modern tools and technologies to gather and learn strategies that can be helpful for you. Use online bookseller resources, such as Amazon, to quickly look up the authors and books mentioned in these pages, to gain more information about the topics you're reading about here. Even if you don't end up buying these books, the online information about each one can greatly expand your understanding.

Also use online video resources, such as YouTube, to locate videos made by the authors and theorists referenced here. Most of these authors have modernized the information they wrote into their original books, presenting them in video format to expand their power, and make them more understandable and user-friendly. You can also use online apps and websites to help you apply the principles taught here—for example, to help you with time management, physical exercise, and healthy food preparation.

On the other hand, don't forget to balance these modern technologies with the basic wisdom of the ages. The elements that will prove most powerful to you in your healing process are the natural resources provided by the earth itself—natural food, sunlight, activity, and connections to real-life people, not just screen images. Don't be so enamored with technology that you spend your days and nights in front of a screen. Use modern resources to give you ideas and guidance—then go out into the real world every day to apply them.

The modern world we live in contains many advantages and conveniences that can benefit us—but these are so often overused, crowding out natural resources, that they end up working *against* us, rather than working *for* us. In many ways, throughout the world, physical and emotional health are becoming counter-cultural, because of the habits engrained in modern lifestyles—excessive screen time, artificial food, "virtual" relationships, and sedentary living that continues late into the night, interrupting natural sleep-wake patterns.

Just imagine—if you are wise, you can live even in today's world, enjoying not just the benefits of modern technologies, but also life-sustaining benefits of age-old wisdom and health strategies. You and your loved ones can carve out happy, productive lives, even in an environment where more and more people are now struggling. You can even become an inspiration and support to others, as you apply these principles to help yourself. As you heal and recover, others will wonder what you are doing. Share the principles and strategies you have learned, to help others grow and recover as you are learning to do. This will expand your joy and resilience even further, increasing your mastery of these ideas, as you find ways to share them with others.

Powerful Tips and References, for Your Continued Growth and Progress

The last few pages of this book pull together all that you have learned over the earlier chapters. Use these pages as referencing resources to help you find information you've already read, and want to apply to help yourself or someone else. These pages also include references to the original works drawn from, in the ideas gathered here. If there is an idea you feel you need more information or detail about, refer to these original works to expand your understanding. Return to these ideas again and again, over the process of time, to continually build your understanding and skills. In the process, you will become and remain depression-free, and enjoy a life of rich fulfillment, satisfaction, and joy.

ACKNOWLEDGMENTS

————

GIVING CREDIT WHERE CREDIT IS DUE

I n concluding the writing of this book, I now understand what so many other authors have written about the difficulty and demands of this process. Though writing is a lonely and arduous task, it is never one done truly alone. I am deeply grateful to all of those who have facilitated and supported the writing of this book.

First and foremost, I am grateful to my husband, Steve, who has weathered so many storms with me over the thirty-plus years we have spent together. First, through the storms of my own personal challenges, as I sought answers to my own struggles, with his kind and tireless support. Then later, through the many demands of sharing these healing ideas—through classes, music, videos, and now through this book. He is my partner in life, in raising our family, and in every creative process I have ever undertaken. He has always been my head cheerleader, my top encourager, and the one who keeps everything afloat at home when I need to burrow into my creative tunnel to write. None of this would have been possible without him.

Second, to my five amazing children, who bring such joy and satisfaction into my life, and who constantly delight me with their own remarkable gifts and accomplishments.

Third, to my sixth child, my angel baby, who has watched over this process since his departure from this world in 2001. Losing him was the deepest pain I ever experienced, prompting the deepest healing work I have ever had to do. And his continuing angelic influence in my life, and in my life's work, has been substantial and irreplaceable. It took both heaven and earth to get this book written and published. Fortunately, friends in heaven, as well as friends on earth, have now made that possible.

Fourth, to the many authors and teachers whose ideas permeate these pages. These were true torchbearers in my own life. As I now pass the torch onwards, I am deeply grateful for the healing and inspiring impact of their innovative and restorative ideas.

Fifth, to my insightful editors, writing coaches, designers, and to all of those who proofread the manuscript and provided helpful feedback.

Sixth, to my clients and students over the years, who have tested and implemented these ideas, and taught me so much about the healing process.

Finally, to the Source of all this light and goodness, of whom it was long ago written:

*The Spirit of the Lord God is upon me, because the Lord hath anointed me to preach good tidings unto the meek; he hath sent me to **bind up the broken-hearted**, to proclaim liberty to the captives; and the opening of the prison to them that are bound…*

To comfort all that mourn… *to give unto them beauty for ashes, the oil of joy for mourning, the garment of praise for the spirit of heaviness; that they might be called trees of righteousness, the planting of the Lord, that he might be glorified.*

And they shall build the old wastes, *they shall raise up the former desolations, and they shall repair the waste cities, the desolations of many generations.*

—Isaiah 61:1-4

I am one of those whose mourning has been comforted—whose prison doors have been opened—whose broken heart has been bound up, with infinite tenderness and care, by Him who truly is the **Ultimate Healer.**

To Him I express my eternal and undying gratitude—singing with songs of everlasting joy.

Carrie Maxwell Wrigley
Sandy, Utah, USA
Christmas Day, December 25, 2018

REFERENCES TO SOURCE MATERIALS BY CHAPTER

SECTION I—Quick Start:

Chapter 1: Your Happiness Toolkit: What It Is, How To Build It, And Why

Doidge, Norman. *The Brain That Changes Itself: Stories of Personal Triumph from the Frontiers of Brain Science.* New York: Penguin Books, 2007.

Doidge, Norman. *The Brain's Way of Healing: Remarkable Discoveries and Recoveries from the Frontiers of Neuroplasticity.* New York: Penguin Books, 2015.

Yapko, Michael D. *Hand-Me-Down Blues: How to Stop Depression from Spreading in Families.* New York: St. Martin's Press, 1999.

Yapko, Michael D. *Depression Is Contagious: How the Most Common Mood Disorder Is Spreading Around the World and How to Stop It.* New York: Free Press, 2009.

Covey, Stephen R. *The 7 Habits of Highly Effective People: Restoring the Character Ethic.* New York: Simon & Schuster, 1989.

Chapter 2: OVERCOMING DEPRESSION: What Helps, What Doesn't, and How to Choose a Healing Course

Seligman, Martin E.P. *Authentic Happiness: Using the New Positive Psychology to Realize Your Potential for Lasting Fulfillment.* New York: Simon & Schuster, 2002.

Seligman, Martin E.P. *Flourish: A Visionary New Understanding of Happiness and Well-Being.* New York: Simon & Schuster, 2011.

Brogan, Kelly. *A Mind of Your Own: The Truth About Depression and How Women Can Heal Their Bodies to Reclaim Their Lives.* New York: HarperCollins, 2016.

Glenmullen, Joseph. *The Antidepressant Solution: A Step-by-Step Guide to Safely Overcoming Antidepressant Withdrawal, Dependence, and "Addiction."* New York: Simon & Schuster, 2005.

Moncrieff, Joanna. *The Myth of the Chemical Cure: A Critique of Psychiatric Drug Treatment.* New York: Macmillan, 2008.

Angell, Marcia. *The Truth About Drug Companies: How They Deceive Us and What to Do About It.* New York: Random House, 2004.

Barber, Charles. *Comfortably Numb: How Psychiatry Is Medicating a Nation.* New York: Random House, 2008.

Breggin, Peter R. *Toxic Psychiatry: Why Therapy, Empathy, and Love Must Replace the Drugs, Electroshock, and Biochemical Theories of the "New Psychiatry."* New York: St. Martin's Press, 1991.

Carlat, Daniel J. *Unhinged: The Trouble with Psychiatry—A Doctor's Revelations about a Profession in Crisis.* New York: Simon & Schuster, 2010.

Glenmullen, Joseph. *Prozac Backlash: Overcoming the Dangers of Prozac, Zoloft, Paxil, and Other Antidepressants with Safe, Effective Alternatives.* New York: Simon & Schuster, 2001.

Kirsch, Irving. *The Emperor's New Drugs: Exploding the Antidepressant Myth.* New York: Basic Books, 2010.

Valenstein, Elliot S. *Blaming the Brain: The TRUTH about Drugs and Mental Health.* New York: Simon & Schuster, 1998.

Chapter 3: UNIQUE TO YOU: Understanding Your Depression and Your Happiness Toolkit

Cousens, Gabriel. *Depression-Free for Life: A Physician's All-Natural, 5-Step Plan.* New York: Harper-Collins, 2000.

Emmons, Henry. *The Chemistry of Joy: A Three-Step Program for Overcoming Depression Through Western Science and Eastern Wisdom.* New York: Simon & Schuster, 2006.

Nedley, Neil. *Depression: The Way Out.* Oklahoma: Nedley Publishing, 2001.

Yapko, Michael D. *Breaking the Patterns of Depression.* New York: Random House, 1997.

Chapter 4: 21st-CENTURY DEPRESSION: An Expanding Worldwide Epidemic— How to Survive and Thrive

Abramson, John. *Overdosed America: The Broken Promise of American Medicine.* New York: Harper-Collins, 2004.

Moynihan, Ray, and Cassels, Alan. *Selling Sickness: How the World's Biggest Pharmaceutical Companies Are Turning Us All into Patients.* New York: Nation Books, 2005.

NAMI (National Alliance on Mental Illness). *Depression.* (Statistics gathered from various pages on official website, nami.org).

NIMH (National Institute of Mental Health). *Depression.* (Statistics gathered from various pages on official website, nimh.nih.gov).

Waters, Ethan. *Crazy Like Us: The Globalization of the American Psyche.* New York: Simon & Schuster, 2010.

Whitaker, Robert. *Anatomy of an Epidemic: Magic Bullets, Psychiatric Drugs, and the Astonishing Rise of Mental Illness in America.* New York: Random House, 2010.

WHO (World Health Organization). *Depression.* (Statistics gathered from various pages on official website, who.int).

Chapter 5: BUILDING YOUR HAPPINESS TOOLKIT: *The Ultimate, Lifelong Do-It-Yourself Adventure!*

Seligman, Martin. *Authentic Happiness* and *Flourish.* (Same as chapter 2)

Smith, Hank. *Be Happy: Simple Secrets to a Happier Life.* American Fork, Utah: Covenant Communications, 2017.

SECTION II—Inborn Traits:

TOOL #1: ACTION: Do What You Love— And Do What Loves You Back!

Schwartz, Tony. *The Way We're Working Isn't Working: The Four Forgotten Needs That Energize Great Performance.* New York: Simon & Schuster, 2010.

Covey, Stephen R. *7 Habits of Highly Effective People.* (Same as chapter 2)

TOOL #2: FEELING: Feel and Express Your Actual Feelings

(same references as Tool #14)

TOOL #3: POSITIVITY: Notice and Enjoy the Good Things

Seligman, Martin. *Learned Optimism: How to Change Your Mind and Your Life.* New York: Simon & Schuster, 1990. *(Also, Seligman titles from chapter 2)*

Williams, Mark, Teasdale, John, Segal, Zindel, and Zabat-Zinn, Jon. *The Mindful Way Through Depression: Freeing Yourself from Chronic Unhappiness.* New York: Guilford Press, 2007.

TOOL #4: LEARNING: Develop New Abilities and Skills

Doidge, Norman. *The Brain That Changes Itself* and *The Brain's Way of Healing.* (Same as chapter 1)

Robbins, Anthony. *Unlimited Power: The New Science of Personal Achievement.* New York: Simon & Schuster, 1986.

Robbins, Anthony. *Awaken the Giant Within: How to Take Immediate Control of Your Mental, Emotional, Physical, and Financial Destiny.* New York: Simon & Schuster, 1991.

TOOL #5: CREATIVITY: Focus on Creating Rather Than Consuming

Hollins, Peter. *Think Like da Vinci: Practical Everyday Creativity for Idea Generation, New Perspectives, and Innovative Thinking.* Independently Published, 2018.

Winn, Marie. *The Plug-In Drug: Television, Computers, and Family Life.* New York: Penguin Books, 2002. (originally 1977)

SECTION III—Learned Skills:

TOOL #6: IDENTITY: Know and Value Your Unique Traits and Gifts

Keirsey, David, and Bates, Marilyn. *Please Understand Me: Character and Temperament Types.* Prometheus Nemesis Book Company, 1978.

Tieger, Paul D., and Barron, Barbara. *Do What You Are: Discover the Perfect Career for You Through the Secrets of Personality Type.* New York: Little, Brown, and Co. 1992.

Tieger, Paul D., and Barron, Barbara. *Nurture by Nature: Understand Your Child's Personality Type—And Become a Better Parent.* New York: Little, Brown, and Co., 1997.

Tieger, Paul D., and Barron, Barbara. *Just Your Type: Create the Relationship You've Always Wanted Using the Secrets of Personality Type.* New York: Little, Brown, and Co., 2000.

Myers, Isabel Briggs. *Gifts Differing: Understanding Personality Type.* Palo Alto, CA: Consulting Psychologists Press, 1980.

————

Hartman, Taylor. *The Color Code.* Taylor Don Hartman, 1987.

Helgoe, Laurie. *Introvert Power: Why Your Inner Life Is Your Hidden Strength.* Naperville, IL: Sourcebooks, 2013.

Laney, Marti Olsen. *The Introvert Advantage: How to Thrive in an Extrovert World.* New York: Workman Publishing, 2002.

TOOL #7: RECORDING: Write and Preserve Your Life Experience

Covey, Stephen R. *The 7 Habits of Highly Effective People.* (*Same as chapter 2*)

Eyre, Linda and Richard. *Lifebalance: How to Simplify and Bring Harmony to Your Everyday Life.* New York: Simon & Schuster, 1997. (originally 1987)

TOOL #8: SEEKING: Reach Out for Guidance, Support, and Insight

Erikson, Erik H. *Childhood and Society.* W.W. Norton and Company, 1950.

Clinton, Tim, and Sibcy, Gary. *Attachments: Why You Love, Feel, and Act the Way You Do.* Orange County, CA: Yates and Yates, 2002.

Jeffers, Susan. *Feel the Fear . . . And Do It Anyway.* New York: Ballantine Books, 1987.

Jeffers, Susan. *Dare to Connect: How to Create Confidence, Trust, and Loving Relationships.* Platkus, 2001.

Johnson, Sue. *Hold Me Tight: Seven Conversations for a Lifetime of Love.* New York: Little, Brown, and Company, 2008.

TOOL #9: SOCIALITY: Engage in Meaningful Social Connections

Leman, Kevin. *The Birth Order Book: Why You Are the Way You Are.* Grand Rapid, MI: Platkus, 1985.

Carnegie, Dale. *How to Win Friends and Influence People.* New York: Simon & Schuster, 1936.

Covey, Stephen R. *The 7 Habits of Highly Effective People.* (Same as chapter 2)

Gabor, Don. *How to Start a Conversation and Make Friends.* New York: Simon & Schuster, 1983.

Gottman, John. *The Relationship Cure: A 5-Step Guide to Strengthening Your Marriage, Family, and Friendships.* New York: Random House, 2001.

TOOL #10: SERVICE: Joyfully Share What You Have and Are with Others

Pipher, Mary. *The Shelter of Each Other: Rebuilding Our Families*. New York: Random House, 1996.

SECTION IV—Advanced Strategies:

TOOL #11: HEALTH: Care Wisely for Your Body—And Your Brain

Price, Weston. *Nutrition and Physical Degeneration*. La Mesa, CA: The Price-Pottenger Nutrition Foundation, Inc., 1939.

———

Barnard, Neal. *Dr. Neal Barnard's Program for Reversing Diabetes: The Scientifically Proven Program for Reversing Diabetes Without Drugs*. Rodale, Inc. 2006.

Campbell, T. Colin, and Campbell, Thomas M. *The China Study: The Most Comprehensive Study of Nutrition Ever Conducted and the Startling Implications for Diet, Weight Loss, and Long-Term Health*. Dallas, TX: BenBella Books, Inc., 2006.

Crawley, Chris, and Lodge, Henry S. *Younger Next Year: A Guide to Living Like 40 Until You're 80 and Beyond*. New York: Workman Publishing Company, 2004.

Esselstyn, Caldwell B. *Prevent and Reverse Heart Disease: The Revolutionary, Scientifically Proven, Nutrition-Based Cure*. New York: Penguin Group, 2007.

Fuhrman, Joel. *Eat to Live: The Amazing Nutrient-Rich Program for Fast and Sustained Weight Loss.* New York: Little, Brown, and Company, 2003.

Hyman, Mark. *The UltraMind Solution: Fix Your Broken Brain by Healing Your Body First—The Simple Way to Defeat Depression, Overcome Anxiety, and Sharpen Your Mind.* New York: Simon & Schuster, 2009.

MacDougall, John. *The Healthiest Diet on the Planet: Why the Foods You Love—Pizza, Pancakes, Potatoes, Pasta, and More—Are the Solution to Preventing Disease and Looking and Feeling Your Best.* New York: HarperCollins, 2016.

Moss, Michael. *Salt, Sugar, Fat: How the Food Giants Hooked Us.* New York: Random House, 2013.

Murkoff, Heidi, and Mazel, Sharon. *What to Expect When You're Expecting.* New York: Workman Publishing, 1984.

Ornish, Dean. *Dr. Dean Ornish's Program for Reversing Heart Disease: The Only System Scientifically Proven to Reverse Heart Disease Without Drugs or Surgery.* New York: Ballantine Books, 1990.

Roizon, Michael F. *Real Age: Are You as Young as You Can Be?* New York: Harper Collins, 1999.

Wark, Chris. *Chris Beat Cancer: A Comprehensive Plan for Healing Naturally.* Hay House, Inc., 2018.

———

Gabriel, John. *The Gabriel Method: The Revolutionary DIET-FREE Way to Totally Transform Your Body.* Atria Books, 2008.

Minirth, Frank, and Meier, Paul. *Love Hunger: Recovery from Food Addiction—10 Stage Life Plan for Your Body, Mind, and Soul.* New York: Random House, 1990.

TOOL #12: ACTIVITY: Enjoy Daily Health-Promoting Movement

Duke University. https://today.duke.edu/2000/09/exercise922.html. Duke Today, September 22, 2000.

Ratey, John J. *Spark: The Revolutionary New Science of Exercise and the Brain.* New York: Little, Brown, and Company, 2008.

———

Levine, James A. *Move a Little, Lose a Lot.* New York: Random House, 2009.

Levine, James A. *Get Up! Why Your Chair Is Killing You and What You Can Do About It.* New York: Palgrave MacMillan, 2014.

Vernikos, Joan. *Sitting Kills, Moving Heals: How Simple, Everyday Movement Will Prevent Pain, Illness, and Early Death—And Exercise Alone Won't.* Fresno, CA, Linden Publishing, 2011.

Vernikos, Joan. *Designed to Move: The Science-Backed Program to Fight Sitting Disease and Enjoy Lifelong Health.* Fresno, CA, Linden Publishing, 2016.

———

Breus, Michael. *The Power of When: Discover Your Chronotype—And the Best Time to Eat Lunch, Ask for a Raise, Have Sex, Write a Novel, Take Your Meds, and More.* New York: Little, Brown, and Company, 2016.

Huffington, Ariana. *The Sleep Revolution: Transforming Your Life One Night at a Time.* New York: Penguin Random House, 2016.

Panda, Satchin. *The Circadian Code: Lose Weight, Supercharge Your Energy, and Transform Your Health from Morning to Midnight.* New York: Penguin Random House, 2018.

TOOL #13: ORDER: Organize Your Time, Resources, and Living Space

Covey, Stephen R. *The 7 Habits of Highly Effective People.* (Same as chapter 2)

Eyre, Linda and Richard. *Lifebalance.* (Same as chapter 2)

———

DeGraaf, John, Wann, David, and Naylor, Thomas B. *Affluenza: The All-Consuming Epidemic.* San Francisco, CA: Berrett-Koehler Publishers, Inc., 2002.

Aslett, Don. *Clutter's Last Stand: It's Time to Dejunk Your Life!* Avon, MA: Adams Media, 2005 (1984.)

Kondo, Marie. *The Life-Changing Magic of Tidying Up: The Japanese Art of Decluttering and Organizing.* Berkeley, CA: Ten Speed Press, 2014.

Mills, Sherie. *I Almost Divorced My Husband, But I Went On Strike Instead.* Springville, UT: Cedar Fort, Inc., 2011.

TOOL #14: THINKING: *Direct Your Thoughts in Positive, Productive Ways*

Seligman, Martin. *Learned Optimism: How to Change Your Mind and Your Life.* New York: Simon & Schuster, 1990.

Seligman, Martin. *The Optimistic Child: A Proven Program to Safeguard Children Against Depression and Build Lifelong Resilience.* New York: Harper Collins, 1995.

Burns, David D. *Feeling Good: The New Mood Therapy.* New York: Harper Collins, 1980.

Burns, David D. *The Feeling Good Handbook.* New York: Penguin Books, 1990.

Burns, David D. *When Panic Attacks: The New Drug-Free Anxiety Therapy That Can Change Your Life.* New York: Broadway Books, 2006.

Ellis, Albert, and Harper, Robert A. *A Guide to Rational Living.* Wilshire Book Co., 1975.

Helmstetter, Shad. *The Self-Talk Solution.* New York: Simon & Schuster, 1987.

McKay, Matthew, Rogers, Peter D., and McKay, Judith. *When Anger Hurts: Quieting the Storm Within.* Oakland, CA: New Harbinger Publications, 1989.

Schwartz, Jeffrey M. *Brain Lock: Free Yourself from Obsessive-Compulsive Behavior—A Four-Step Self-Treatment Method to Change Your Brain Chemistry.* New York: Harper Perennial, 1996.

Schwartz, Jeffrey M., and Gladding, Rebecca. *You Are Not Your Brain: The 4-Step Solution for Changing Bad Habits, Ending Unhealthy Thinking, and Taking Control of Your Life.* London: The Penguin Group, 2011.

TOOL #15: CONNECTION: *Communicate and Relate Well with Others*

Gottman, John. *Why Marriages Succeed or Fail and How YOU Can Make Yours Last.* New York: Simon & Schuster, 1994.

Gottman, John, and Silver, Nan. *The Seven Principles for Making Marriage Work: A Practical Guide from the Country's Foremost Relationship Expert.* New York: Random House, 1999.

Gottman, John. *The Relationship Cure: A 5-Step Guide to Strengthening Your Marriage, Family, and Friendships.* New York: Random House, 2001.

Gottman, John, and Gottman, Julie Schwartz. *Ten Lessons to Transform Your Marriage: America's Love Lab Experts Share Their Strategies for Strengthening Your Relationship.* New York: Random House, 2006.

Markman, Howard J., Stanley, Scott M., and Blumberg, Susan L. *Fighting for Your Marriage: Positive Steps for Preventing Divorce and Preserving a Lasting Love.* San Francisco, CA: John Wiley and Sons, 2001.

———

Burns, David D. *The Feeling Good Handbook.* New York: Penguin Books, 1990.

Covey, Stephen R. *The 7 Habits of Highly Effective People. (Same as chapter 2)*

TOOL #16: HEALING: Repair Old Wounds and Move On with Joy!

Bradshaw, John. *Homecoming: Reclaiming and Championing Your Inner Child.* New York: Bantam Books, 1990.

Capacchione, Lucia. *Recovery of Your Inner Child: The Highly Acclaimed Method for Liberating Your Inner Self.* New York: Simon & Schuster, 1991.

Dusay, John. *Egograms: How I See You and You See Me.* New York: Harper and Row, 1977.

———

Bridges, William. *Transitions: Making Sense of Life's Changes.* Lifelong Books, 2004. (reprint)

Colgrave, Melba, Bloomfield, Harold, and McWilliams, Peter. *How to Survive the Loss of a Love: 58 Things to Do When There Is Nothing to Be Done.* New York: Bantam Books, 1976.

Kubler-Ross, Elizabeth. *On Death and Dying.* Scribner, 1969.

———

Gil, Eliana. *Outgrowing the Pain: A Book for and About Adults Abused as Children.* New York: Dell Publishing, 1983.

Lew, Mike. *Victims No Longer: The Classic Guide for Men Recovering from Sexual Child Abuse.* New York: Harper Perennial, 2004.

Nakazawa, Donna Jackson. *Child Disrupted: How Your Biography Becomes Your Biology and How You Can Heal.* New York: Simon & Schuster, 2015.

Van Der Kolk, Bessel. *The Body Keeps the Score: Brain, Mind, and Body in the Healing of Trauma*. New York: Penguin Group, 2014.

———

Hari, Johann. *Chasing the Scream: The First and Last Days of the War on Drugs*. New York: Bloomsbury, 2015.

Hari, Johann. *Lost Connections: Uncovering the Real Causes of Depression—And the Unexpected Solutions*. New York: Bloomsbury, 2018.

Trimpey, Jack. *Rational Recovery: The New Cure for Substance Addiction*. New York: Pocket Books, 1996.

OVERVIEW OF TOOLS AND TOPICS BY CHAPTER

SECTION I—Quick Start

Chapter 1: YOUR HAPPINESS TOOLKIT: What It Is, How to Build It, and Why

TOOLS	TOPICS
1–3 The Four "Whys" **1–5 Wellness Grid**	**1–1** What Is *Your* Happiness Toolkit? **1–2** How to Build *Your* Happiness Toolkit **1–3** Why *You* Should Build *Your* Happiness Toolkit **1–4** People-Pleasing, Perfectionism, and "Productivity" **1–5** Transformational Tool #1: **The Wellness Grid**

Chapter 2: OVERCOMING DEPRESSION: What Helps, What Doesn't, and How to Choose a Healing Course

TOOLS	TOPICS
2–4 Four Basic Stages of Healing **2–5 Five Ineffective Strategies** **2–6 Up-or-Down Spiral**	**2–1** Overcoming Depression with Positive Action **2–2** How You Think About Depression Impacts Its Course **2–3** Choose an Individualized Approach, Not Standardized **2–4** Pursue Healing from the Inside Out, Not Just "Treatment" **2–5** Avoid These Five Ineffective Strategies for Depression **2–6** Transformational Tool #2: **The Up-or-Down Spiral**

Chapter 3: UNIQUE TO YOU: Understanding Your Depression and Your Happiness Toolkit

TOOLS	TOPICS
3–2 The Diamond **3–3 IRA** **3–5 Unique Causes of YOUR Depression**	**3–1** Integrative Wellness Training, Not Symptom Management **3–2** The Diamond: An Integrative Tool for Individualized Assessment **3–3** Using the Diamond to Plan Your Recovery Strategy (IRA) **3–4** From Depression to Happiness—Why Every Recovery Is Unique **3–5** Transformational Tool #3: **The Diamond**

Chapter 4: 21st-CENTURY DEPRESSION: An Expanding Worldwide Epidemic—How to Survive and Thrive

TOOLS	TOPICS
4–4 The Cure for Everything **4–5 Patterns Promoting Disease/Health** **4–6 More-or-Less Grid**	**4–1** You're Not Alone; Increase of Depression in the World We Live In **4–2** To Actually Get Better, Actually Fix What's Wrong **4–3** To Fix What's Wrong, You Need to Know What's Wrong **4–4** What Works Works—What Doesn't Work Doesn't Work **4–5** Disease-Promoting Patterns vs. Health-Promoting Patterns **4–6** Transformational Tool #4: **The More-or-Less Grid**

Chapter 5: BUILDING YOUR HAPPINESS TOOLKIT: The Ultimate, Lifelong Do-It-Yourself Adventure!

TOOLS	TOPICS
5–5 16 Strategies List **5–5 16 Contrasting Lifestyle Patterns** **5–5 3 Levels Upward/Downward**	**5–1** Happiness Is Not Something to Be Pursued—But to Be Built! **5–2** Take Joy in Incremental Growth and Progress, Over Time **5–3** Three Basic Levels of Development and Recovery **5–4** The 16 Tools (And Their Opposites)—A Brief Overview **5–5** Transformational Tool #5: **Your Happiness Toolkit**

SECTION II—Toolkit, Level One—*Inborn Traits*

Tool #1—*ACTION: Do What You Love—And Do What Loves You Back!*

TOOLS	TOPICS
1–1 *Recreational Survey* 1–4 *Implementing "As If"* 1–5 *Finding a Balance*	1–1 Positive Action—Foundation of Wellness and Happiness 1–2 Why Do We Stop Doing What We Love? 1–3 Positive, Proactive, and Productive—Choosing Actions 1–4 Don't Wait Until You "Feel Like It"—Implementing "As If" 1–5 Finding a Balance: Doing What You Love, What is Required

Tool #2: *FEELING: Feel and Express Your Actual Feelings*

TOOLS	TOPICS
2–3 *Three-Factor Mood Log* 2–3 *Feelings Survey* 2–5 *"I" Message Formulas*	2–1 Expressing Genuine Feelings—An Inborn Ability 2–2 Why Do We Stop Expressing Our Actual Feelings? 2–3 Building Self-Awareness: What Are You Feeling Today? 2–4 Developing an Expanded Vocabulary for Expressing Feelings 2–5 Expressing Your Actual Feelings to Others

Tool #3: POSITIVITY: Notice and Enjoy the Good Things

TOOLS	TOPICS
3–2 Gratitude Journal 3–2 Expressing Gratitude 3–4 Mindfulness	3–1 Noticing and Enjoying the Positive—A Simple but Powerful Skill 3–2 Building Positive Awareness— What Do You Appreciate Today? 3–3 Gratitude/Resentment— You Decide Which Perspective to Adopt 3–4 Mindfulness—A Path to Expanded Appreciation and Enjoyment 3–5 Positive Psychology—Opening New Doors for a New Millennium

Tool # 4: LEARNING: Develop New Abilities and Skills

TOOLS	TOPICS
4–4 Three Learning Styles 4–4 Five Ways to Learn	4–1 The Joy of Lifelong Learning and Development 4–2 Neuroplasticity—The Brain's Lifelong Ability to Change Itself 4–3 How We Get Stuck, and Why We Might Remain Stuck 4–4 Your Learning Style—Visual, Auditory, or Kinesthetic? 4–5 Learning in a Balanced and Manageable Way

Tool #5: CREATIVITY: Focus on Creating Rather Than Consuming

TOOLS	TOPICS
5–3 Creative Expression— Options **5–3 Review: Level 1 Tools**	**5–1** Creativity—Why It Is So Important for Emotional Health **5–2** Consuming, Passive Entertainment—A Modern Scourge **5–3** Expression—A Path of Discovery, A Road Through Pain **5–4** Your Worst Nightmare Can Become Your Greatest Inspiration **5–5** Mobilizing Your Inborn Traits for Recovery and Wellness

SECTION III—Toolkit, Level Two—*Learned Skills*

Tool #6—IDENTITY: Know and Value Your Unique Traits and Gifts

TOOLS	TOPICS
6–3 *Personality Type* 6–4 *Temperament*	**6–1** "Who Am I?"—Mobilizing the Power of Self-Awareness **6–2** Comparative Worth vs. Innate Worth **6–3** Personality Typing to Understand and Value Self/Others **6–4** Temperament—Why We Are All Needed Just As We Are **6–5** Type Development—How We Change and Grow Over Time

Tool #7: RECORDING: Write and Preserve Your Life Experience

TOOLS	TOPICS
7–3 *Recording Techniques*	**7–1** Building Positive Awareness by Recording Your Life Experience **7–2** Dangers of Reactivity, The Fragmentation of Experience **7–3** Varieties of Techniques for Recording Life Experience **7–4** Using Writing to Soothe and Channel Strong Emotions **7–5** Preserving Your Personal Legacy for Yourself and Others

Tool #8: SEEKING: Reach Out for Guidance, Support, and Insight

TOOLS	TOPICS
8–4 Three Attachment Styles **8–5 Ten Strategies for "Seeking"**	**8–1** Seeking for Help—A Crucial, Life-Sustaining Skill **8–2** What Goes Wrong—How We Learn *Not* to Seek Help **8–3** The Tendency to Turn to Screens and Machines **8–4** Three Styles of Attachment and Their Lifelong Impact **8–5** Building the Capacity to Reach Out in Times of Need

Tool #9: SOCIALITY: Engage in Meaningful Social Connections

TOOLS	TOPICS
9–3 Birth Order **9–4 Six Strategies for "Sociality"** **9–5 The 4 "Ts"**	**9–1** Peer Relationships at Home, Play, School, Dating, and Work **9–2** What Gets in the Way of Meaningful Social Connections? **9–3** Personality, Attachment Styles, Birth Order—Impact on Sociality **9–4** Six Strategies for Finding Your Tribe, Building Your Social Network **9–5** The "4 Ts": Elements of Relationship Building, Erosion, Repair

Tool #10: SERVICE: Joyfully Share What You Have and Are with Others

TOOLS	TOPICS
10–4 *"Service"* **Ideas** **10–5 Level 2 Summary**	**10–1** Giving Back—The Most Joyful Expression of Ourselves **10–2** How Service Expands Our Happiness, Over Our Lifetime **10–3** What Happens When Service Becomes a Lost Art? **10–4** Finding Service Opportunities, Balanced with Self-Care **10–5** Pulling Together All You've Learned So Far

SECTION IV—Toolkit, Level Three—*Advanced Strategies*

Tool #11—HEALTH: Care Wisely for Your Body—And Your Brain

TOOLS	TOPICS
11–5 Depression-Fighting Nutrition Tips	**11–1** Healthy Body, Healthy Brain—Foundation of Wellness **11–2** 3 Health-Killers in the Modern World; Reversing Them **11–3** Food is Fuel: Choosing Wellness-Promoting Nutrition **11–4** Identifying and Correcting a Depressed Eating Pattern **11–5** 15 Nutritional Tips to Overcome Depression and Disease

Tool #12: ACTIVITY: Enjoy Daily Health-Promoting Movement

TOOLS	TOPICS
12–3 Exercise Types and Benefits **12–4 Non-Exercise Activity; Walk Types** **12–5 Sleep/Sunlight Tips**	**12–1** Movement and Activity: Building Positive Energy, Vitality **12–2** How Inactivity Contributes to Depression and Illness **12–3** The Transformative Power of Physical Exercise **12–4** Non-Exercise Activity: A Powerful New Wellness Tool **12–5** Sleep and Sunlight: Natural Cycles for Daily Renewal

Tool #13: ORDER: Organize Your Time, Resources, and Living Space

TOOLS	TOPICS
13–3 *Time Management* 13–5 *Three-Box Dejunking* 13–5 *Home Management*	13–1 Bringing Order to Your Life, Increasing Positive Control 13–2 How Disorder Interferes with Emotional Wellness 13–3 Time Management—Your Most Valuable Resource 13–4 Resource Management—Manage Finances/Belongings 13–5 Home Management—Dejunk/Organize Your Home

Tool #14: THINKING: Direct Your Thoughts in Positive, Productive Ways

TOOLS	TOPICS
14–3 *3 Ps (Learned Optimism)* 14–4 *Ten Forms of Twisted Thinking; Five-Factor Mood Log* 14–5 *Ten Antidotes for Twisted Thinking*	14–1 Thoughts, Beliefs, Moods—How They Affect Each Other 14–2 A-B-C Response Pattern—Putting You in the Driver's Seat 14–3 Interpretive Style—Choose an Optimistic Mindset 14–4 Cognitive Therapy—Thoughts That Feed Depression 14–5 Positive Self-Talk –Silencing the Negative Chatterbox

Tool #15: CONNECTION: Communicate and Relate Well with Others

TOOLS	TOPICS
15–4 Good and Bad Communication **15–4 Danger Signs** **15–5 Connection/ Disconnection Patterns**	**15–1** Relationship Building— Important But Demanding **15–2** Turn Toward Others, Not Against or Away From Them **15–3** Know and Respect Others' Needs, As Well As Your Own **15–4** Building Effective Communication, Foster Understanding **15–5** Patterns of Connection or Disconnection: A Summary

Tool #16: HEALING: Repair Old Wounds and Move On with Joy!

TOOLS	TOPICS
16–2 Timelines **16–2 Other Past-Resolution Strategies** **16–3 Grief: Five Stages; 4 Fs; Transition** **16–4 Tri-Partite Brain** **16–5 Abuse/ Trauma/Addiction Recovery**	**16–1** How Old Wounds Get in the Way, Impede Happiness **16–2** Original Pain—Finding the Courage to Face, Overcome It **16–3** Grief, Loss, and Transition— Finding New Meaning **16–4** Why All of This Matters— Balancing the Tri-Partite Brain **16–5** Abuse, Trauma, Addiction— Breaking Old Chains

ABOUT THE AUTHOR

C arrie Maxwell Wrigley, LCSW, has been a counselor for over thirty years, specializing in the treatment of depression, anxiety, addiction, grief, trauma, and relationship challenges. She currently works in her private practice, Morning Light Counseling, in Sandy, Utah.

Carrie has also been a public health educator for over twenty years, providing education on emotional recovery, and teaching courses on marriage and family enrichment. She has developed several websites to share information on these various topics, including counselinglibrary.org.

Carrie received her formal education at the University of Utah, obtaining first a BFA in Theatre, and then returning later for her MSW (Master of Social Work) degree. Carrie has a particular interest in prevention, and is passionate about sharing practical strategies that individuals can use to create and maintain emotional wellness over time, with a strong emphasis on self-help, and building self-efficacy.

Carrie also uses her artistic gifts to spread a message of hope, healing, and wellness. Trained as an actor, she is an engaging and dynamic presenter, who uses storytelling and original music to amplify her teaching. She is a prolific songwriter, whose music has been used in school, church, and community settings.

Her inspirational and religious music has been heard by thousands, and is now available on her website, morninglightmusic.org, and on iTunes, Amazon, and CD Baby. She spent twelve years developing and sharing a Character Education Through Music program for elementary and middle school students, creating fun original music (available at impactmusic4kids.org) to teach values such as responsibility, caring, inclusion, anti-bullying, and community.

Carrie also continues to love acting on stage and on film; her acting credits can be found on IMDB.com. Music and acting continue to be an integral and joyful part of her personal **"Happiness Toolkit."**

Carrie has been married for over thirty years to her husband, sweetheart, and business partner, Steve Wrigley. They are the parents of five amazing children; and Carrie is the oldest of seven children. Lessons from her family life permeate this book, and these relationships remain the most central, enduring, and joyful core of her life.

Carrie is also sustained by her faith, which is the anchoring foundation for her life and work. The material in this book was presented first in a religious context, as "Christ-Centered Healing from Depression." Repurposed later for a more inclusive audience, this material continues to reflect that "*light which shineth in darkness*" (*John 1:5*). Years of experience truly affirm: "***Weeping may endure for the night, but joy cometh in the morning***" (*Psalm 30:5*).

I f you'd like to contact Carrie for speaking engagements, performances, counseling services, or simply to offer feedback or ask additional questions, she can be reached at her email—carrie@morninglightcounseling.com—or through any of her websites:

- **MORNINGLIGHTCOUNSELING.COM**— private counseling practice

- **COUNSELINGLIBRARY.ORG**—online resource library on counseling topics

- **IMPACTMUSIC4KIDS.ORG**—character education music, including lyrics

- **MORNINGLIGHTMUSIC.ORG**—religious and inspirational music, including lyrics

- **CARRIEWRIGLEY.COM**—updates, performance information, and bookings

Additional Products Include:

 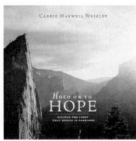 

Made in United States
North Haven, CT
09 October 2021